The Five Steps to Buying a Computer

1. Decide what you want your computer to do.
2. Find the software that will get you the result you want.
3. Find the hardware to run your software.
4. Shop for service and support.
5. Buy that computer!

Where to Spend Extra Money

Buy a faster microprocessor. Nothing beats a fast microprocessor. Also, because it's the most difficult item to upgrade later, it's better to spend more money here first.

Get a bigger hard drive. Although it's easy to add more storage later, most folks typically underestimate their storage needs. Too much space is great!

Maximize your memory! Ensure that as much memory as possible is in one "bank."

Jumbo-size your monitor. Those 19-plus-inch screens are *dreamy*.

Words of Wisdom

- Don't buy brand names, but rather a solution to your software problem.

- Ignore part numbers: It's an 8GB hard drive, not an 8ZRc4012C-x.

- Avoid untested technology. Unless you see an item in numerous computer ads, it's probably not worth getting.

- Software drives the hardware. Without software to take advantage of a fancy computing device, the device is useless.

- Over the lifetime of your PC, you will spend as much on software as you do on hardware — and maybe more.

- Most PCs have a useful life of about four years. After that, it's cheaper to buy a new PC than to upgrade your existing model.

Don't Forget to Buy These Items Too

- A mousepad
- A wristpad
- A power strip, or surge protector, or UPS
- A printer cable
- Paper for your printer
- Extra printer toner or ink
- A modem cable
- A few floppy disks or zip disks
- Backup tapes
- A roll of paper towels
- A nice reference book, such as *PCs For Dummies,* 6th Edition (published by IDG Books Worldwide, Inc.)

...For Dummies: #1 Computer Book Series for Beginners

Important Questions to Ask a Potential Dealer (And Some Ideal Answers)

Q: Where do you fix your computers?

A: Right here or in your home or office!

Q: Can I phone up someone to ask questions?

A: Sure! At any time. Here's our 800 number!

Q: Do you offer classes?

A: Yes, we have our own classroom, and classes are free to anyone who buys our PCs!

Types of Support

Vanilla: You pay not only for the phone call but also for the support.

Chocolate: You pay only for the phone call.

Carob: You get free support, but you pay for the phone call for 90 days; after that, you pay for the support.

Fudge: Free phone call, free support, no time limit.

Questions to Help You Decide What You Want a Computer to Do

- ✔ What do you see yourself doing with your computer?
- ✔ How do you spend most of your time?
- ✔ Which activities are the most repetitive?
- ✔ Do you do anything that involves lists or organizing information?
- ✔ Do you ever sit with a calculator or typewriter for more than a few minutes each week?

...For Dummies: #1 Computer Book Series for Beginners

BUYING A
COMPUTER
FOR
DUMMIES®

BUYING A COMPUTER FOR DUMMIES®

by Dan Gookin

IDG Books Worldwide, Inc.
An International Data Group Company

Foster City, CA ♦ Chicago, IL ♦ Indianapolis, IN ♦ New York, NY

Buying A Computer For Dummies®

Published by
IDG Books Worldwide, Inc.
An International Data Group Company
919 E. Hillsdale Blvd.
Suite 400
Foster City, CA 94404
www.idgbooks.com (IDG Books Worldwide Web site)
www.dummies.com (Dummies Press Web site)

Library of Congress Catalog Card No.: 98-85845

ISBN: 0-7645-0313-8

Printed in the United States of America

10 9 8 7 6 5 4 3 2 1

1B/SZ/QW/ZY/IN

Distributed in the United States by IDG Books Worldwide, Inc.

Distributed by Macmillan Canada for Canada; by Transworld Publishers Limited in the United Kingdom; by IDG Norge Books for Norway; by IDG Sweden Books for Sweden; by Woodslane Pty. Ltd. for Australia; by Woodslane (NZ) Ltd. for New Zealand; by Addison Wesley Longman Singapore Pte Ltd. for Singapore, Malaysia, Thailand, Indonesia and Korea; by Norma Comunicaciones S.A. for Colombia; by Intersoft for South Africa; by International Thomson Publishing for Germany, Austria and Switzerland; by Toppan Company Ltd. for Japan; by Distribuidora Cuspide for Argentina; by Livraria Cultura for Brazil; by Ediciencia S.A. for Ecuador; by Ediciones ZETA S.C.R. Ltda. for Peru; by WS Computer Publishing Corporation, Inc., for the Philippines; by Unalis Corporation for Taiwan; by Contemporanea de Ediciones for Venezuela; by Computer Book & Magazine Store for Puerto Rico; by Express Computer Distributors for the Caribbean and West Indies. Authorized Sales Agent: Anthony Rudkin Associates for the Middle East and North Africa.

For general information on IDG Books Worldwide's books in the U.S., please call our Consumer Customer Service department at 800-762-2974. For reseller information, including discounts and premium sales, please call our Reseller Customer Service department at 800-434-3422.

For information on where to purchase IDG Books Worldwide's books outside the U.S., please contact our International Sales department at 650-655-3200 or fax 650-655-3297.

For information on foreign language translations, please contact our Foreign & Subsidiary Rights department at 650-655-3021 or fax 650-655-3281.

For sales inquiries and special prices for bulk quantities, please contact our Sales department at 650-655-3200 or write to the address above.

For information on using IDG Books Worldwide's books in the classroom or for ordering examination copies, please contact our Educational Sales department at 800-434-2086 or fax 317-596-5499.

For press review copies, author interviews, or other publicity information, please contact our Public Relations department at 650-655-3000 or fax 650-655-3299.

For authorization to photocopy items for corporate, personal, or educational use, please contact Copyright Clearance Center, 222 Rosewood Drive, Danvers, MA 01923, or fax 978-750-4470.

is a trademark under exclusive license to IDG Books Worldwide, Inc., from International Data Group, Inc.

IDG BOOKS WORLDWIDE

About the Author

Dan Gookin got started with computers back in the post-vacuum-tube age of computing: 1982. His first intention was to buy a computer to replace his aged and constantly breaking typewriter. Working as slave labor in a restaurant, however, Gookin was unable to afford the full "word processor" setup and settled on a computer that had a monitor, keyboard, and little else. Soon his writing career was under way with several submissions to fiction magazines and lots of rejections.

His big break came in 1984, when he began writing about computers. Applying his flair for fiction with a self-taught knowledge of computers, Gookin was able to demystify the subject and explain technology in a relaxed and understandable voice. He even dared to add humor, which eventually won him a column in a local computer magazine.

Eventually Gookin's talents came to roost as a ghostwriter at a computer book publishing house. That was followed by an editing position at a San Diego computer magazine. During this time, he also regularly participated in a radio talk show about computers. In addition, Gookin kept writing books about computers, some of which became minor bestsellers.

In 1990, Gookin came to IDG Books Worldwide with a book proposal. From that initial meeting unfolded an idea for an outrageous book: a long overdue and original idea for the computer book for the rest of us. What became *DOS For Dummies* blossomed into an international bestseller with hundreds of thousands of copies in print and in many translations.

Today, Gookin still considers himself a writer and computer "guru" whose job it is to remind everyone that computers are not to be taken too seriously. His approach to computers is light and humorous yet very informative. He knows that the complex beasts are important and can help people become productive and successful. Gookin mixes his knowledge of computers with a unique, dry sense of humor that keeps everyone informed — and awake. His favorite quote is "Computers are a notoriously dull subject, but that doesn't mean I have to write about them that way."

Gookin's titles for IDG Books Worldwide include the best-selling *DOS For Dummies, PCs For Dummies, Word For Windows For Dummies,* and *The Illustrated Computer Dictionary For Dummies.* All told, he has written more than 80 books about computers. Gookin holds a degree in communications from the University of California, San Diego, and lives with his wife and four boys in the wilds of Idaho.

You can e-mail Dan on the Internet: dang@idgbooks.com.

ABOUT IDG BOOKS WORLDWIDE

Welcome to the world of IDG Books Worldwide.

IDG Books Worldwide, Inc., is a subsidiary of International Data Group, the world's largest publisher of computer-related information and the leading global provider of information services on information technology. IDG was founded more than 25 years ago and now employs more than 8,500 people worldwide. IDG publishes more than 275 computer publications in over 75 countries (see listing below). More than 90 million people read one or more IDG publications each month.

Launched in 1990, IDG Books Worldwide is today the #1 publisher of best-selling computer books in the United States. We are proud to have received eight awards from the Computer Press Association in recognition of editorial excellence and three from *Computer Currents'* First Annual Readers' Choice Awards. Our best-selling *...For Dummies*® series has more than 50 million copies in print with translations in 38 languages. IDG Books Worldwide, through a joint venture with IDG's Hi-Tech Beijing, became the first U.S. publisher to publish a computer book in the People's Republic of China. In record time, IDG Books Worldwide has become the first choice for millions of readers around the world who want to learn how to better manage their businesses.

Our mission is simple: Every one of our books is designed to bring extra value and skill-building instructions to the reader. Our books are written by experts who understand and care about our readers. The knowledge base of our editorial staff comes from years of experience in publishing, education, and journalism — experience we use to produce books for the '90s. In short, we care about books, so we attract the best people. We devote special attention to details such as audience, interior design, use of icons, and illustrations. And because we use an efficient process of authoring, editing, and desktop publishing our books electronically, we can spend more time ensuring superior content and spend less time on the technicalities of making books.

You can count on our commitment to deliver high-quality books at competitive prices on topics you want to read about. At IDG Books Worldwide, we continue in the IDG tradition of delivering quality for more than 25 years. You'll find no better book on a subject than one from IDG Books Worldwide.

John Kilcullen
CEO
IDG Books Worldwide, Inc.

Steven Berkowitz
President and Publisher
IDG Books Worldwide, Inc.

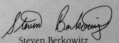

VIII WINNER
Eighth Annual Computer Press Awards ≥1992

IX WINNER
Ninth Annual Computer Press Awards ≥1993

X WINNER
Tenth Annual Computer Press Awards ≥1994

XI WINNER
Eleventh Annual Computer Press Awards ≥1995

IDG Books Worldwide, Inc., is a subsidiary of International Data Group, the world's largest publisher of computer-related information and the leading global provider of information services on information technology. International Data Group publishes over 275 computer publications in over 75 countries. More than 90 million people read one or more International Data Group publications each month. International Data Group's publications include: **ARGENTINA:** Buyer's Guide, Computerworld Argentina, PC World Argentina; **AUSTRALIA:** Australian Macworld, Australian PC World, Australian Reseller News, Computerworld, IT Casebook, Network World, Publish, Webmaster; **AUSTRIA:** Computerwelt Osterreich, Networks Austria, PC Tip Austria; **BANGLADESH:** PC World Bangladesh; **BELARUS:** PC World Belarus; **BELGIUM:** Data News; **BRAZIL:** Annuário de Informática, Computerworld, Connections, Macworld, PC Player, PC World, Publish, Reseller News, Supergamepower; **BULGARIA:** Computerworld Bulgaria, Network World Bulgaria, PC & MacWorld Bulgaria; **CANADA:** CIO Canada, Client/Server World, ComputerWorld Canada, InfoWorld Canada, NetworkWorld Canada, WebWorld; **CHILE:** Computerworld Chile, PC World Chile; **COLOMBIA:** Computerworld Colombia, PC World Colombia; **COSTA RICA:** PC World Centro America; **THE CZECH AND SLOVAK REPUBLICS:** Computerworld Czechoslovakia, Macworld Czech Republic, PC World Czechoslovakia; **DENMARK:** Communications World Danmark, Computerworld Danmark, Macworld Danmark, PC World Danmark, Techworld Danmark; **DOMINICAN REPUBLIC:** PC World Republica Dominicana; **ECUADOR:** PC World Ecuador; **EGYPT:** Computerworld Middle East, PC World Middle East; **EL SALVADOR:** PC World Centro America; **FINLAND:** MikroPC, Tietoverkko, Tietoviikko; **FRANCE:** Distributique, Hebdo, Info PC, Le Monde Informatique, Macworld, Reseaux & Telecoms, WebMaster France; **GERMANY:** Computer Partner, Computerwoche, Computerwoche Extra, Computerwoche FOCUS, Global Online, Macwelt, PC Welt; **GREECE:** Amiga Computing, GamePro Greece, Multimedia World; **GUATEMALA:** PC World Centro America; **HONDURAS:** PC World Centro America; **HONG KONG:** Computerworld Hong Kong, PC World Hong Kong, Publish in Asia; **HUNGARY:** ABCD CD-ROM, Computerworld Szamitastechnika, Internetto online Magazine, PC World Hungary, PC-X Magazin Hungary; **ICELAND:** Tolvuheimur PC World Island; **INDIA:** Information Communications World, Information Systems Computerworld, PC World India, Publish in Asia; **INDONESIA:** InfoKomputer PC World, Komputek Computerworld, Publish in Asia; **IRELAND:** ComputerScope, PC Live!; **ISRAEL:** Macworld Israel, People & Computers/Computerworld; **ITALY:** Computerworld Italia, Macworld Italia, Networking Italia, PC World Italia; **JAPAN:** DTP World, Macworld Japan, Nikkei Personal Computing, OS/2 World Japan, SunWorld Japan, Windows NT World, Windows World Japan; **KENYA:** PC World East African; **KOREA:** Hi-Tech Information, Macworld Korea, PC World Korea; **MACEDONIA:** PC World Macedonia; **MALAYSIA:** Computerworld Malaysia, PC World Malaysia, Publish in Asia; **MALTA:** PC World Malta; **MEXICO:** Computerworld Mexico, PC World Mexico; **MYANMAR:** PC World Myanmar; **NETHERLANDS:** Computer! Totaal, LAN Internetworking Magazine, LAN World Buyers Guide, Macworld Netherlands, Net, WebWereld; **NEW ZEALAND:** Absolute Beginners Guide and Plain & Simple Series, Computer Buyer, Computer Industry Directory, Computerworld New Zealand, MTB, Network World, PC World New Zealand; **NICARAGUA:** PC World Centro America; **NORWAY:** Computerworld Norge, CW Rapport, Datamagasinet, Financial Rapport, Kursguide Norge, Macworld Norge, Multimediaworld Norge, PC World Ekspress Norge, PC World Nettverk, PC World Norge, PC World ProduktGuide Norge; **PAKISTAN:** Computerworld Pakistan; **PANAMA:** PC World Panama; **PEOPLE'S REPUBLIC OF CHINA:** China Computer Users, China Computerworld, China InfoWorld, China Telecom World Weekly, Computer & Communication, Electronic Design China, Electronics Today, Electronics Weekly, Game Software, PC World China, Popular Computer Week, Software Weekly, Software World, Telecom World; **PERU:** Computerworld Peru, PC World Profesional Peru, PC World SoHo Peru; **PHILIPPINES:** Click!, Computerworld Philippines, PC World Philippines, Publish in Asia; **POLAND:** Computerworld Poland, Computerworld Special Report Poland, Cyber, Macworld Poland, Networld Poland, PC World Komputer; **PORTUGAL:** Cerebro/PC World, Computerworld/Correio Informático, Dealer World Portugal, Mac*In/PC*In Portugal, Multimedia World; **PUERTO RICO:** PC World Puerto Rico; **ROMANIA:** Computerworld Romania, PC World Romania, Telecom Romania; **RUSSIA:** Computerworld Russia, Mir PK, Publish, Seti; **SINGAPORE:** Computerworld Singapore, PC World Singapore, Publish in Asia; **SLOVENIA:** Monitor; **SOUTH AFRICA:** Computing SA, Network World SA, Software World SA; **SPAIN:** Communicaciones World España, Computerworld España, Dealer World España, Macworld España, PC World España; **SRI LANKA:** Infolink PC World; **SWEDEN:** CAP&Design, Computer Sweden, Corporate Computing Sweden, Internetworld Sweden, it.branschen, Macworld Sweden, MaxiData Sweden, MikroDatorn, Nätverk & Kommunikation, PC World Sweden, PCaktiv, Windows World Sweden; **SWITZERLAND:** Computerworld Schweiz, Macworld Schweiz, PCtip; **TAIWAN:** Computerworld Taiwan, Macworld Taiwan, NEW ViSiON/Publish, PC World Taiwan, Windows World Taiwan; **THAILAND:** Publish in Asia, Thai Computerworld; **TURKEY:** Computerworld Turkiye, Macworld Turkiye, Network World Turkiye, PC World Turkiye; **UKRAINE:** Computerworld Kiev, Multimedia World Ukraine, PC World Ukraine; **UNITED KINGDOM:** Acorn User UK, Amiga Action UK, Amiga Computing UK, Apple Talk UK, Computing, Macworld, Parents and Computers UK, PC Advisor, PC Home, PSX Pro, The WEB; **UNITED STATES:** Cable in the Classroom, CIO Magazine, Computerworld, DOS World, Federal Computer Week, GamePro Magazine, InfoWorld, I-Way, Macworld, Network World, PC Games, PC World, Publish, Video Event, THE WEB Magazine, and WebMaster; online webzines: JavaWorld, NetscapeWorld, and SunWorld Online; **URUGUAY:** InfoWorld Uruguay; **VENEZUELA:** Computerworld Venezuela, PC World Venezuela; and **VIETNAM:** PC World Vietnam. 5/7/98

Author's Acknowledgments

This book has existed in many forms over the past ten years. Originally it was a pamphlet published by *Byte Buyer,* in San Diego, California. My thanks go to Jack Dunning and Tina Rathbone, for their assistance with that edition, called *How to Understand and Buy Computers*.

Several years ago, it became another book, *Buy That Computer!* (published by IDG Books Worldwide). I'd like to thank John Kilcullen, for picking up the idea. Thanks also go to David Solomon, for his input and wisdom.

Other thanks go to Chris Wagner, Jerry Hewett, Al Telles, Ken Jacobson, and Sandy Gookin (wife unit), for various contributions through the years. Thanks also to Takara, for the best sushi in northern Idaho. Finally, thanks to all the readers through the years who have written to me or phoned me up on the radio to ask questions about computers. It's those questions that keep me in touch with what people really need. I hope this book doesn't disappoint.

Publisher's Acknowledgments

We're proud of this book; please register your comments through our IDG Books Worldwide Online Registration Form located at http://my2cents.dummies.com.

Some of the people who helped bring this book to market include the following:

Acquisitions, Editorial, and Media Development

Project Editor: Rebecca Whitney

Acquisitions Editor: Michael Kelly

Technical Editor: Bill Karow

Editorial Manager: Mary C. Corder

Editorial Assistant: Paul E. Kuzmic

Production

Project Coordinators: Regina Snyder, Karen York

Layout and Graphics: Lou Boudreau, Linda M. Boyer, J. Tyler Connor, Angela F. Hunckler, Anna Rohrer, Brent Savage, Michael A. Sullivan

Proofreaders: Kelli Botta, Vickie Broyles, Nancy Price, Rebecca Senninger, Janet M. Withers

Indexer: Ann Norcross

General and Administrative

IDG Books Worldwide, Inc.: John Kilcullen, CEO; Steven Berkowitz, President and Publisher

IDG Books Technology Publishing: Brenda McLaughlin, Senior Vice President and Group Publisher

Dummies Technology Press and Dummies Editorial: Diane Graves Steele, Vice President and Associate Publisher; Mary Bednarek, Director of Acquisitions and Product Development; Kristin A. Cocks, Editorial Director

Dummies Trade Press: Kathleen A. Welton, Vice President and Publisher; Kevin Thornton, Acquisitions Manager

IDG Books Production for Dummies Press: Michael R. Britton, Vice President of Production; Beth Jenkins Roberts, Production Director; Cindy L. Phipps, Manager of Project Coordination, Production Proofreading, and Indexing; Kathie S. Schutte, Supervisor of Page Layout; Shelley Lea, Supervisor of Graphics and Design; Debbie J. Gates, Production Systems Specialist; Robert Springer, Supervisor of Proofreading; Debbie Stailey, Special Projects Coordinator; Tony Augsburger, Supervisor of Reprints and Bluelines

Dummies Packaging and Book Design: Robin Seaman, Creative Director; Jocelyn Kelaita, Product Packaging Coordinator; Kavish + Kavish, Cover Design

◆

The publisher would like to give special thanks to Patrick J. McGovern, without whom this book would not have been possible.

◆

Contents at a Glance

Introduction 1

Part I: Buy That Computer! 5
Chapter 1: Some Questions to Get Out of the Way 7
Chapter 2: How to Buy a Computer 13
Chapter 3: "What Can a Computer Do for Me?" 23
Chapter 4: Understanding Hardware and Software 29

Part II: Understanding Hardware 37
Chapter 5: All about Mr. Microprocessor 39
Chapter 6: Memory Stuff (Temporary Storage) 47
Chapter 7: Disks of Every Type(Permanent Storage) 55
Chapter 8: The Monitor, Keyboard, and Mouse 67
Chapter 9: Expansion Options 77
Chapter 10: Gizmos Galore 87
Chapter 11: All about Printers 93
Chapter 12: Put It in a Box 101

Part III: Software Overview 109
Chapter 13: Your Computer's Operating System 111
Chapter 14: Everything You Wanted to Know about Software
(But Were Afraid to Ask) 119

Part IV: The Buying Process 135
Chapter 15: Shopping for Software 137
Chapter 16: Matching Hardware to Your Software 151
Chapter 17: Where to Buy? 161
Chapter 18: Shopping for Service and Support 175
Chapter 19: Buying Your Computer — Go for It! 181

Part V: You and Your New PC 187
Chapter 20: Setting Up Your New PC 189
Chapter 21: When to Buy, When to Sell, When to Upgrade 197

Part VI: The Part of Tens 205
Chapter 22: Ten Common Mistakes First-Time Computer Buyers Make ... 207
Chapter 23: Ten Warning Signs 211
Chapter 24: Ten Other Things You Should Buy 215
Chapter 25: Ten Tips and Suggestions 221

*Appendix: Commonly Asked Questions and
Their Answers* 225

Index 263

Book Registration Information .... *Back of Book*

Cartoons at a Glance

By Rich Tennant

Fax: 978-546-7747 • E-mail: the5wave@tiac.net

Table of Contents

• •

Introduction 1
About This Book 1
And Just Who Are You? 2
Icons Used in This Book 2
Where to Go from Here 3

Part I: Buy That Computer! 5

Chapter 1: Some Questions to Get Out of the Way 7
"Just Tell Me Which Type of Computer I Need!" 7
"Why Not Let Me Have One of Your Computers?" 8
"Where Can I Buy a Computer Really Cheap?" 8
"Which Brands Do You Recommend?" 8
"Which Brands Do You Recommend Staying Away From?" 8
"How Much Will My Computer Cost?" 8
"Shouldn't I Just Buy the Most Expensive Computer I Can Afford?" 9
"Then Shouldn't I Buy the Fastest Computer I Can Afford?" 9
"Should I Get a Used Computer?" 9
"What about Refab Computers?" 9
"How about Buying a Laptop?" 9
"How Much Less Than the 'Sticker Price' Should I Expect to Pay?
   (Or Can I Get 'a Deal'?)" 10
"Where Can I Get More Information beyond What's Covered in
   This Book?" 10
"Does This Book Offer a Buyer's Guide?" 10
"Can You Recommend Any Buyer's Guides?" 10
"Isn't There an Easy Way to Do This? Can't I Just Go Out and Buy
   a Computer?" 11

Chapter 2: How to Buy a Computer 13
The Five Steps to Buying a Computer 14
Step 1: What Do You Want to Do with Your Computer? 15
Step 2: Looking for Software 16
Step 3: Finding Hardware 16
Step 4: Shopping for Service and Support 19
Step 5: Buying Your Computer 20
Don't Sit Around Waiting for the Technology Bus! 20
Stuff to Remember 20

Chapter 3: "What Can a Computer Do for Me?" 23

Knowing Which Questions to Ask 23
  The best question to ask 24
  Another, worthy question 24
  The "Okay, I'm really stuck" questions 25
Understanding Your Computer's Potential 26
Stuff to Remember 27

Chapter 4: Understanding Hardware and Software 29

Hardware: The Hard Stuff 29
  The microprocessor (the main piece of hardware) 30
  Basic hardware 31
Software, the Other Hard Stuff 32
  The operating system 32
  Applications and other programs 33
Putting It All Together 34
Stuff to Remember 34

Part II: Understanding Hardware 37

Chapter 5: All about Mr. Microprocessor 39

Get Yourself the Latest Pentium Microprocessor 39
Microprocessor Speed (Or "If Mega Stubs His Toe, Then Megahertz") 40
The Whole MMX Deal 41
Some Microprocessor Q&A for You 42
  What does "386 or greater" mean? 42
  If software says that it requires a 486 or later, does that include
    a Pentium? 43
  Are all Pentium processors the same? 43
  Should I buy an upgradable microprocessor option? 43
  What about those "math coprocessors?" 44
  What's the "OverDrive" chip? 44
  What's Turbo? 44
  What's the cache? 45
Stuff to Remember 45

Chapter 6: Memory Stuff (Temporary Storage) 47

Say Hello to Mr. Byte 47
Banks o' Memory (RAM) 49
  Some unimportant technical memory terms 50
  Back to the memory banks 51
Stuff to Remember 52

Chapter 7: Disks of Every Type (Permanent Storage) 55

All about Disk Storage 56
Get Yourself a Hard Disk Drive 56
How much stuff does it hold? 58
How fast does it go? 59
The secret hard drive controller 60
Gotta Have a Floppy Drive Too 61
CD-ROMs 62
CD-ROM speeds 62
Other CD-ROM stuff 63
Stuff to Remember 65

Chapter 8: The Monitor, Keyboard, and Mouse 67

The Monitor ("Look at Me! I'm As Pretty As a Trinitron TV!") 67
Judging a monitor by its size 68
Selecting the proper graphics adapter 69
Read them labels! 71
Keyboards 72
Standard keyboards 73
Nonstandard keyboards 73
Mice and Other Nonfurry "Pointing Devices" 74
Types of computer mice 74
Mouse software 76
Stuff to Remember 76

Chapter 9: Expansion Options 77

Connecting Stuff by Using Ports 77
The printer port 78
The serial port 79
The joystick/MIDI port 81
The SCSI port 81
A Full House of Cards 82
Slots-a-fun 83
A special bus-port thing for laptops 84
Stuff to Remember 85

Chapter 10: Gizmos Galore 87

Modems 87
Will your modem live inside or outside your PC? 88
Going faster and faster 89
Sound Options 90
Tape Backup Gizmos 91
Stuff to Remember 92

Chapter 11: All about Printers **93**

Different Printers for Different Printing 93
    How much? 94
    Things that affect a printer's price 94
    Printers do not come with cables (or paper)! 96
Laser Printers Go "Fwoom Pkt Shhh!" 97
Ink Printers Go "Thwip, Sft-Sft-Sft, Clunk!" 98
Impact Printers Go "Rrrrrrrrtttttteeee!" 98
Fax Printers Go "Slowly" 99
Stuff to Remember 100

Chapter 12: Put It in a Box **101**

Computers for Every Mood 101
    The standard desktop model 102
    The small-footprint PC 102
    The tower 103
    The minitower 104
Not Really PCs 105
    Too small to see or type on 105
    Laptops and notebooks 106
Stuff to Remember 108

Part III: Software Overview *109*

Chapter 13: Your Computer's Operating System **111**

Understanding Operating Systems 111
Choosing an Operating System 112
    Check that software base! 113
    How friendly is it? 114
    Windows 98 versus Windows NT 115
    Operating systems other than Windows 116
Stuff to Remember 117

**Chapter 14: Everything You Wanted to Know about Software
(But Were Afraid to Ask)** **119**

Applications, Categories, and Programs 120
Word Processors 120
Desktop Publishing 122
Spreadsheets 122
Databases 123
Graphics 124
Bundled Software Packages 125
    Meanwhile, the back-at-the-office type of integrated program 126
    Bundled software 126

Communications and Internet Software 127
    Doing the Internet 127
    Regular old telecommunications 128
Recreation and Education 129
    Games 129
    Education 130
Utility Programs 130
Programming 131
Software for Free and Almost Free 132
    Public-domain software 133
    Freeware 133
    Shareware 133
    Demo software 134
Stuff to Remember 134

Part IV: The Buying Process 135

Chapter 15: Shopping for Software 137

How to Buy Software 137
    Taking a test-drive 138
    Other sources for test-driving 139
Helpful Hints 139
    Types of help you find in software 140
    Don't forget support! 140
After You Find What You Want. 142
    Stuff you find on the software box 142
    Things to look out for in software descriptions 143
    Filling in the form example #1 144
    Filling in the form example #2 146
    At last: The software worksheet 148
Stuff to Remember 150

Chapter 16: Matching Hardware to Your Software 151

The ...*For Dummies* Hardware Worksheet 151
Filling in the Worksheet (Step-by-Step) 153
    Choose an operating system 153
    Pick a microprocessor 154
    Calculate your memory needs 154
    Calculate your hard drive storage 155
    Do you need SCSI? 156
    More storage decisions 156
    Various stuff 157
    Pick a printer 158
A Sample for You to Review 159
Stuff to Remember 159

Chapter 17: Where to Buy? **161**

Reading a Computer Ad 161
Finding computer advertisements 162
Dissecting an ad 162
Looking at a buying grid 164
Recognizing common tricks used to make an advertised price
look really cheap 164
Some Q&A before You Rush Out to Buy 166
"Should I get a quote?" 166
"Can I haggle?" 166
"Should I get a discount off the manufacturer's suggested
retail price?" 166
"Isn't there any way to get a deal on a computer?" 167
"Is it better to buy from a noncommissioned salesperson?" 167
"What about buying a used computer?" 167
"What about refurbished stuff?" 167
"You didn't say anything about the swap meet" 168
Where to Buy.. 168
Your locally owned and operated computer store 168
National chains 169
The megastore 170
Mail-order brand names 170
Mail-order pieces' parts 171
Buying on the World Wide Web 172
Stuff to Remember 173

Chapter 18: Shopping for Service and Support.................................... **175**

How to Find Service and Support 175
Service Questions 176
"How long is your warranty?" 176
"Do you fix the computers here?" 176
"Do you fix the computer at my home or at the office?" 176
Support Questions 177
"Can I phone someone to ask questions?" 177
"Do you offer classes?" 178
Stuff to Remember 179

Chapter 19: Buying Your Computer — Go for It! **181**

A Review 181
What to Spend "Extra" Money On 182
"When Do I Get My PC?" 183
Don't Ever Put a "Deposit" on a Computer!............................... 183
Hey, Bud! You're Ready to Buy 184
A few last-minute buying tips 184
The final step is to. 185
Stuff to Remember 185

Part V: You and Your New PC *187*

Chapter 20: Setting Up Your New PC 189

Setting Up Your PC 189
    Finding all the pieces' parts 190
    "Do I have to read the manuals?" 190
Finding a Place for Mr. PC 190
Putting the PC Together 191
    Preparing to plug things in 191
    Plugging things in 192
    Turning it on for the first time 192
    Turning it off 193
Breaking It In: The "Burn-In" Test 195
Understanding Your System 195

Chapter 21: When to Buy, When to Sell, When to Upgrade 197

Unlike Wine, PCs Don't Age Well 197
Should You Upgrade? 198
    Which hardware to upgrade first 198
    My $.02 on upgrading your microprocessor 200
    Upgrading software 200
    Upgrading your operating system 201
Should You Sell Your Beloved PC? 201
Buying a Used Computer 202

Part VI: The Part of Tens *205*

Chapter 22: Ten Common Mistakes First-Time
Computer Buyers Make 207

Not Knowing What It Is That You Want the Computer to Do 207
Buying Hardware Rather Than Software 208
Shopping for the Cheapest Computer System in Town 208
Being Unprepared for the Sale 208
Forgetting Some Extra Items 208
Not Paying By Credit Card 209
Not Reading the Setup Manuals 209
Forgetting That Software Is Expensive 209
Not Looking for a Printer 209
Buying Too Much 210
Not Counting Learning Time 210

Chapter 23: Ten Warning Signs **211**

Industry "Standards" versus the Ads 211
Out-of-Date Stock 212
Money Down Required 212
Missing Pieces 212
No Address in the Mail-Order Ad 213
Salespeople Too Busy to Help or Answer Questions 213
Salespeople in the Store Ignore You 213
No Classroom 214
No Software Documentation Is Sold with the Computer 214

Chapter 24: Ten Other Things You Should Buy **215**

Mousepad and Wristpad 215
Power Strip 216
Surge Protector 217
UPS 217
Printer Cable 217
Printer Paper 218
More Ink Stuff 218
Modem Cable 219
Floppy Disks 219
Backup Tapes 219
A Roll of Paper Towels 220

Chapter 25: Ten Tips and Suggestions **221**

Your Computer Has a Clock 221
Get a Second Phone Line 222
After a Spell, Reread Your Manuals 222
Put a Timer on That Internet 222
Get Internet Antiporn Software 223
Subscribe to a Computer Magazine 223
Join a Computer Users' Group 223
Buy a Great Book 223
Don't Let the Computer Ruin Your Life 224
Don't Let the Computer Run Your Life 224

Appendix: Commonly Asked Questions and Their Answers **225**

Software 225
Operating Systems 226
Bits and Bytes and RAM 226
Disk Drives 227

Monitors and Keyboards 227
Printers and Peripherals 228
Computer Systems 229
General 231

Index *263*

Book Registration Information .... *Back of Book*

Introduction

· ·

Welcome to *Buying A Computer For Dummies* — a book which assumes that you know *nothing* about a computer but are strangely compelled to buy one. If that's you, you have found your book!

This book is not a buyer's guide. In it, you won't find endless, boring lists of prices and products and useless part numbers. Instead, this book assumes that you need a computer for some reason. You'll discover that reason and then read about how to find software to carry out that task. From there, you'll match hardware to your software and end up with the PC that's perfect for you.

Because this is a *...For Dummies* book, you can expect some lively and entertaining writing — not boring computer jargon. Nothing is assumed. Everything is explained. The result is that you'll have your own computer and actually enjoy the buying process.

About This Book

Unlike most typical *...For Dummies* books, this one really is meant to be read from front to back. Everything follows in a logical progression when you buy a PC. Although you can skip over chapters or start reading at any point, the information in later chapters does build on the stuff explained earlier.

Buying a computer is a five-step process, which this book fully explains. Along the way, you'll read about computer hardware and software and fill in some worksheets that help you configure a computer just for you.

The five steps to buying a computer are outlined in Chapter 2. Before that, Chapter 1 answers some questions you may have before you decide to embark on a computer-buying mission. After that, the book is divided into several parts, each of which occurs at a different stage in the buying process:

Part I overviews the buying process.

Part II discusses computer hardware: what it is and why you need it.

Part III covers computer software, which is more important than the hardware when it comes to buying a PC.

Part IV details the buying process: where to buy, how to read a computer ad, and how to find service and support before the sale.

Part V deals with setting up your new PC.

Part VI is the traditional ...*For Dummies* "Part of Tens" — various lists for review or to help you get on your way.

This book also has a Q&A appendix for any lingering questions you may have.

And Just Who Are You?

Let me assume that you're a human being who wants to own a computer. You probably don't have one now, or, if you do, it's very, *very* old and you desire a new one. Other than that, your experience with a computer is very limited. You've heard the jargon and know some brand names, but that's about it. If that's you, then this is your book.

This book concentrates on buying a PC, otherwise known as an IBM-compatible computer or a Windows computer. Although all the information does apply to buying *any* computer, the main thrust involves buying a PC. Some Macintosh information is scattered throughout, and I urge everyone to try Mac software when they go software hunting. Aside from that, 85 percent of this book is about buying a PC.

Icons Used in This Book

Lets you know that something technical is being mentioned. Because it's technical, and written primarily as nerd trivia, you can freely skip the information if you want.

Flags useful information or a helpful tip. When you're visiting the computer store, for example, make sure that you leave with the same number of children you had when you arrived.

Something to remember, like all computers need a monitor or else you'll never see what it is you're doing.

Oops! Better watch out. You have lots of warnings to heed when you're buying a computer. This icon lets you find them right quick.

Check out this nutshell summary of the important points in each chapter.

Where to Go from Here

Steadily grab this book with both hands, and start reading at Chapter 1. Then continue reading. Occasionally, you may be asked to visit a computer store or find a computer advertisement. Do so when asked. Fill in the worksheets that are offered. Then get ready to go out and buy yourself a computer.

Part I
Buy That Computer!

The 5th Wave   By Rich Tennant

"I don't think this new salesman is going to work out."

In this part . . .

*I*t wasn't hard to buy the toaster. And the microwave oven was easy: It had a Cook Popcorn button on it. The VCR was harder because the salesman told me that I really need SurroundSound yet our TV has only one speaker hole. And cars, well, you just kick the tires and ask for about $1,000 off or a higher price on your trade-in. But a computer?

Unlike other stuff you may buy, a computer has lots of uses. And lots of uses means (unfortunately) lots of buttons, none of which says Write Report or Get on the Internet or even Cook Popcorn. So you don't even need me to tell you that finding a computer to match your needs won't be easy. It's possible, but you need some help and soothing words of advice along the way. That's why this book was written.

Finding a computer that works best with you is what this book is all about. And, as long as you absorb the information in this book, buying yourself a computer will be a snap. This part of the book provides an overview of the simple five-step process and offers some necessary background information. That's enough to get you started on your way to owning your own computer.

Chapter 1

Some Questions to Get Out of the Way

In This Chapter

▶ Answers to your most important questions

▶ Nothing more

*I*f you're like me, you hate to wade through page after page of mindless drivel about this or that — you just want to get to the meat of the situation. In this case, you probably have some questions you want answered right away. Well, here are the answers. (The mindless drivel starts in the next chapter.)

"Just Tell Me Which Type of Computer I Need!"

Sorry, can't do that. Because everyone is different, everyone needs something a little different in their computers. Although it's true that you could get by with just about any computer, why settle for something less than what you need? This book shows you how to find a computer especially for you.

Think of it like a car. You may say, "I want a new car." But which type? A sedan? A truck? How big of an engine do you want? What about good gas mileage? Do you want to pay extra for power seats or heated outside mirrors? And — most importantly — what *color* do you want? Because computers are more complex than cars, you have even more personal decisions to make.

"Why Not Let Me Have One of Your Computers?"

Because you probably don't do what I do. Also, I can't send you any of my old computers because I'm fresh out of stamps.

"Where Can I Buy a Computer Really Cheap?"

All over. But do you *want* cheap? How about getting service and support instead? You need that more than you need to save a few bucks off the purchase price.

"Which Brands Do You Recommend?"

None. Brands are irrelevant in buying a computer. And brand names and part numbers change all the time. Looking at a brand name for a computer should be the *last* thing you do when you buy one. This book explains why. If you feel better buying a major brand-name computer, however, then by all means go ahead.

"Which Brands Do You Recommend Staying Away From?"

Specifically those companies that would take me to court for mentioning their names! Seriously, brand names are irrelevant. Some do have ugly reputations. Ask around or read the paper for some companies that produce crap, if that's what you're trying to avoid.

"How Much Will My Computer Cost?"

Anywhere from $600 on up to several thousand dollars, depending on which options you need or the size of your credit limit. Obviously, if you're spending someone else's money, you want to pay more for your computer.

"Shouldn't I Just Buy the Most Expensive Computer I Can Afford?"

No. Why pay for something you won't use? Expensive computers tend to fall into a category known as "file server." These beefed-up monsters are designed to run full computer networks for small- to medium-size businesses. You probably don't need one.

"Then Shouldn't I Buy the Fastest Computer I Can Afford?"

Yes, although speed is only a small part of the overall computer equation that includes storage, peripherals and other options, plus all the software you need to get your work done. Besides, this question of speed doesn't need to be answered until just before you're ready to buy. Although the advertisements boast of a computer's speed, you need to ignore that part for now.

"Should I Get a Used Computer?"

I don't recommend getting a used computer as a first computer purchase.

"What about Refab Computers?"

They're okay, as long as they come with a warranty and proper service and support.

"How about Buying a Laptop?"

I know many people who buy laptops as a second PC, primarily because they're portable. (And it's fun to take your work to a coffee shop once in awhile.) Some businesses have their sales force or folks who travel frequently use laptop PCs. A laptop is a niche computer, however, designed for specific purposes. If your travel is related to your business, odds are that your company will give you a laptop. Otherwise, I recommend buying a normal, desktop computer first. Worry about getting a laptop later.

"How Much Less Than the 'Sticker Price' Should I Expect to Pay? (Or Can I Get 'a Deal'?)"

The days of wheeling and dealing computers are long over — unless you're buying several dozen of them at a time. The advertised price is most often the price you pay, though if you can find a competitor who offers a lower price, some dealers will give you a discount. You really shouldn't be shopping price, though. This book tells you why.

"Where Can I Get More Information beyond What's Covered in This Book?"

Three places. First, ask your friends or coworkers who are into computers. Second, look in your newspaper for local computer users' group meetings. These meetings are geared toward beginners and not technical people (which is what you would expect). Third, pick up an informative magazine to find out what's new and gather some how-tos. Unlike books, magazines offer current information. A good one to try is *PC Novice* magazine. Try to avoid the techy magazines for now; the large magazines that are all ads don't help you until you're ready to buy.

"Does This Book Offer a Buyer's Guide?"

Nope.

"Can You Recommend Any Buyer's Guides?"

Not really. Buyer's guides are for the old hands at buying a computer, folks who really care about part numbers and bolt sizes. Unless you know of a buyer's guide that says "Hey! I'm perfect for you" after one of the entries, you don't really need one.

"Isn't There an Easy Way to Do This? Can't I Just Go Out and Buy a Computer?"

Sure, why not? But you bought this book because you wanted to buy the best personal computer for you — not just an off-the-shelf unit that may not meet your needs or (worse) a computer that's packed with stuff you pay for but never use.

Chapter 2
How to Buy a Computer

• •

In This Chapter

▶ The five steps to buying a computer

▶ Step 1: Decide what you want the computer to do

▶ Step 2: Find software to get that job done

▶ Step 3: Find hardware to make the software go

▶ Step 4: Shop for service and support

▶ Step 5: Buy that computer!

• •

*H*ollywood may not have done it yet, although I'll bet that a really scary movie could be made about the typical computer-buying experience. I'm talking true, solid horror here. The tragic part of it all is that it doesn't have to be that bad.

Sure, computer jargon will always exist. You can easily avoid the uncertainty and doubt surrounding the computer-buying process, however. Just like buying anything, the more you know about what you're buying, the better a buyer you are. That's the purpose of this book, although the essence of buying a computer is explained in the five simple steps outlined in this chapter.

✔ I should tell you up front that the biggest mistake people make in buying a computer is shopping price and not service. Although lots of places will sell you the cheapest PC in the universe, don't expect them to offer much after-sale support.

✔ Yes, you need support.

✔ The second biggest mistake is shopping for hardware before shopping for software. (Chapter 3 explains why that is true.)

✔ Though you can use this book to help you find a nice used computer, I don't recommend buying one as your first PC. Why? No support. (See Chapter 18.)

The Five Steps to Buying a Computer

If you want to buy the perfect computer, the one Santa would have given you had you been good all year, then you should follow these five simple steps:

1. Decide what you want the computer to do.

2. Find the software that will get you the result you want.

3. Find the hardware to run your software.

4. Shop for service and support.

5. Buy that computer!

As many reasons exist for considering buying a personal computer as people to think up the reasons. And owning a computer brings more benefits to you than could possibly be listed — even by a computer. So you have no excuse for not having completed Step 1. When you have that task done, the rest of the steps fall nicely into place.

Most people confuse Steps 2 and 3. A common mistake is looking at computer hardware rather than software. The truth is that you buy a computer to get work done, not to support some major brand-name manufacturer. It's the software part of a computer that gets the work done.

Step 4 is the most important — more important than buying the computer (which is Step 5). Too many computer buyers overlook service and support and regret it later.

Finally, Step 5 involves buying the computer. Although this statement would seem obvious, I know lots of folks who put off the purchase, holding out for a better deal or newer technology that's just "moments away." Bah! When you're ready to buy, buy. 'Nuff said.

- ✔ If you haven't already decided what a computer can do for you, browse through Chapter 14 to see what the little beasties are capable of.

- ✔ The *software* gets the work done. You buy hardware to support the software you've chosen.

- ✔ "Service" means getting the computer fixed. Support means getting H-E-L-P when you need it. *Everyone* needs service and support with a new PC. Everyone.

- ✔ The rest of this chapter amplifies the five basic steps. The rest of this book tells you how to accomplish them and end up with your own, very best personal computer.

Step 1: What Do You Want to Do with Your Computer?

The first step toward buying your own computer is to decide what you want to do with it. You buy a car to avoid the burden of walking long distances. You buy a phone so that you don't have to live near everyone you know. And you buy dental floss because you're over 30. But a computer?

Well? What do you see yourself doing on a computer?

Computers aren't like aquariums or the television: They come with no prepackaged entertainment value (though the fish on a computer screen never seem to die). Instead, it's up to *you* to figure out what it is you want the computer to do. Only when you know what the computer will do for you do all the other steps in the buying process fall into place.

- ✔ Some people know instantly what they want a computer to do. I want a computer to help me write. My son wants a computer to play games. My grandmother doesn't have a computer, although she could use one to help her with her church flock and to write up her meeting notes. Chapter 3 helps if you're a little lost at this stage.

- ✔ It helps to picture yourself in the future, working on a PC. What are you doing (besides swearing at it)?

- ✔ If you ever work with lists, numbers, 3-x-5 cards, home finances, stocks, bonds, or Swiss bank accounts or if you trade in plutonium from the former Soviet Union, you need a computer.

- ✔ If you're buying a computer to complement the one at your office, you probably need something similar at home.

- ✔ If you're buying a computer for your kids in school, ask their teachers what types of computers are being used in school. Buy something similar for home.

- ✔ If you still don't think that you need a computer, you probably don't. The biggest excuse people give for not having a computer is that they can't figure out what to do with it. (Price is the second excuse.) Those people probably have lists, write letters, do home finance, pay bills, and buy and sell Soviet plutonium on a weekly basis. Face it: Those folks are going nowhere fast.

Step 2: Looking for Software

When you know what you want the computer to do, you go out and look for software to get the job done. This chore involves going to the software stores and seeing what's available or asking friends who have computers what they recommend.

When you've found the software you need, take notes. On each software package, on the side, are its hardware requirements — like the nutritional contents on a box of cereal. Write that information down, using a form similar to the one shown in Figure 2-1. (The forms are in the back of this book.)

Chapters 15 and 16 show you how to fill out the forms for yourself. That's your ticket for the next step: buying hardware to run your software.

✔ It's best to try software before you buy it. Just about any computer store lets you try it: Sit down at the computer, and play with the software you plan to buy. See how much you like it. See whether it works the way you would expect it to. Does it make sense? If not, try something else.

✔ Remember: You're not buying anything in this step. You're just looking at various software packages you'll purchase later and jotting down their PC hardware appetite. That information — the stuff on the side of the box — helps you assemble your perfect PC system.

Step 3: Finding Hardware

After assembling your software lineup, your next step is to match your computer's hardware to the software's requirements. The idea is to find a computer that can run your software. The software knows what it needs (on the side of the box); you simply have to fill the order.

The task is simple: After gathering all the forms you filled in for the software you plan to buy (the various copies of the forms you filled out in Step 2), work the Hardware Worksheet, as shown in Figure 2-2.

Thanks to the worksheet, you will know exactly what type of computer hardware you need. You'll never be steered to the wrong machine.

But don't buy anything yet!

Software Worksheet

Category: Office   Word processing   Spreadsheet
Recreation   Database   Graphics
Utility   Communications   Internet
Education   Programming   Personal finance
Multimedia   Reference   Productivity

Product name: _____

Developer: _____

Price: _____

Type of support: Vanilla   Chocolate   Carob   Fudge

Operating system: Windows 98   Windows NT   Version: _____
Windows 95   Mac   OS/2
Windows 3.1   DOS   Other: _____

Microprocessor: 486/better   Pentium MMX   Pentium: _____
Speed:_____ MHz

Memory needed: _____ Megabytes

Hard disk storage: _____ Megabytes

CD-ROM: Yes   No

Graphics: SVGA   No special requirements   Other: _____
Graphics memory: _____ Megabytes

Sound: SoundBlaster   AdLib   None   Other: _____

Special printer: Nope   Recommended:_____

Special peripherals: Scanner   Modem   Microphone
MIDI   Joystick   Special mouse: _____

Other stuff: _____

Figure 2-1:
The *...For
Dummies*
software
requirements
worksheet.

Hardware Worksheet

Operating system: Windows 98   Windows NT
OS/2   Mac   Other: _____

Microprocessor: Pentium _____   Speed:_____ MHz

Memory: _____ Megabytes

Hard drive storage: _____ Gigabytes

SCSI: Yes   No

Floppy drive(s): Drive A   3½-inch   1.44MB
Drive B   5¼-inch   1.2MB

Removable: Zip drive   Jaz drive   MO drive

Tape backup: Capacity: _____   DAT

CD-ROM: Speed:____ X   Tray   Cartridge

Graphics: SVGA   Other: _____
Graphics memory: _____ Megabytes

Monitor: Diagonal: _____ inches   Dot pitch: _____ mm
Multiscanning

Modem: Internal   External
Speed:_____ bits per second

Mouse: Standard mouse   Trackball   Other: _____
"Wheel" mouse

Sound: SoundBlaster   AdLib   Other: _____
External speakers   Subwoofer

Ports: Serial: COM1   COM2   COM3   COM4
Parallel: LPT1   LPT2
USB   FireWire
Joystick   MIDI

Other options: _____

Printer: IBM/Lexmark   Hewlett-Packard   Epson   Canon
Other: _____
Laser   Ink jet   Dot matrix
Color

Figure 2-2:
The *...For Dummies* hardware requirements worksheet.

✔ Most people make the mistake of shopping hardware first and software second. After all, what you're buying is a *computer*. What the computer *does,* however, is more important.

✔ As another example, you may go shopping for a car when what you're really buying is transportation.

✔ If you match your software to your hardware, you won't be one of the sorry people who has to return to the computer store weeks later to upgrade your memory or hard drive or something else that they should have taken care of *before* they bought.

Step 4: Shopping for Service and Support

Crazy Omar and Discount Tong may have deals on PCs, but what kind of support do they offer? Especially if you're a first-time buyer, no substitute exists for after-sale support. This consideration far outweighs getting a deal or finding the cheapest PC in the land.

✔ It's easy to forget service and support because it's not sold prominently in the ads. Instead, you see prices and deals and sales. Ignore them!

✔ *Service* is the ability to fix your PC if something goes wrong with it. The best service is on-site, where someone comes to you and fixes your PC right where it lives. The worst service is when you have to box up your PC and ship it to some overseas factory.

✔ *Support* is help. It can be in the form of classes, phone support, or training.

✔ The trade-off for a cheap PC is little service and no support.

✔ Chapter 18 goes into more detail about shopping for service and support.

TIP

Have a little class

I don't steer any of my friends to a local computer store that doesn't have a classroom attached. It's wonderful to know that a store is so dedicated to happy users that it devotes floor space to a classroom.

Some people take classes *before* they buy their computer. I recommend buying the computer first and taking the classes later. That way, you have something to go home and practice on. Also, with the computer in your possession, you'll be able to ask more useful questions than had you never used one.

Step 5: Buying Your Computer

When you're ready to buy your computer, buy it. You know what you need the computer for, you know what software to buy, you know what hardware to buy, and you've found a proper dealer with service and support. So buy it!

- ✔ The buying process is covered in Part IV of this book.

- ✔ I would like to say that no lousy computer dealers exist, but they do. Never put money down on a computer. Always pay by credit card — never with cash or a check. Always make sure that you get what you paid for: Check the invoice and, if you're suspicious, have a third-party repair place check your computer.

Don't Sit Around Waiting for the Technology Bus!

Before moving on, some hesitation always occurs when you're ready to buy your computer. In fact, Step 5 (buying your computer) is the hardest of all the steps.

It's not the money that keeps some people from buying a computer. No, it's the rapid advancement of technology. Computer technology zooms ahead quickly. A computer you buy today is guaranteed to be obsolete in three years and nearly useless in five. People see this situation as a warning: Don't buy today's computer; wait for the next generation.

Although it's true that the next generation of computers will be better, faster, and probably less expensive, it's also true that waiting for it gets you nowhere. It's like not catching a bus because you assume that the next bus will have fewer people on it or be cleaner. That may be the case, but while you're waiting, you're not going anywhere.

The bottom line is when you're ready to buy, buy.

Stuff to Remember

Five important steps are involved in buying a computer:

1. Decide what you want the computer to do.
2. Find the software that will get you the result you want.
3. Find the hardware to run your software.
4. Shop for service and support.
5. Buy that computer!

The most important of these steps is the first one: having a purpose in mind for the computer. You don't have to think hard about how a computer can help you. In fact, anyone who uses a calculator or a typewriter has an immediate use for a computer.

After you find a way a computer can help you, the rest is just following the steps and becoming well informed. This book will make you well informed. You must follow the steps on your own.

Chapter 3

"What Can a Computer Do for Me?"

. . . .

In This Chapter

▶ Asking yourself a few questions

▶ Discovering a computer's potential

. . . .

*M*ore important than which computer you buy is the *software* you plan to use. The software controls the hardware — the computer. Before you ever consider a brand name, such as IBM or Compaq or Gateway or Ugly Bob's Discount PC, the key question to ask yourself is, "What do I plan to do with my computer?"

The goal of this book is not to sell you a computer. After all, the slim — very tiny — chance exists that you cannot benefit from owning a computer. For most people, however, finding a computer is easy. They know what a computer can do for them, so they take off to get one. Others may need more help in discovering how a computer can help them. For those folks, it helps to ask yourself some questions.

This chapter is for people who are still wondering exactly why they need a computer. The sections in this chapter help you discover just exactly what it is a computer can do for you. That way, when you buy one, you don't get stuck with something you don't really need.

Knowing Which Questions to Ask

The odds are pretty good that you know what you want a computer for. If so, great. Please review the questions at the end of this chapter and move on to Chapter 4. If you don't really know what you want your computer for, keep reading and (trust me) it will come to you.

Thanks to software, computers can do just about anything. Heck, if they had arms and legs, they could mop the floor. Even so, computers most often help you to do work; repetitive tasks are what a computer is all about. And they never complain. Computers also educate and entertain, which means that they can do just about anything for anyone. (Oh, and computers can frustrate you too. But that's really beyond the point you're at right now.)

Before you ask yourself the questions, take a good look at your job, your hobbies, and your life. What do you spend time on? What do you dabble with? What would you like to do or explore? Never start by saying, "I have a computer — now what?"

The best question to ask

The first and best question to ask yourself is

> What do I see me doing with a computer?

Notice that the question isn't "What am I doing with this new IBM technological powerhouse?" Instead, the focus is on your work. What will the computer help you do?

- For me, the answer was easy. I wanted to write. The software that helps me do that is word-processing software.
- Parents can use computers to help educate their kids.
- Kids ignore all the educational software and play games like Bug Stomper, Alien Blaster, and Don't Tell Mom and Dad.
- Most small businesses need a computer to run the business. Anything financial is a breeze for a computer.
- If you're an artist, you must have a computer! Most university art departments now have dozens of computer-related courses. Nearly all graphic design done today is made by computer.
- Anything you do on paper or with a calculator can be done better with a computer.
- Have a list? Then you're probably better off putting that information in a computer where it can be stored, sorted, sifted, spindled, folded, and mutilated.
- Verily I say unto you, for everything you do, there is some way a computer can help you do it.

Another, worthy question

The questions you need to ask yourself often deal with computers that may already influence your life:

What do I do on other computers that I would want to do on my home computer?

For example, if you already have a computer at the office, what do you do with it? Furthermore, what do you do on the office computer that you would also need a home computer for? (If you're buying a computer for the office and already have one at home, you need to go back to the first question: What will you be doing with the computer at the office?)

If you're buying a computer for your kids, what do they do with it at school? Find out what software they use. Talk with the school's computer manager or computer science teacher. They probably have some wonderful suggestions for you. (Keep in mind that you're in the software stage; put off their "this is a great place to shop" suggestions for now.)

The "Okay, I'm really stuck" questions

Not everyone will be blessed by finding that one software package right on the shelf, the package that screams, "I'm everything you ever wanted to do on a computer." Sure, it may happen, although most of the time it doesn't.

When the answers to these questions don't give you the name of a specific type of software program, you need to think more generally about what you do and how a computer can help.

Here are a few questions you should mull over in your head:

- ✔ What do I spend the most time on?
- ✔ What activities are the most repetitive?
- ✔ Do I do anything that involves making lists or organizing information?
- ✔ Do I ever sit with a calculator to work out problems for more than a few minutes?
- ✔ Do I ever sit with a typewriter for more than a few minutes each week?
- ✔ Do I sometimes get angry enough at an inanimate object to swing a baseball bat at it?

Don't let even the smallest excuse steer you away from the computer. No matter what it is you do, a computer can help you do it better, faster, and much more easily. Trust me: Software exists to do just about anything. It's up to you to match your needs to that software.

Some inspiring thoughts

Most of the time, computers are used for business functions. The word processors work over the words, the spreadsheet programs crunch the numbers, and the databases store, sort, and print information. What if you're not in business? Then you just need to take a close look at what you do.

My grandmother doesn't think that she needs a computer. Yet she spends a great deal of time doing some tasks for which a computer would be ideal. As the librarian at her church, she could use a computer to keep track of the books, by tracking which of them are on loan and which are overdue. Good-bye, index cards! She could also use a computer to type and print the minutes of her meetings. Better still, she could hook up to the Internet and send me e-mail, which would save on my long-distance phone bills.

My music teacher uses a computer for scheduling and billing her students. More than that, she has a program that lets her compose, play, and print music. If you're into genealogy, you *must* have a computer. No matter what your hobby, a computer aspect of it probably exists that you're unaware of.

For business, the computer can do just about anything. It works with numbers, words,

records, and on and on. Even if you spend all day glued to a phone, having a computer nearby can be handy: Computers keep track of phone numbers and can even dial the phone for you. Special "tickler" software is available that enables you to keep current with those you talk to. For example, imagine that a client calls and you don't remember anything about him. Type his name into the computer, and instantly the tickler software displays all his past ordering information plus any notes you made the last time you spoke. Impress him by asking how Helga and the children are — all thanks to the computer.

In the home, computers are used primarily to entertain and educate. Everyone enjoys computer games. Computer encyclopedias and learning games can help the kids. Calendar programs can help organize the family schedule, and mail lists can make printing labels for Christmas or birthday parties a snap.

Although I could go on and on, you should get the idea by now. Discovering what a computer can do for you is the first step you take toward buying the ideal personal computer.

Understanding Your Computer's Potential

A computer is capable of just about anything. What makes it so capable is the software that controls it. The primary duty of software is to tell a computer what to do, and it can tell the computer to do anything the computer is capable of (and even "fake" some things the computer isn't capable of). The reason that a single computer can be used as a word processor, a graphics design workstation, and even an arcade game is that the different software programs tell the computer what to do.

Don't buy anything less than a computer as a substitute. For example, although a home game machine is nice, a computer can also play games (many of them better than what's available on the game machine), and it can do your income taxes. Although those fancy typewriters with display screens may process your words, a computer can also process words and cruise the Internet for you to look for handy quotes or relevant graphics.

The bottom line: Computers are the solution to *many* of your problems. Don't go out hunting for several other devices when one computer will do the job.

Stuff to Remember

Before you even start thinking about buying a computer, you need to think about what you'll be doing with it. That task will be carried out by computer software, and that software is what controls the computer hardware you eventually buy.

Here are a few of the questions you should mull over before you start shopping for computer software:

- ✔ What do you see yourself doing with your computer?
- ✔ How do you spend most of your time?
- ✔ What activities are the most repetitive?
- ✔ Do you do anything that involves making lists or organizing information?
- ✔ Do you ever sit with a calculator or typewriter for more than a few minutes each week?

Chapter 4

Understanding Hardware and Software

- -

In This Chapter

▶ All about hardware

▶ The microprocessor

▶ Basic PC hardware

▶ All about software

▶ The operating system

▶ How everything works together

- -

*T*he old alchemists believed that everything was composed of water, air, earth, or fire. They also believed, of course, that you could turn lead into gold. Computer scientists, looking much like alchemists but without the funny hats, believe that all computers are composed of two parts: hardware and software. If you can figure out how those two elements work, you can use a computer to turn silicon into gold.

This chapter covers the basics of all computer systems: hardware and software. You gotta know which is which because one is far, far more important than the other. It's when you don't know which is more important that you end up buying a computer that may not be right for you.

Hardware: The Hard Stuff

Computer hardware is easy to identify: It's anything you can touch. If you can touch it, it's hardware. The monitor, computer box, keyboard, printer, modem, doodads inside the box — it's all hardware.

✔ Hardware is anything you can touch.

✔ If you drop it on your foot and you go "ouch," it's probably hardware.

✔ Here's one that baffles most people: Floppy disks and CD-ROM disks are hardware. Even though they store software, the disks themselves are hardware. The software — like music on a cassette tape — is not the hardware on which it is stored.

✔ The most important piece of hardware is the computer's microprocessor.

The microprocessor (the main piece of hardware)

All hardware in any computer is geared to work best with one single chip. That chip is the computer's *microprocessor*. All the computer's circuitry is designed to work with and behave for a certain type of microprocessor.

You probably wouldn't think that this issue would be important. Different types of microprocessors exist, however, just as different engines for an automobile exist. Like a car, microprocessors come in different speeds and with different horsepower. Unlike a car, however, a microprocessor determines the design and potential of the rest of the computer more than the engine determines, for example, what type of stereo you have in your car.

In keeping with years of computer industry tradition, microprocessors are given silly names: Pentium, Power PC, and Alpha, for example. Also, microprocessor names look like numbers: 80386, 486, and 68040. You also see combinations of the two: K6, Pentium II, i486. The names do have some significance, although it's nothing to fret over now. Just know that Pentium is the name of a microprocessor chip and not some building you would visit when you're in Rome.

All the details of the microprocessor are presented in Chapter 5. At this point, all you need to know is that the microprocessor is the most important piece of hardware in a computer.

✔ The microprocessor is not the computer's brain; the brain part (if it has any) is the software, which is covered in the latter part of this chapter.

✔ The microprocessor is also called the CPU, or central processing unit.

✔ A "specific type of microprocessor" refers to its name, not individual microprocessors one-by-one. For example, the PC I'm writing this book on has a Pentium Pro microprocessor. It's the same as all Pentium Pro microprocessors, except that I probably paid more for it because I bought it from someone I know.

✔ Some folks call the microprocessor "processor," for short. They're probably the same folks who call McDonald's "Mickey Dee's," even though they're not saving any syllables.

Basic hardware

The microprocessor isn't the computer. Though the microprocessor tells you a great deal about the computer and the rest of the hardware, it is merely the center of attention. Supporting the microprocessor are many other items inside and outside the computer's box. Here's the short list:

BIOS: To make sure that each part of the computer talks to all the other parts (the printer, keyboard, monitor, memory, and so on), a special program is burned onto a silicon chip and called the BIOS, or Basic Input/Output System. Although this tiny program controls the basics of the computer, it doesn't run everything (you need an operating system — software — for that).

Memory: By itself, the microprocessor doesn't remember much. It's like an absentminded professor: smart and quick but forgetful. To help the micro-processor store information, RAM or memory is used (Chapter 6 discusses memory).

Storage devices: Computer memory is short-term; its contents are erased when you turn off the power. For long-term storage, other devices are used, including hard disks, CD-ROMs, floppy disks, and other media and storage devices (Chapter 7 covers this topic).

Keyboard and mouse: Two must-have pieces of hardware are the keyboard and the mouse. These items provide input — information from you — to the computer. The days of talking to the thing are fast approaching, although even when you can talk to your computer, you still need a keyboard to help you back up and erase.

Monitor: Providing output for all the wonderful information the computer has to offer is the monitor. Unlike buying a TV set, buying a computer monitor is tricky stuff. It's easy to be misled. (Chapter 8 straightens things out.)

Printer: Not normally considered part of a basic computer purchase, a printer is still something everyone needs. More is involved in choosing a printer than just looking at a sample page in the store. (Chapter 11 has oodles of hints to help you buy.)

Modem: Fast becoming part of the basic computer is the modem, a device for communicating with other computers over the phone lines. (Modems are covered in Chapter 9.)

Other gizmos: Oh, there's really no end to the differing types of hardware in and around a computer. They have tape-backup devices, magneto-optical drives, scanners, digital cameras, and loads and loads of stuff you can forever buy and add to your computer. You see, buying is an endless pro-cess . . . especially if you become too attached to your new computer.

All this stuff is hardware, and all of it works with the microprocessor to create the hardware side of your computer system. By itself, hardware is unimportant. Only with the proper software driving everything do you get the most from your hardware.

✔ About half the computer hardware lives inside the computer box, officially known as the *console*. The other half sits outside, connected to the box with cables. In fact, cables are a very big and ugly part of any computer — something they don't show you in the ads.

✔ Some external devices are called *peripherals*. For example, the printer is a peripheral. Although the keyboard and monitor could be considered peripherals, they're too important to the computer's basic operation to be called that. (It's a thing for semanticists and college professors to debate.)

✔ You'll notice that all computer hardware either produces input (sends information to the microprocessor) or generates output (receives or displays information from the microprocessor). Some devices, such as a modem, do both. This process is all part of something called I/O, or Input/Output, which is the basic function of all computers. It's nerdy stuff.

Software, the Other Hard Stuff

Software is the brains of the operation. Some people claim that the micro-processor is the computer's brain. No. No. No. No. No. The microprocessor is just a big, flat, expensive piece of technology — like a Keebler fudge cake with metal legs. You need software to make the microprocessor seem like it has any sort of intelligence.

The operating system

The main piece of software controlling your computer is called the *operating system*. It's the operating system — not the microprocessor — that tells the whole computer what to do. All hardware, including the microprocessor, must obey the operating system. And all software must work with the operating system.

The operating system has three important jobs: controlling the hardware, controlling all the software, and giving you (the human) a way to ultimately control everything yourself.

Control that hardware! The operating system tells the computer what to do and how to do it. Although the microprocessor inside the computer may be doing the work, the operating system is giving the orders.

Closely linked to the operating system is a special piece of hardware called the BIOS (see the section "Basic hardware," earlier in this chapter). The operating system gives instructions, in the course of its duties, to *both* the microprocessor and the BIOS.

Supervise that software! All the software you use (everything — all the applications, programs, utilities, and games) must work with the operating system. In fact, software is written for the operating system, not for the computer or microprocessor. Only a few games are written directly to the computer's hardware. Just about every other program is designed for a specific operating system.

The key to a successful operating system is a large software base (lots of computer programs that work under that operating system). That base is what makes the traditional operating systems so successful. Even though everyone hated DOS, it could run millions of programs. That's what made it so common (albeit unpopular).

Work with humans! Finally, the operating system has to present you, the person ultimately in charge of the computer, with a reasonable method of controlling things. DOS did that with a command-line interface, which everyone hated. Windows uses graphics, which people hate too, but not as much.

The operating system has to show you ways to run programs and ways to control the computer's hardware. Chapter 13 discusses various operating system types in detail and shows why some operating systems do this final job better than others.

 ✔ The operating system and the microprocessor must work together to give you the best possible computer. When they work together, they're said to be *compatible*.

 ✔ You'll likely be using only one operating system: Windows. (Chapter 13 has more info on why that is true.)

 ✔ DOS stands for Disk Operating System, which seems rather silly until you consider that when it was developed, not every computer came with a disk. In fact, early microcomputers had no disk drives; their operating system was merely the BIOS plus maybe a built-in version of the BASIC programming language.

Applications and other programs

Like a general without an army, an operating system by itself merely looks impressive. The operating system's army in this case is all the programs you have on your computer, which is how you get work done. (Operating systems merely control things; they don't do any real work for you.)

In the Big Picture, the application programs are the reasons you buy your computer. You find yourself a nice and tidy word processor, which runs under a specific operating system, which requires a certain amount of hardware to help it do your stuff. That's the true chain of command.

(This book discusses various applications programs in Chapter 13.)

Putting It All Together

Everything in your computer must work together if you ever expect to get anything from it. Operating systems are written toward specific microprocessors, BIOSes, and other hardware. Programs are written toward specific operating systems, as well as specific hardware. It all works together.

When hardware doesn't work with software, you have an incompatibility. (That's bad.) For example, you cannot run the Macintosh operating system on a PC. Why? Because the Macintosh uses a different type of microprocessor and has an utterly different BIOS. Different hardware and software just don't work together.

The hardware must obey the software. The software must work under the operating system. And everything has to work well with you. Figure 4-1 illustrates this concept graphically.

- ✔ Remember that *you* are in charge. You pick the software, which then tells you which hardware to get. That's the best way to buy a computer.

- ✔ All the pieces must fit together well for you to end up buying the best computer you can.

- ✔ What's the most important piece (besides you)? The software. That's why Step 2 in the buying process is looking for software. When you find it, the rest of the pieces fall naturally into place.

Stuff to Remember

Did you read any subtle hints about the *software* being more important than hardware? Good! When you have that information nailed into your brain's memory banks, you're free to understand the entire buying process.

Here's the rundown of what you should have gleaned from this chapter:

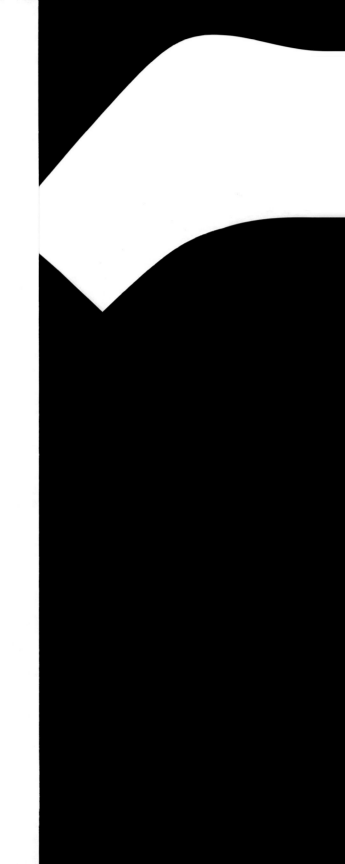

- ✔ Although hardware is impressive, it's nothing without the proper software to drive it.

- ✔ The chief piece of software is the operating system. It controls everything: all the hardware and all the other software in your computer.

- ✔ You use software to get work done on your computer.

- ✔ Both the hardware and the software have to work well together, and everything has to work well for you.

- ✔ You, the human, are ultimately in charge of the operating system, which means that you run the computer.

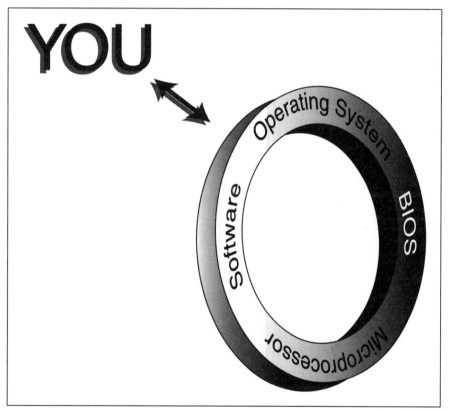

Figure 4-1:
The "how
your
computer
system
works"
donut.

Part II
Understanding Hardware

"A PORTABLE COMPUTER? YOU'D BETTER TALK TO OLD BOB OVER THERE. HE'S OWNED A PORTABLE LONGER THAN ANY ONE HERE."

In this part . . .

It's the software that drives the hardware, which should have been drilled into your skull by now if you've read through Part I of this book. Yet, to understand the buying process, you must first know about some computer hardware. After all, if you buy software that says "Non-SCSI compatible," it helps to know what that phrase means before you decide whether it's for you. It's like being able to understand the devastating effects of water before you buy a boat.

The chapters in this part of the book cover computer hardware. This part has two purposes. The first is to familiarize you with various hardware doodads, especially the items you find in a computer ad. The second is to let you know how to buy those items, in case you want to upgrade your hardware in the future. Read this stuff lightly first, and then get into the dirty details later, if the urge strikes you.

Chapter 5
All about Mr. Microprocessor

In This Chapter

▶ Just buy the latest Pentium

▶ Microprocessor speeds

▶ All about MMX

▶ Microprocessor Q&A

*A*t the center of everything in your computer's hardware is the microprocessor. It's your PC's traffic cop, the conductor for a mad electronic orchestra. Because all the other hardware in your computer depends on the capabilities of the microprocessor, your computer needs a good, fast microprocessor to make everything run smoothly and sweetly.

Get Yourself the Latest Pentium Microprocessor

In the olden days, you actually had a choice when it came time to pick a microprocessor for your PC. In 1990, for example, you could buy a 386 or spend more to get a faster 486 microprocessor. Each 386 or 486 had other flavors: 386SX for an "entry" system or a 486DX4 for a top-of-the-line model. Decisions, decisions.

All new computers of the PC type now come with Intel Pentium microprocessors. Numbers are (mostly) a thing of the past. The Pentium chip comes in three varieties:

✔ Pentium (the original)

✔ Pentium Pro

✔ Pentium II

The original chip was the Pentium, or what would have been called a 586 had Intel kept with its fine tradition of naming microprocessors after famous numbers. (Rumor has it that the chief scientist at Intel calls his dog "4837.")

After the Pentium came the Pentium Pro. Then came the Pentium II, which would be equivalent to a 686 in the famous-numbers category. Most computers now have a Pentium II microprocessor.

✔ Sure, older Pentium microprocessors may still be available in some computers. The microprocessors are probably low-end models or some older lines, typically for sale at a discount.

✔ As far as you're concerned, a Pentium or Pentium Pro and a Pentium II have two differences: The Pentium II is faster and *more expensive* than either of its predecessors.

✔ All Pentium microprocessors are 32-bit processors. This statement doesn't really mean anything — until someone makes a 64-bit microprocessor.

✔ Manufacturers other than Intel also make Pentium-class microprocessors. They have names like K5 or K6 or even 686 and so on. These microprocessors are simply inexpensive alternatives to the Intel stuff.

Microprocessor Speed (Or "If Mega Stubs His Toe, Then Megahertz")

The only truly technical rating of a microprocessor you should pay attention to is its speed. All microprocessors have a speed rating. Each chip whizzes along at a specific, regulated speed measured in megahertz, which is abbreviated as MHz. The higher a MHz value, the faster the chip. The faster the chip, the more expensive it is.

Fast microprocessor = Better ☺ = More expensive ☹

The first Pentiums zoomed along at about 75 to 90 MHz. (That's *fast* when you consider that the first IBM PC had a microprocessor that chugged along at 4.77 MHz.) Today's Pentium II chips are rated between 200 MHz and 300 MHz, with newer models breaking the 400 MHz rating.

Yes, you pay much more for the fastest chip. But do you need it? Your software often tells you. Again, the speed is what you can afford beyond the minimum requirements of your software.

✔ Buy the fastest microprocessor you can afford.

✔ The larger the MHz value, the faster the microprocessor.

✔ Your brain has a speed rating of only about 2 MHz. (Not *you* individually — everyone in general.) The human brain can do several million things at a time, however, whereas the microprocessor does only one thing at a time, which is why humans consider themselves to be superior to most computers.

My computer's faster than yours! Nya! Nya! Nya!

Computer nerds aren't satisfied with the mere megahertz rating of a microprocessor. No, they've devised several tests — like a microprocessor SAT — to determine exactly how fast a computer can whiz along.

Computer speed ratings are a complete and total joke, of course, because any "test" they try to pull can be fooled into giving a faster result (as long as you know which switches to throw). Yet this fact doesn't stop the advertisers from boasting how much faster their model is than the competition.

Oh, you see bar graphs and charts in the magazines when they compare computer speeds. The truth is that speed is relative because the computer sits around idle most of the time waiting for you to type something. Anyway, the following list of various speed-rating tests explains what they mean, if anything:

Norton SI: The original computer speed rating, where a 1.0 equals the speed of the first IBM PC. The bigger the number, the faster the computer; the speed rating, however, depends directly on the microprocessor's horsepower and not on the computer's actual performance (which means that this test can be fooled).

Whetstones: A speed test that measures how fast a computer can do math (which the nerds call "floating-point operations"). Because this test is somewhat inconsistent, the "punish Dhrystone" test is often used instead.

Dhrystones: A real-world test of a computer's performance. Rather than measure just processor speed (like Norton SI), this test is a much better judge of how fast a computer performs. Unfortunately, it too can be fooled.

Winstones: Another "punish" name, this one dealing with specific computer speeds in Windows. As with every other test, it can be fooled.

The bottom line: Who cares! As long as you match your microprocessor's speed to what your software needs, you'll do nifty-keen.

The Whole MMX Deal

The latest fad in microprocessors is something called MMX. It doesn't stand for *anything* — and I have this information from high sources from within Intel. What MMX does is to provide the microprocessor with special *humph* for making computer games and graphics go faster.

That's H-U-M-P-H, and it's a technical term — one that's dear to computer scientists. Don't bandy it about carelessly.

Do you need MMX? Not really. Only if your software was written to support the MMX instructions do you *need* it. Not all software is written with MMX in mind. If it is, it says so on the box. (It may even use that *humph* word.)

Still, all this MMX nonsense is moot: Almost every new PC now sold comes with an MMX microprocessor. You get it whether you need it or not. Because you will have one, however, you should scan the shelves for MMX software just to take advantage of it.

- ✔ MMX could stand for *multi*media *ex*tensions, but *naaaa!*

- ✔ MMX software includes a number of games and also some multimedia stuff, educational software, and anything with animation or intense graphics.

- ✔ My high source at Intel tells me that it's "MMX Technology" (which is how you're supposed to say it because it's trademarked). Intel can't say that MMX stands for something specific because if it does, it can't trademark the name, or something like that.

Some Microprocessor Q&A for You

The following common questions crop up when normal people attempt to understand computer microprocessors. The answers provided in this section educate you without converting you into a Jolt-cola-swilling computer geek.

What does "386 or greater" mean?

Computer hardware is always developed before computer software is. As an example, consider that someone had to invent the bassoon before anyone could write music for it. For that reason, a lag always occurs between the time software written specifically for a new microprocessor becomes available.

To deal with the lag time, software developers take advantage of the fact that older PC microprocessors are compatible with the recent stuff. Software that ran on an archaic IBM PC with an 8088 microprocessor still runs now on a Pentium II. (It runs very fast.)

The common denominator of microprocessors was the old 80386, or 386, chip. All the stuff written for that chip works on all later 486 and Pentium microprocessors. This capability is described on a software box by using the term "386 or greater" or "386 or later."

If software says that it requires a 486 or later, does that include a Pentium?

Yes. The "or laters" stack up this way:

386 or later includes all 386, 486, and Pentium microprocessors.

486 or later includes all 486 and all Pentium microprocessors but no 386.

Pentium or later just means Pentiums (no numbered microprocessors).

Pentium II means all Pentium II microprocessors, not any Pentium Pros or plain Pentiums.

Are all Pentium processors the same?

No. Some software programs require a Pentium II microprocessor. It says so right on the box. If you have anything less, the program does not run. This situation rarely happens, but because you're a smart shopper, it's a mistake you'll never make.

Should I buy an upgradable microprocessor option?

Some manufacturers boast that you'll never have to buy another computer because their model enables you to "plug in" a new microprocessor. Golly, that sounds nice. . . .

My advice is to skip paying extra for a computer with an upgradable micro-processor. The reason is simple: When it comes time to upgrade to a new microprocessor, it's just better to go ahead and buy a whole new computer. Why? Because computer motherboards and other components are built to take advantage of the new microprocessor.

Another reason: It's often cheaper. A new microprocessor may cost 50 to 70 percent of the cost of a whole new computer. PC manufacturers buy micro-processors by the truckload, which means that the microprocessors are cheap. One microprocessor at a time is expensive.

(Also see Chapter 21, about upgrading your equipment, for more ranting on this topic.)

What about those "math coprocessors?"

A *math coprocessor* is a special companion chip for the microprocessor, kind of like a pocket calculator. Its job is to do mathematical computations, and it's engineered to do them more swiftly than the microprocessor can do on its own.

All Pentium microprocessors have built-in math coprocessors. If your software demands a math coprocessor, you're all set. Only if you somehow buy a used computer would you otherwise have to question whether it had a math coprocessor.

   ✓ The math coprocessor is often called an FPU, or floating-point unit. Same thing.

   ✓ All Pentiums come with a built-in math coprocessor.

   ✓ If, for some bizarre reason, you get a 486 PC, note that the 486SX version of that microprocessor lacks a math coprocessor.

What's the "OverDrive" chip?

The OverDrive chip is a special option, available on some computers, that enables you to quickly upgrade an older microprocessor to a more recent model. You plug the OverDrive chip into a special socket on your computer's motherboard. The OverDrive then takes over, and your computer runs faster.

What's Turbo?

Turbo means "two speeds" — fast and slow. Most microprocessors have this feature: Although they can run at their normal, zippy-zip-zip speed of a gazillion MHz or so, they also have a second, slow speed of about 8 MHz. A switch on your PC's console changes the speed.

Why run at the slow speed? Mainly, to be totally compatible with the original IBM equipment; the first IBM PC/AT model ran at only 8 MHz. In the old days, some software — specifically, computer games — didn't function at faster speeds.

Turbo mode is no longer used. In fact, most new PCs lack a turbo switch, and older PCs that have a turbo switch don't have it connected to anything.

What's the cache?

An obscure attribute of a microprocessor is something called the cache (pronounced "cash"). A *cache* is a storage place. In a microprocessor, the cache is used to store instructions a software program gives the computer. The larger that cache storage area, the faster the microprocessor goes.

You may occasionally see a cache value used in describing a microprocessor. For example, a salesperson may boast that his computer model has a "2MB L2 cache." This abbreviation means that the microprocessor has two million bytes of memory to help speed it up.

What's the point? The larger the cache, the better the microprocessor performs. Use the cache size for comparison when you get around to shopping — if you care to; most of the time, my eyes gloss over when salespeople get technical.

Stuff to Remember

The microprocessor is the most important part of all your computer hardware because it controls the rest of the computer. Here are your priorities when you're looking for a microprocessor:

- Buy the fastest microprocessor you can afford. At minimum, buy the fastest microprocessor your software requires (a 90 MHz Pentium, for example).

- You need a Pentium microprocessor. The best is now the Pentium II.

- Ensure that you get an MMX Pentium or compatible microprocessor.

- Non-Intel microprocessors are okay, although if having a K6 or 686 or other non-Pentium microprocessor concerns you, don't buy it. (These microprocessors generally appear in low-end, or "home," machines.)

- Don't pay extra for a computer with an upgradeable microprocessor; most people upgrade their entire computer, which is often cheaper and better than just buying another microprocessor.

Chapter 6
Memory Stuff (Temporary Storage)

. . . .

In This Chapter

▶ Bytes, kilobytes, megabytes, and gigabytes

▶ Memory (RAM) in your computer

▶ Memory terms

▶ Filling your memory banks

. . . .

*T*wo types of storage are in every computer: temporary and permanent. Although you may think that permanent storage would be better (and it is), you still need both. You need temporary storage for the stuff you work on *right now* and permanent storage to save it for later.

In your PC, permanent storage is provided by disk drives, which are covered in Chapter 7. This chapter covers memory (RAM), which is temporary storage because, without power, the contents of memory are erased.

This chapter covers the basics of computer memory. It also contains a discussion of the terms *byte, kilobyte, megabyte,* and *gigabyte* — if you're unfamiliar with those yardsticks of computer storage.

Computer storage is one area where more isn't necessarily better. Sure, if you can afford it, lots of storage is wonderful! If you don't *need* all that storage, however, you're wasting a ton of money.

Say Hello to Mr. Byte

With videotape, the storage unit is a minute. You buy a videotape that records, for example, 120 minutes of stuff. The gas tank in your car stores fuel by the gallon. The storage unit for beer is the 12-ounce can. You don't buy 72 fluid ounces of beer; you buy a six-pack. In a computer, the basic unit of storage is a *byte*.

What a byte is and how it works aren't important. What's important to know is what a byte stores:

One byte stores one character of information.

The word *byte*, for example, contains four letters, or four characters. A computer uses 4 bytes of storage to store that word. The word *closet* requires 6 bytes. The sentence above requires 45 bytes of storage, which includes all the letters, spaces between the words, and the period at the end of the sentence.

To make a large number of bytes easy to describe, modern scientists have stolen some ancient Greek words: *kilo, mega,* and *giga,* which sound like bad guys the Power Rangers would fight but are really terms used to describe the size of something. Bytes are measured in the following terms:

- ✔ **Kilobyte:** 1,024 bytes, or about a thousand bytes
- ✔ **Megabyte:** 1,048,576 bytes, or about a million bytes
- ✔ **Gigabyte:** 1,099,511,628 bytes, or about a billion bytes

These terms are used to describe both temporary as well as permanent storage in a PC — how much room you have for the stuff you create. It's okay to round these oddball numbers to the nearest big numbers. From now on, that's what I will do:

- ✔ **Kilobyte:** 1,000 bytes
- ✔ **Megabyte:** 1,000,000 bytes
- ✔ **Gigabyte:** 1,000,000,000 bytes

To give you a better understanding, think of a kilobyte of storage as enough room to store all the text on this page (about half a page of single-spaced typewritten text). That's 1,000 characters — a *kilobyte* of storage.

A *megabyte* is one million bytes of storage. That's enough room to store a small novel or a detailed graphic picture of your cousin's family (including the dogs).

A *gigabyte* is an awesome amount of computer storage — one billion bytes, or 1,000 megabytes. Rarely does any single thing require a gigabyte of storage. Instead, you use gigabytes to store the multiple-megabyte files you and your computer collect.

You need to know about these sizes because two types of computer storage use them for measurement: the computer's memory and the computer's disk storage.

- A byte stores one character.
- One thousand bytes are in a kilobyte ("kill-uh-bite").
- One million bytes are in a megabyte ("meg-uh-bite").
- One billion bytes are in a gigabyte ("gig-uh-bite").
- The abbreviation for kilobyte is K or KB.
- The abbreviation for megabyte is M or MB.
- The abbreviation for gigabyte is G or GB.

- Beyond the gigabyte is the *terabyte,* which is one trillion bytes of storage. Outrageous? Perhaps. Consider, however, that having a PC with a 2GB hard drive would have been considered outrageous just ten years ago, when 20MB hard drives were the rage.
- Twenty-four cans of beer are in a case, and 24 hours are in a day. Coincidence?

Banks o' Memory (RAM)

Science fiction TV shows typically feature computers with "banks" of memory. Although that term isn't inaccurate, because even your own PC has banks of memory, it's a poor measurement.

Memory in your computer is most often measured in *megabyte* units because personal computers come with a few millions of bytes of memory. The standard quantity for most new computers is 16MB of memory, or RAM. Some come with more memory, typically 32MB or 64MB.

Some inexpensive PCs may have only 8MB of RAM. You most likely want to avoid anything with less memory than that amount.

How much memory do you need? The answer depends on your software. For now, you have to remember only two things: You need memory (or RAM) in your computer, and memory is measured by the megabyte.

- *RAM* is an acronym for Random-Access Memory, which distinguishes it from ROM, or Read-Only Memory. In common computer parlance, the terms "memory" and "RAM" refer to the same thing. Forget about ROM.
- Really, I'm serious: Forget about ROM. You don't need to buy more of it. Your computer comes with enough ROM. Don't worry about it.

- Watch out for computers advertised with no memory or 0K or 0MB of RAM. This sales ploy makes a computer look cheaper than other models sold with memory included. All computers need memory, so you have to pay for it one way or another.

✔ Older computers measure memory by the kilobyte. If you intend to buy an older machine, it may have only 640K of memory in it or claim to have 1MB total. That's not enough!

✔ Your computer's operating system (Windows 95 or Windows 98) requires *at least* 8MB of memory to function. That's the bottom line for memory in all PCs.

✔ Sometimes memory may be described as *extended* memory. That's an archaic term. All memory in a PC is just memory. If an ad says "16MB extended memory," it's the same thing as "16MB memory" or "16MB RAM."

Some unimportant technical memory terms

Memory isn't simply memory. Just when the computer industry reaches the point where memory *could* be just "memory," they invent a new type of memory. So along comes a new acronym or technical description to distinguish the New Memory from the Old Memory. Ugh.

DRAM: Another term for RAM. Same thing.

ECC: An acronym for Error Checking and Correction, which could mean extra circuits to ensure that memory is being properly written to and read from.

EDO: An acronym for Extended Data Out. Whatever it really means, all it indicates is a special type of fast or more efficient memory. Whatever. Advertisers love the term (primarily because marketing types love three-letter acronyms).

Memory speed: Memory is gauged by its speed, similar to a microprocessor. With memory, the speed is measured in *nanoseconds* (abbreviated *ns*), or billionths of a second.

Parity: Another nerdy term, this one refers to a self-check that memory chips can perform on themselves every time the memory is accessed. Do you need parity? Maybe. A computer manufacturer decides whether it wants to put parity in its PCs. Other than that information, anything else I could say about parity would put you to sleep.

SRAM: An even faster type of RAM, but not as fast as EDO.

SIMM: An acronym for single in-line memory module. It's essentially a bunch of memory chips all soldered to a handy little expansion card — about the size of a pocket comb. Many variations exist: DIMM, DIP, SIP, and others. They all describe the same thing with subtle differences that shouldn't concern you.

Back to the memory banks

The PC you buy will indeed have banks of memory. The memory cards plug into these slots inside the computer. (The memory chips live on the memory cards.) Each slot is known as a *bank,* and they're purely technical. However, the way your memory is configured in each bank may be important.

When you order your computer, try to get the manufacturer to install all your computer's memory into as few banks as possible. For example, Figure 6-1 shows a setup with four banks of memory. A 4MB SIMM card is plugged into each bank, which gives that computer a total of 16MB of RAM — a good amount.

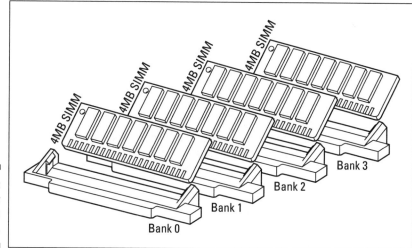

Figure 6-1:
Memory
banks in
a PC.

Suppose that someday you want to add another 16MB of memory to this same computer. Because it has only four banks and each bank is full, you have only one option: Toss out all your memory (for which you paid dearly), and replace it with 16MB of new memory. Yes, that's a waste of money.

A better situation is shown in Figure 6-2: All 16MB of memory are plugged into one bank. If you want to upgrade to 32MB, all you need is another 16MB SIMM, which plugs into another, open bank. And, you still have more banks available for future upgrades.

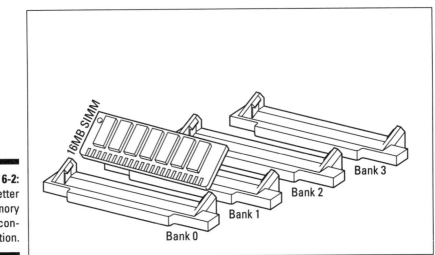

Figure 6-2:
A better
memory
bank con-
figuration.

16MB SIMM

Bank 0

Bank 1

Bank 2

Bank 3

✔ Try to put as much memory as possible into a single bank.

✔ Yes, as you may have guessed, one 16MB SIMM may cost more than eight 4MB SIMMs. You save money on upgrades, though.

✔ Yes, this information is technical! For example, some computers insist that *all* memory banks have the same amount of memory in them. If you have three 16MB SIMMs in three banks and want to add a 64MB SIMM to the last bank, you can't do it. (Hey! Don't blame me! Beat up an engineer!) Also, some systems require you to install SIMMs in pairs, which requires some additional thinking when you're buying additional memory.

Stuff to Remember

You need both permanent and temporary storage to hold the stuff you work on and create in your computer. For temporary storage, you need memory (RAM) — and a great deal of it. Here are the important things to remember about memory (which sounds kind of redundant):

✔ Memory in a computer is measured by the byte. A typical PC has millions of bytes of memory, called megabytes.

✔ The total amount of memory you need depends on your software requirements.

✔ Generally speaking, most PCs are sold with a minimum of 8MB of memory. More is better. Too much, if you don't need it, however, is a waste of money. (You find out how much you need in Part IV of this book.)

✔ Permanent storage is provided by disk drives, which are covered in Chapter 7.

Memory is cheap, cheap, cheap!

It's been a while since I've bought memory for a computer, so I was utterly shocked when I saw how ridiculously *cheap* computer memory really is.

The following chart shows the average cost per megabyte of computer memory for the past several years.

Memory is cheaper now because so much of it is available on a single chip. Back in 1984, it took eight or nine 4-kilobit memory chips to

make one 4K bank of memory. That may have cost you $40. I remember paying $150 for a 64K bank of memory.

You can now get eight or nine 64-megabit chips to make a bank of 64MB of memory and pay only $150. (My old TRS-80 computer wouldn't know what to do with 64MB of memory, of course, but that's beside the point.) Memory is cheap!

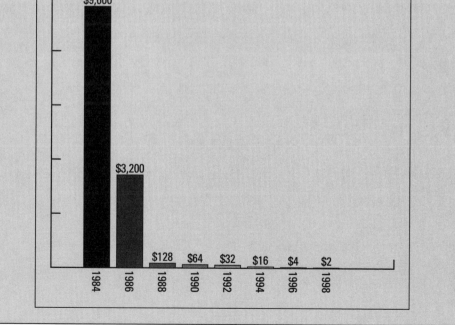

Chapter 7

Disks of Every Type (Permanent Storage)

. . . .

In This Chapter

▶ Disk storage basics

▶ The hard disk drive

▶ Hard drive capacities and speeds

▶ IDE and SCSI controllers

▶ Floppy disk information

▶ CD-ROM information

. . . .

*W*hy is memory (RAM) temporary storage? Because it needs a constant flow of electricity to maintain its information. When a computer is switched on, memory is available and ready to store information. When the power is turned off, memory is off, and all the data stored there is lost — poof!

Obviously, what you do on the computer is important. You need a permanent place to store the stuff you do, a place that isn't subject to "poof!" every time you switch off your PC. That permanent storage is provided by your computer's disk drives, of which two main types exist: The hard drive and the floppy drive. Other types exist as well, all covered here.

✔ Disk storage is measured by the byte. See the section "Say Hello to Mr. Byte" in Chapter 6 for a discussion of what a byte is and what the terms kilobyte, megabyte, and gigabyte mean.

✔ Don't confuse the terms RAM memory and disk memory. Though both are measured in bytes, the RAM value is memory, which the computer uses when it's working with the program. The disk storage value is storage space — like in a closet. (A program may need more disk space than it needs RAM memory, which is okay, but don't think that the computer's memory and disk space values should match.)

Boring stuff about how disk drives work

Disk drives are the most common devices for storing computer information, programs, and the documents you create. They work like a magnetic record player — except that the record is, in this case, the disk. Floppy disks, for example, are made of essentially the same stuff as cassette tapes — except that the floppy disk is smashed flat, like a pancake. The disk in a hard drive is rigid metal coated with a magnetic oxide, also flat like a pancake.

Each disk drive has a recording "head," like a cassette recorder. This recording head floats back and forth over the flat, magnetic surface of the floppy disk. Because the disk spins 'round and 'round, the recording head can quickly locate any particular point anywhere on the disk. It can then read or write data from that specific point to or from the computer's memory.

All about Disk Storage

Every computer needs disk drives. Specifically, each computer should have at least one each of the three main types of drives: a floppy disk drive, a hard disk drive, and a CD-ROM drive. Each of these different types of drives serves a specific purpose and, though other types of disk drives and disk storage are available, you use those three most of the time.

✔ Disk drives provide permanent storage on your computer.

✔ The disk is what stores information. The *disk drive* is the device that reads the disk. For a hard drive, the disk and disk drive are encased in the same unit. For floppy and CD-ROM drives, however, the disk and the drive are two separate things.

Get Yourself a Hard Disk Drive

Every computer must have a hard disk drive, or hard drive, for short. It's like a huge, electronic closet where your PC stores its stuff. Unlike memory, where you can get by with a few megabytes, you need gigabytes of hard disk storage. Yes, that's a great deal of stuff.

Hard drives are judged in three ways:

✔ Storage capacity, or how many gigabytes (or megabytes) they hold

✔ Speed, or how fast the information can be accessed from the hard disk

✔ Interface, or how the hard drive connects to the motherboard and talks with the microprocessor

You should consider a fourth factor too: cost. On a cost-per-megabyte basis, a hard drive is the best bargain you can buy for your computer; the larger and faster the hard drive, the less expensive it is on a dollar-per-megabyte scale. Figure 7-1 shows the relative average cost, from 1984 through 1998, to store 100 megabytes of information on a computer hard drive.

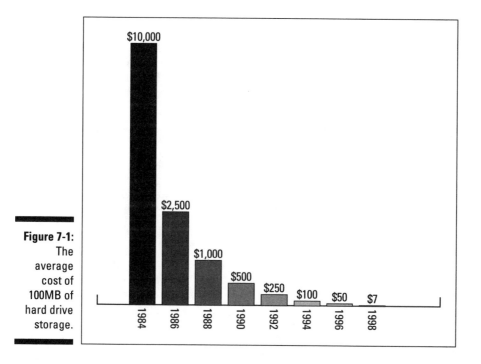

Figure 7-1:
The average cost of 100MB of hard drive storage.

✔ Your computer needs at least one hard drive.

✔ Some computers have more than one hard drive. That's great!

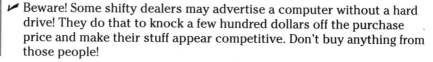

✔ Beware! Some shifty dealers may advertise a computer without a hard drive! They do that to knock a few hundred dollars off the purchase price and make their stuff appear competitive. Don't buy anything from those people!

✔ As with memory, you can always add more hard drives to your computer. The only limitation is the space inside *and* outside your computer.

✔ In the olden days, computers didn't need hard drives. They got by with only floppy drives. The floppy drive is now rarely used. Why? It just doesn't store enough information, and it's slower than a Dostoevski novel.

✔ No, you cannot take the hard drive out of your computer. See the nearby sidebar, "The saga of the 'fixed' disk," for more information.

How much stuff does it hold?

The average hard disk drive sold now can store about 2GB of data. This number is more or less the minimum you need for running today's hoggish programs. Hard drive sizes vary, however; you can buy anything from a 900MB hard drive on up to 10GB — or more!

The saga of the "fixed" disk

In IBM terminology, a hard dive is a *fixed disk*. No, that doesn't mean that it was once broken. It's just the way IBM people think. A "fixed disk" is fixed inside a computer — you cannot remove it. Unlike floppy disks or CD-ROM disks, you cannot yank a hard disk from a hard drive unless you have lots of muscle, time, and ambition. Even then, the result won't be what you want.

Hard disks are fixed to help keep them fast. Inside the protective hard drive shell, the disks can spin without interference from dust, hair, cookie crumbs, or smoke that often rings up around computers. (You can buy removable hard drives, if you want. Although they're expensive, you can swap disks between two computers, both equipped with removable hard disk drives.)

The following list describes other terms used to describe a hard disk drive:

Drive C: The name Windows gives your PC's first hard disk drive.

Drive D: The name Windows gives your PC's second hard disk drive (if you have one). Hard drives are all named after letters, starting with *C.*

Hard drive: The hard disk and its drive or case.

Hard disk: The hard disk itself (used interchangeably with "hard drive").

Fixed disk: The early IBM term for a hard drive.

Hard file: The current IBM term for a hard drive after the 1989 marketing "reorg."

Winchester disk: A nickname given to early IBM hard drives that could store 30MB of information on two disks (30/30, like the rifle).

There really is no rhyme or reason behind hard drive sizes. Your first PC, in fact, may have 2.1GB or a 3.4GB or some odd number. Don't let those numbers faze you. As long as you don't buy a hard drive with too little storage space, you'll be okay.

How big does your hard disk need to be? Popular computer consultant thinking says "Twice as much as you think you need." There's no sense in figuring that you'll have only 10,000 customers in your database and then have business double your expectations and — ta-da! — you need a new hard drive. Major pain.

Using the software worksheets in Chapter 15, you will calculate approximately how much storage space all your software needs. Then, following a simple formula, you'll be able to calculate the exact minimum size hard drive you need. (Anything else I could say right here would be a guess.)

✔ Avoid buying any PC with less than a 1GB hard drive. Although those smaller sizes were popular a few years back, they're just not beefy enough to hold today's software.

✔ The first IBM PC was sold without a hard drive. The IBM PC/XT, introduced in 1983, came with a 10MB hard drive. Yes, that was considered oodles of storage space back then.

✔ The typical PC sold today comes with a 2GB hard drive.

✔ Mid-to-high-end PCs are sold with 4GB hard drives and bigger.

✔ You can always add a second hard drive if you run out of storage on your first one.

How fast does it go?

Lots of speed aspects are involved in buying a hard drive, primarily because computer people love measuring how fast things are. This measurement doesn't mean anything to you as a first-time buyer, unless you're a white lab coat type. One speed measurement is important: access time.

The *access time* is the speed at which a hard drive accesses information on the disk. This speed is measured in milliseconds. One *millisecond* is one thousandth of a second, often abbreviated *ms.*

The faster the hard disk, the smaller its access time value. The smaller the access-time value, the more quickly you can get at your data. Faster is better, obviously; no one wants to wait for a hard drive that feels like it has someone's gum munged into the bearings.

How fast?

The millisecond rating for any hard disk you buy now should be less than 15 ms. Anything larger is considered slow. Speed ratings of 12 ms and slower are considered typical, with any speed in the single digits considered absolute heaven.

✔ Access speed may sound silly because you're measuring time in milliseconds. I mean, how noticeable can ten milliseconds be? Differences in hard disk speeds are very noticeable, however — especially for "disk intensive" applications (databases and graphics programs, for example).

✔ Whenever you're working on a faster or slower hard drive, you notice the speed difference right away.

✔ The first PC/XT hard drive had a speed of 65 ms. Until a few years ago, a 40 ms rating was considered rather zippy.

The secret hard drive controller

The hard drive controller is a special piece of electronics that plugs into your computer, connecting the hard drive mechanism to your PC's motherboard and (eventually) to the microprocessor. You have a choice of which hard drive controller you want, depending on how you use your computer.

Two controller standards exist: IDE and SCSI. Both these terms are used as acronyms, so you have to live with them.

IDE controllers are the most common and least expensive. Using an IDE controller, you can have as many as two hard drives (as well as two CD-ROM drives) inside your computer. Your new computer will most likely have an IDE controller in it with an IDE hard drive sitting there happily obeying its commands.

SCSI controllers are more versatile than IDE controllers but are also more expensive and less common. With a SCSI controller, you can have as many as *seven* hard drives on your computer — two inside and five outside. You could even add *another* SCSI controller to your computer and have as many as 14 hard drives. It's greed city!

✔ Between you and me, no difference really exists between an IDE controller and a SCSI controller. Don't let anyone sway you one way or the other, especially if they look like they haven't bathed in awhile.

✔ IDE stands for Integrated Drive Electronics. No need to memorize that one.

✔ SCSI stands for Small Computer System Interface, which is endearingly pronounced "skuzzy."

✔ In addition to hard drives, SCSI controllers also work with CD-ROM drives, tape backups, removable drives, scanners, and other interesting devices, which makes that type of controller a worthy purchase for someone considering all those devices on their computer. (Read more about this subject in Chapter 10.)

✔ I have only one warning about controllers: Make sure that any hard drives you buy for your computer match the type of controller you have: IDE drives for an IDE controller and SCSI drives for the SCSI controllers.

✔ Nothing is wrong with having both IDE and SCSI hard drives in a computer. The computer I'm using to write this book, in fact, has both IDE and SCSI hard drives (as well as CD-ROM drives). Call me nuts.

Gotta Have a Floppy Drive Too

All computers should have at least one floppy drive. Even with a hard disk, at least one floppy disk drive is required for the transporting, backing up, and initial loading of programs and data to the hard disk.

A few interesting issues surround floppy disks, but nothing overly crucial. I can almost promise you, in fact, that your computer will come with one floppy drive capable of eating floppy disks that are $3^1/_2$ inches square and can hold 1.44MB of information. Still, it's worth bringing up a few issues about the drives:

✔ You have to buy floppy disks for your floppy drive. Buy disks labeled HD or "high density" or "1.44MB."

✔ All floppy disks must be formatted before you can use them. If possible, try to buy the disks preformatted (it says so on the box). Otherwise, you have to format them yourself, which you do by using your PC's operating system.

✔ A PC's operating system refers to the floppy drive as drive A.

✔ Your computer can have *two* floppy drives. (That's the missing drive B, according to the operating system.) No reason for this really exists: In the old days, two floppy drives speeded up the backup process. Hard drive information is now backed up to tape and not to floppy disks (though it can be — if you're into pain).

✔ You may have to buy one of the older $5^1/_4$-inch floppy drives. In case you've been out of circulation for a while or have an older computer with that format, that type of drive is necessary for copying files back and forth. Otherwise, you have no need to bother with the older format.

✔ A super-high-density floppy drive exists. Called the ED drive (for Extended Density or named after the guy who developed it, I'm not sure which), this format never caught on, though some PCs may have the floppy drive as an option. Don't bother.

CD-ROMs

Since 1990 or so, the CD-ROM drive has become a necessary part of every computer system. Before then, new programs came on floppy disks (some still do). With the advent of Windows and the popularity of graphics-intensive games, most new software comes on CD-ROM disks instead. You need a CD-ROM drive to install that software.

✔ Your computer should come with at least one CD-ROM drive.

✔ CD-ROM drives eat CD-ROM discs. Those discs look just like the CD discs you buy at the music store.

✔ You cannot write information to a CD-ROM drive. It's read-only, which is the *RO* in CD-ROM: Compact Disc, Read-Only Memory.

✔ Some types of CD-ROM drives can write information; see the section "Other CD-ROM stuff," later in this chapter.

✔ Oh, yes, you can play musical CDs on your computer (as long as your computer has speakers so that you can hear the music). A special program is required, although it should come with your computer or the operating system.

✔ Unlike a musical CD, a computer CD-ROM disc contains computer files, as much as 650MB worth.

✔ You can get CD-ROM disks in and out of a CD-ROM drive in two ways. I prefer the type of CD-ROM drive that sticks out its tray, into which I place the disk. With the other type of CD-ROM drive, you put the disk into a plastic case (a *caddy*) and then insert the case into the drive. I find that method rather clumsy.

✔ Most CD-ROM drives connect to the motherboard by using the IDE controller — the same one as your hard disk.

✔ Some CD-ROM drives are also SCSI. Make sure that you buy a SCSI CD-ROM if your computer has a SCSI controller.

CD-ROM speeds

I'm sure that lots of technical tidbits about a CD-ROM are out there, stuff that other books would go to great, dry lengths to explain. "Blah-blah-blah," they would say. Down here on planet Earth, though, you should care about only one aspect of a CD-ROM drive: its speed.

CD-ROM drive speed is measured in relation to the first CD-ROM drive on a PC. Call that drive speed one, or 1X. Because the next generation's drive was twice as fast, it was called 2X. Then came the three-times-as-fast break-through, and, lo, 3X CD-ROM drives were created. Do you see where this discussion is headed?

CD-ROM drives now have speeds of 6X, 8X, 12X, 16X, and *more!* Yes, you pay more for a faster CD-ROM drive. The idea is to get a CD-ROM drive that accesses information nearly as fast as a hard drive. Me? I can't really tell, although you should make sure that you get something as fast or faster than a 6X.

✔ Yes, CD-ROM drives are slow when compared to a hard drive.

✔ The 1X speed is actually the speed of the CD player you have in your stereo.

✔ Don't worry: If you put a music CD into a 16X CD-ROM drive, it doesn't play 16 times faster. Somehow, the drive figures it out, and the music sounds okay.

Other CD-ROM stuff

If you're *really* into CD-ROMs, you can get your PC a multi-CD changer. Like the changer you may have in your car or in your home stereo or boom box, a computer CD changer simply handles more than one CD-ROM at a time.

Another type of CD-ROM drive is the writeable CD-ROM, often called CD-R or CD-WR. Although these drives work like regular computer CD-ROM drives, when they're used with special software and CD-ROM disks, they can record information. (After all, CDs have to be created some way.)

The CD-R drive is something best purchased by people who do multimedia or program development. Unlike a hard drive, a CD-R can be written to only once and never changed. That makes it an ideal method for distributing large amounts of information but impractical for typical computer users.

✔ Be careful not to confuse the 8X speed rating with those types of CD-ROMs that hold more than one disk at a time. For example, an 8-disk CD-ROM drive may spin those disks at 16X. It's a strange device, yet people do crave them.

✔ I recommend the multi-CD changer as a purchase only for experienced computer users. If you're just starting out, get a normal CD-ROM drive first. You can always upgrade later.

✔ The same advice goes for a CD-R drive: Get it only if it's part of the purpose for which you bought a computer. Not everyone needs one.

✔ Yes, you can use a CD-R drive to read regular CDs, even music CDs.

✔ CD-R drives have ratings with two speed numbers, such as 2X6. That rating means that the drive writes at the 2X speed and can be used to read CDs at the faster 6X speed. (Writing to a CD-R disk typically takes longer because [fill in complex, useless technical info here].)

Other, oddball forms of storage

The number of ways a computer can store information is unlimited. I've listed some of the other types of disk storage you may find available. As with the special type of CD-ROM drives, consider these types only if they're part of your grand scheme for using your computer:

Magneto-optical drive: A drive that's similar to a CD-ROM drive except that it reads a smaller-format disk, typically 230 megabytes. The disks are about the same size as standard floppy disks (3½ inches square) but thicker. Unlike a CD-R drive, a magneto-optical drive can be written to, read from, and changed at any time. It's popular in the graphic arts community because it holds lots of information and is more flexible than a CD-R.

RAID drive: A stack of several hard drives, typically found in large installations. All the drives work together to ensure that the information stored on the RAID unit isn't corrupted. This type of drive is popular in situations in which the integrity of computer data is highly important. Most individuals do not own RAID drives.

RAM drive: A portion of a computer's memory that behaves like a disk drive. The operating system somehow fools itself into thinking that the RAM drive is just like another disk in the system, except that it's *very* fast. Unfortunately, RAM drives use too much memory to make them practical today.

Removable hard drive: Ever since the first hard drive was "fixed" inside the computer, various people have been working on ways to yank the disk back out. Several different types of hard drives have removable disks. They're all typically very expensive and are used in only specific circumstances.

Zip drive: A popular form of removable storage. Originally known as the *Bernoulli drive,* or *Bernoulli box,* a Zip drive is essentially a very large-capacity floppy drive. For example, a typical Zip disk can store 100MB of data, which is great for storing large files or for backup purposes. Many computer manufacturers offer Zip drives as an option.

Jaz drive: A relative of the Zip drive that stores 1GB of information (ten times the storage space of a Zip drive). Again, this type of drive is a common option for many PCs. It's ideally suited for transporting large files or for backing up your hard drive.

Future watch: DVD disks

The next, best thing on the horizon is the DVD disk. DVD stands for Digital Versatile Disk on a computer and Digital Video Disk when you hook one up to your TV. For now, the DVD is merely another format for playing home movies.

Although a DVD disk is the same size as a CD-ROM disk, it holds lots more information. This size makes it an ideal successor to the CD-ROM for computer data, as well as a way to view movies on your computer. (Yeah, pay $1,000 for a computer to view the same movies you could see on a $200 TV set.)

I mention the DVD disk merely to sate the lusts of my technical peers who claim that DVD disks will one day be as common on computers as CD-ROM drives are today. As my mom used to say, "We'll see. . . ."

Until you see computer ads which say that DVD disks are installed as the standard in most systems, I would put off any thought of buying a DVD player for your PC for now. If they do become popular, all the information you need to know about them will appear right here, in future editions of this book.

Stuff to Remember

Permanent storage requires some busy little devices. Your new computer should come with one each of a hard drive, floppy drive, and CD-ROM drive. Here are the details:

- ✔ You want to buy the fastest hard drive you can afford. Be sure that the speed is around 12 ms or less.

- ✔ Although your new computer's hard drive will have a capacity rated in gigabytes, don't fret over the size until you know what kind of software you're getting.

- ✔ Get an IDE drive. Only if you plan to use other SCSI devices in your computer should you consider a SCSI drive.

- ✔ Your computer should have one 3½-inch, 1.44MB floppy drive.

- ✔ Your computer also needs one CD-ROM drive. Try buying the fastest CD-ROM drive you can afford, although this is not the place to spend extra money if you have it (buy more memory or a larger hard drive instead).

Chapter 8

The Monitor, Keyboard, and Mouse

● ●

In This Chapter

▶ Picking a proper monitor

▶ Choosing a graphics adapter

▶ Picking a keyboard

▶ Musing over a mouse

● ●

*T*here is no need to make a computer any more stubborn than it is. You need to communicate with your PC. To make the computer understand you, it needs a keyboard and a mouse. To see what the computer is telling you, you need a monitor. Without any of those things, your computer would be deaf and mute — worthless.

Unlike computers of old, where the monitor and keyboard were often built-in, PCs now have separate monitors and keyboards (and mice). You have a choice! Making the best choice is what this chapter is about.

The Monitor ("Look at Me! I'm As Pretty As a Trinitron TV!")

A computer can communicate with you in two ways: through its printer (covered in Chapter 9) or the monitor. Though printing is necessary and an important part of what your computer does, the best way for a computer to communicate with you is with its video display, or monitor.

The monitor you choose for your PC has two parts. The first is the monitor itself, which sits on top of or alongside the computer box, or console. The second part is a video controller, which plugs into your computer's mother-board inside the box. You need both these items to create the graphics system for your PC.

✔ No personal computer is complete without a monitor.

✔ All PCs now sold have their monitors as options (as opposed to each model PC having its own monitor). You get to choose the monitor type and size. Although some computers may have a same-label monitor, it's still possible to pick and choose from a wide variety of monitors for your own needs.

✔ What you see on the glassy part of the monitor is called the *screen,* or *display.* The term *monitor* refers to the hardware itself.

✔ The circuitry inside the computer that controls the monitor is referred to as the *graphics adapter.* If you want to be a real nerd, call your monitor a CRT (cathode-ray tube).

✔ No, you cannot use your TV set as a monitor for your computer. Although TV sets are good for watching TV, their resolution isn't good enough for watching computer information.

✔ All PC monitors now sold are color monitors. Only if you have special needs should you bother with a monochrome, or black-and-white, computer monitor. A special variation of the monochrome monitor called the "paper white" monitor also is available, although most people opt for color.

Judging a monitor by its size

Monitors are measured like TV sets: diagonally in inches. Oh, other technical measurements exist too, which you can read about in the sidebar "Other technical measurements," later in this chapter. The monitor's size really should be first and foremost, though.

A typical monitor measures about 17 inches diagonally. Cheaper models measure 15 and 14 inches diagonally. If you want to spoil yourself, consider a 19-, 20-, or 21-inch monitor. Those sizes are nice, but they also tend to cost as much as the computer itself!

✔ Beware! A monitor's diagonal measurement may *not* be the same as its viewing area. The size of the screen is occasionally a few inches smaller than the glass.

✔ If you want to spend a little more money, get a *flat-screen* monitor. Unlike most PC monitors, the flat screen has a flat viewing surface, which makes the image look really nice. (It looks concave if you're not used to it.)

✔ Large monitors are *very nice.* I bought one on a whim and now have *three* of them! They're spendy, and they're also *heavy.* I threw my back out lugging one up the stairs. If you get a large monitor, make sure that someone else is around to carry it so that they wreck their back and you don't wreck yours.

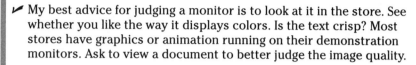

✔ If you're vision impaired, a 21-inch monitor is the answer to your prayers! It shows text nice and big.

✔ My best advice for judging a monitor is to look at it in the store. See whether you like the way it displays colors. Is the text crisp? Most stores have graphics or animation running on their demonstration monitors. Ask to view a document to better judge the image quality.

✔ You can mix and match computers and monitors. Just because one monitor is sitting by another computer in the store doesn't mean that it can't be the monitor you buy.

Selecting the proper graphics adapter

A graphics adapter (or "card") goes along with your monitor. The adapter is the part of your graphics system that lives inside your computer box, which controls the image displayed on the monitor's screen.

Several yardsticks measure PC graphics cards. Most are trivial at this stage of the game. One you may pay attention to, however, is how much video memory is on the card.

Yes — more memory!

Video memory is special memory (RAM) used to help your PC's graphics controller display lots of colors and high graphics resolution. The more video memory your computer has, the better your graphics card — and the more expensive.

SVGA cards typically have 1MB or 2MB of video memory. That's fine for most of us. Four megabytes is good for graphics artists and those who can afford it. Eight megabytes is best suited for people who demand a great deal from their graphics.

What about them thar 3-D graphics adapters?

Glad you asked. Another technical description that's important to graphics hounds is the *3-D* moniker. It means that the graphics card contains special circuitry to speed up the creation and animation of 3-D images — just more stuff to buy.

Does the 3-D stuff mean that you see everything three-dimensionally? Nope. Although a few graphics applications may take advantage of the 3-D circuitry, most software programs don't need it. (Again, it all boils down to what your software needs.)

Other technical measurements

Oh, I could spend all day muttering over the various technical aspects of a computer monitor. Instead, I've jotted down some terms and descriptions that should help you if the need to know arises:

Bandwidth (frequency): The speed at which information is sent from a computer to a monitor, measured in megahertz (MHz). The higher this value, the better.

Dot pitch: The distance between each dot (or *pixel*) on the graphics screen (measured from the center of each dot). The closer the dots, the better the image. A dot pitch of 0.28 millimeters is really good, and smaller values are even better.

Interlaced/non-interlaced: The method by which a monitor paints an image on a screen. An interlaced monitor paints the image twice, which tends to cause the image to flicker. What you want is a non-interlaced monitor, which doesn't flicker (as much).

Multiscanning/multisync: A type of monitor that automatically adjusts itself to several different graphics modes and frequencies. In fact, you may even see the frequency values displayed on the screen when the modes change. Very nice.

Scan rate: The rate at which a monitor's electron gun paints an image on the screen, as measured in kilohertz (kHz). The higher the scan rate value, the better.

✔ Various PC graphics cards have many acronyms and numbers, along with a slew of technical information. The card you get will be essentially some form of SVGA graphics adapter.

✔ SVGA stands for Super VGA, which stands for Super Video Gate Array, which is the name IBM gave the original standard back in 1987.

✔ For shopping purposes, anything that claims to be VGA-compatible also works with SVGA.

✔ Beyond SVGA is the XGA card, which you may see advertised. Everything the SVGA can do, the XGA does. However, it's not required unless your software demands it.

✔ Video memory is not the same as normal RAM memory (as discussed in Chapter 6). You need both.

✔ No, having more video memory doesn't improve computer games. Only advanced graphics applications may require that type of memory; if so, the application claims on the side of the software box how much memory is best.

✔ The same thing holds true for video cards with 3-D capabilities; that stuff works only if your software can somehow exploit it.

✔ Beware of video cards with zero video memory! You need video memory, and installing it "later" shouldn't be an option. Buy your video memory when you buy the card.

✔ The terms VRAM and Video RAM are also used to describe video memory. Watch out for them.

Read them labels!

Sometimes, the way a PC graphics card is described in a computer ad can drive you nuts. Look at these examples:

Matrox Millennium II 8MB WRAM video card

4MB EDO ViRGE 3-D video card

PCI 64-bit 3-D video, MPEG, 4MB EDO RAM

Yes, those are all real examples I pulled from a magazine ad. Sorta looks like someone's trying to incant a spell, eh? Whatever — each of them describes PC graphics, probably SVGA graphics along with some additional options that (golly) sure sound impressive. In fact, your only clue that these items are graphics cards and not the name of prediluvial kings is the word *video* in each of them.

In addition to the brand names, you should be able to determine the following tidbits from these examples:

✔ Each of the cards comes with a specific amount of video memory: 8MB in the first example and 4MB each for the other two.

✔ Refer to Chapter 6 for more information about EDO RAM.

✔ Can you guess what WRAM is? Yes, it's some type of memory, which is the RAM part. The *W? Window!* It's Window RAM to the rescue! WRAM is faster than typical VRAM, though only the Matrox cards use it.

✔ Although Matrox is a brand name, it could also be the name of a queen who betrayed Conan the Barbarian.

✔ Millenium II is a brand name.

✔ The term *3-D* in the second example refers to special circuitry on the card designed to accelerate certain 3-D graphics applications.

✔ The term *PCI* in the third example refers to the way the card plugs into your PC's motherboard. See Chapter 9 for more information about PCI.

✔ The *64-bit* item refers to the way the graphics card works internally. A 64-bit card is twice as capable as a 32-bit card. (And you would pay more for that.)

✔ Don't freak out over the term *64-bit* either; if your software needs it, you'll know about it after reading this book. Otherwise, your software doesn't need it, and you don't have to pay for it.

✔ *MPEG* refers to video hardware designed to improve the performance of movies and other animation played on a computer.

Keyboards

Keyboards, like monitors, come in a variety of types and styles. It can almost be said that no two keyboards are exactly alike. Fortunately, they're all similar enough that you can find one you like without it's being too much of an oddball.

✔ Most new computers come with keyboards. The keyboard is in the box when you first set up the PC. (See Part V of this book.)

✔ Some manufacturers give you a choice of keyboards. Even if they don't, you can always buy another keyboard to replace the one that comes with your PC.

✔ Beware of some dealers who advertise their computers without a keyboard. These dealers are usually mom-and-pop stores that build their own computers. They make their PCs look less expensive than the competition's by leaving out the keyboard. You need a keyboard! Plan to pay at least $30 to $80 extra for the keyboard.

✔ Before personal computers became popular, computer terminals had these incredible keyboards. They had the basic keyboard layout on a typewriter, and then they added a number of specific function keys. Some terminals had keys that actually said Insert Line, Move Block, Close File, and Get Me Chips. These days, computer keyboards are a little more conservative.

Going faster than the eye can see

Buying the best graphics card with lots of memory should be a priority for anyone who plans to use graphical software. One additional way of speeding up your graphics is to buy a *graphics accelerator,* either hardware or software designed to make your graphics go really fast. Make a note to inquire about a graphics accelerator if you plan to use graphical software.

Standard keyboards

The standard computer keyboard sold with just about every computer is called the 101-key Enhanced keyboard, as shown in Figure 8-1. It really does have 101 keys on it; the extras are scattered about the standard typewriter keys like so many weeds in a garden.

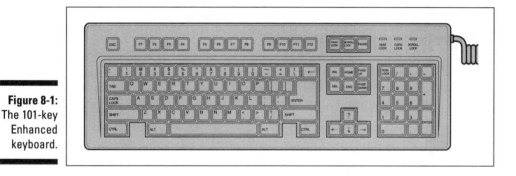

Figure 8-1:
The 101-key
Enhanced
keyboard.

Little deviation from this standard keyboard layout exists. Some computer makers put their name on the keyboards. Sometimes you see lights on various keys (Caps Lock and Num Lock, for example). Each keyboard has a different touch and feel. These minor considerations don't really affect how the keyboard is used. If you want to get unique and funky, though, you're allowed to.

Nonstandard keyboards

The most popular deviation on the standard keyboard is the ergonomic keyboard. This keyboard has a funky shape, designed primarily to be easy on your wrists.

The typical ergonomic keyboard looks like a regular keyboard (refer to Figure 8-1) that has been left out in the sun too long. Ergonomic keyboards are curved, some have a bump in the middle, and some actually break apart. The idea is to have your hands on the keyboard in a position that's as natural as possible. This position supposedly makes you more productive.

 ✔ Aside from ergonomic variations, some keyboards come with special features. The most popular feature is the built-in computer mouse, or "thumbball," for controlling a mouse pointer on the screen.

 ✔ I've seen keyboards with built-in calculators, clocks, and even stereo speakers.

✔ All this bonus, funky stuff costs more money, of course. If you feel that your wrists could benefit from an ergonomic keyboard, look into one. Or, if you opt for a funky keyboard, look into that as well. See what your dealer has to offer. Some places let you substitute keyboards; find out before you buy.

Mice and Other Nonfurry "Pointing Devices"

A mouse is an input device, like your keyboard. It's a required device for nearly all of today's graphical software; you cannot use your computer without a mouse. For that reason, nearly every PC sold has a mouse in the box — the computer mouse kind.

✔ Just like the keyboard that comes with your computer, if you don't like your computer's mouse, you can buy yourself another one.

✔ Some dealers let you choose which mouse you want.

✔ The standard PC mouse is the Microsoft mouse, though other manufacturers seem to be more creative with their mice, especially Logitech.

✔ The current mouse craze is the IntelliMouse, from Microsoft. It has a third button, or "wheel," between the two standard buttons. As with all hardware, however, to make the best use of the IntelliMouse, you need software that works with it.

✔ If you're into graphics, you probably want a specialized mouse, such as a pen mouse or trackball. These types of mice are covered in the next section.

✔ The plural of "computer mouse" is "computer mice," though you need only one mouse for your computer.

Types of computer mice

The computer mouse has three common variations: traditional mouse, trackball mouse, and funky mouse, as shown in Figure 8-2.

Traditional: A palm-size device with one or more "buttons" and a cable trailing up and into the computer. The number of buttons can vary from one to three; two is typical. (I've seen a 28-button mouse.) The cable is also optional because infrared mice communicate with the PC by using telepathy and other magic. Oh, and right-handed and left-handed mice are available, and they come in a variety of shapes and styles.

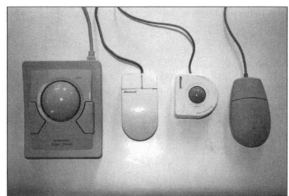

Figure 8-2:
Different
types of PC
mice.

Trackball: A very non-mouselike mouse (refer to Figure 8-2) that has a large, easily manipulated ball and doesn't roll around on your desktop. Artists and graphical types love this type of mouse. Try one out before you buy.

Funky: Any mouse that isn't in the traditional or trackball style (for example, a mouse shaped like a pen, or *stylus*). Tiny, joystick-like mice and pointing devices use a touch-sensitive pad to move the cursor on the screen. Some laptops use a special key on the keyboard or a tiny stick or wand between two keys to move the cursor. It's a strange world.

The dangers of carpal tunnel syndrome

One of the reasons ergonomic keyboards (and the "wristpads" that elevate your wrists with standard keyboards) are so popular is that they help alleviate the threat of carpal tunnel syndrome, or CTS. This painful nerve affliction prevents you from wiggling your fingers as you do when you type on a computer keyboard.

The *carpal tunnel* is a tube-like thing on the underside of your wrist. All the muscles and nerves that control your fingers pass through this tube, or tunnel. (Your fingers are moved by muscles in your arm — betcha didn't know that!) When you move your fingers in a repetitive manner and when your wrist sits at just the right angle, some agitation occurs in the carpal tunnel because the carpal tunnel

begins to collapse. The nerves become inflamed, and you feel a tingly or numb sensation. Eventually, typing becomes impossible because of the pain.

A good way to prevent carpal tunnel syndrome is to type with your hands and arms at the proper angle (flat from your elbow to your wrist). Ergonomic keyboards also help.

If you feel the onset of carpal tunnel syndrome, you can restore the arch in your carpal tunnel by surgery (bad idea) or by wearing around the back of your hand a special wrap that tucks your thumb under your palm (the best idea). Please see a doctor or chiropractor who's dear to you for more medical information.

Mouse software

Because you're probably buying a computer that has Windows 95 or Windows 98 as its operating system, you're all set to use your computer's mouse. Some mice may come with special software that helps you use the mouse's special features. Even so, you should buy a specialty mouse only if the software you use requires it.

For example, some mice look like a pen and pad of paper, though the pen and pad are electronic. Although you can use this type of mouse (or *pointing device*) like a normal mouse, it's ideally suited for people who use the PC to create graphics. Even then, only if your graphics software requires that type of mouse do you really need one.

Another, more practical example is the Microsoft IntelliMouse (or "wheel" mouse). It originally appeared with Microsoft Office 95 — which was the only program that used the mouse's wheel button. If you didn't have Office 95, the mouse's wheel didn't do anything.

The bottom line: Buy a specialty mouse only if your software can understand and appreciate the mouse's special capabilities.

Stuff to Remember

Your computer needs devices in order to communicate with you. To speak to the computer, you use a keyboard and a mouse. To hear the computer, you need a monitor. Here are the things you should consider when you're shopping for this hardware:

- ✔ The monitor is something you can choose for your PC. Even if your PC comes with a monitor "included," you can swap it for something you like better.

- ✔ Judge a monitor by its size, as measured diagonally across its screen. If you can afford to, get a 17-inch or larger monitor. The 21-inch monitors are very nice but are also *very* expensive.

- ✔ Keyboards are a touch typist's best friend. If typing is important to you, test-type a few keyboards before you buy. Remember that you can always buy your PC another keyboard.

- ✔ In addition to a keyboard, all PCs now sold come with a mouse. Just about any mouse will do you, though if you have special needs, you should consider one of the alternative mice instead.

Chapter 9

Expansion Options

● ●

In This Chapter

▶ The printer port

▶ The serial port

▶ The joystick and MIDI port

▶ The SCSI port

▶ Internal PC expansion options

● ●

*E*very computer has flashy and nonflashy parts. The flashy stuff (micro-processor, memory, disk drives, monitors, and so on) has been covered in the preceding few chapters. Now it's time to discuss all the other stuff, the nitty-gritties, the unappealing, the miscellaneous things that don't appear in the ads but that are important to the computer's operation — and expansion in the future. This chapter covers them all.

The items discussed in this chapter include the ports on a computer, which are connections for communicating with a variety of devices as well as internal expansion options.

You can skip this chapter if you're in a hurry; come back here later, though, when you encounter terms like SCSI, PCI, and RS-232.

Connecting Stuff by Using Ports

A *port* is a connector on the back of your main computer box. It's a hole! Into the hole you can plug a variety of cables to connect a variety of devices to your computer.

Ports enable you to add basic items to your computer — stuff that doesn't fit inside the computer box, such as printers and modems. Ports also enable you to connect more exotic things to your computer, such as scanners, external hard drives, and CD-R drives.

- The two most popular ports are the printer and serial ports. Another popular item is the analog-to-digital (A-to-D) port, used for scientific applications such as connecting a joystick to your computer.

- Your computer should come with at least one printer and one serial port. Most come with one printer and two serial ports.

- You need the printer port in order to connect your PC to a printer.

- Your computer may also come with a joystick/MIDI port.

- Adding extra ports to your PC later is entirely possible. (That's why PCs come with expansion slots inside, which are covered in the second half of this chapter.)

- Another type of port not mentioned in this chapter is the mouse/keyboard port. Both these ports (one each for the mouse and keyboard) look the same on the back of a PC, though one is labeled for the mouse and another for the keyboard. That's about all you can do with either one, so there's no point in blabbing on about it here.

- Oh: Except that some computers may refer to the mouse port as an "inport," whatever that means.

The printer port

Shockingly enough, a printer port is the hole in the back of your computer where you plug in your printer. That's easy. The tough part is dealing with some of the other names for the printer port. Here's a sampling:

Parallel port: Describes the way your computer sends each character to a printer; parallel ports work by sending each character to the printer eight bits at a time (each character, or *byte,* is composed of eight bits). The bits all travel side by side, as in a parade, with each bit traveling down its own wire. It's called "parallel" because everything moves side by side.

ECP/EPP port: A fancy name for the second-generation printer port now found in all PCs. This type of printer port offers better two-way communications between the computer and the printer. (The acronym is rarely used anymore because all PCs are sold with this type of printer port, as opposed to the old type that lacked a spiffy six-letter-acronym-with-slash.)

Centronics port: Because Centronics made one of the first microcomputer printers, the cable that connected your computer to the printer was, obviously, a Centronics cable.

LPT1 port: IBM called its printer port LPT1, for "line printer one" printer port. The second printer port was LPT2, and then came LPT3. This term may still be used to label the printer port on the back of some PCs.

✔ All computers need at least one printer port, which enables a printer to be hooked up to your PC.

✔ Your computer can have as many as *three* printer ports, and, yes, it can work with as many as three printers at a time. To add the second and third printer ports, however, you often have to buy a special expansion card.

✔ The most common nickname for a printer port is *parallel port*. Don't let that confooze you.

The serial port

More versatile than the parallel port, the serial port was originally one of the only expansion options for a microcomputer. Because the serial port dealt with two-way communications, it could connect to a variety of devices: modems, printers, scanners, digitizers, and even other computers.

The serial port is now humbled and typically serves only one purpose: to connect a computer to an external modem or to another computer directly. Because most PCs are sold with an internal modem, they don't bother using the serial port for anything. Still, your PC should have one or two — just in case!

Like the printer port, the serial port has other names:

Modem port: A name that obviously refers to the fact that the modem is the primary device plugged into a serial port.

COM1: As with LPT1 for a printer port, the moniker IBM chose for the first serial port. Your computer can have as many as four serial ports, which are dubbed COM1 through COM4.

AUX: Another name for the COM1 port, used primarily by programmers.

Mouse port: Used because the original PC mouse plugged into a serial port. This term no longer applies because computer mice plug into their own port on the back of nearly every PC.

RS-232 port: Serial ports are often referred to as RS-232 or some other RS-numbered port. It's not a Radio Shack part number. Rather, RS stands for Recommended Standard, and 232 is the number of the standard. (I suppose that it was the 232nd standard the engineers could come up with that year.) No matter what the compu-jockeys call it, it's a serial port.

Other uses for the tired old printer port

Other devices, in addition to a printer, can plug into a printer port. Here's a quick rundown of some of the other gizmos you can attach to your PC's printer port:

Network adapter: Some network adapters plug into the printer port, enabling your PC to access a Local Area Network (LAN). This type of adapter is ideal for some low-end PCs that lack internal expansion options.

Sound synthesizer: Some early PCs that lacked complete expansion options could attach a sound synthesizer to their printer ports and get full stereophonic sound. This option is still available, though most PCs come with built-in sound.

Video-capture unit: To quickly grab images from the TV or a videocamera, attach a video-capture unit to your PC's printer port.

External disk drive: Some CD-R, Zip, or other external disk drives can connect to your PC by using the printer port. This option lets you avoid having to open your computer box to add an expansion card and makes it easy to transport the drive between computers.

These devices may occasionally "steal" your printer port, preventing it from being used with your printer. In most cases, however, the device attached to the printer port does not interfere with the printer. Be sure to check before you buy the device so that you don't get gypped out of a printer.

✔ Your computer should have at least one serial port, and most new PCs are automatically sold with two serial ports: COM1 and COM2. That's about all you need.

✔ It's possible to have as many as four serial ports in a single PC, COM1 through COM4. Extra expansion boards enable you to add even more, if the whim hits you.

✔ See Chapter 11 for more information about modems — internal and external.

✔ Some printers hook up to the serial port. Surprisingly enough, they're called *serial printers.* They include some specialized, high-speed printers, but nothing you'll probably find at your local Computer-o-Rama store.

✔ Serial ports work by sending each character from the computer one bit at a time. The serial port disassembles each character and squirts that character's bits out through the port. All the information travels in single file as opposed to bits traveling eight abreast from a printer port. Because the serial port can also receive bits from another device, it's well suited for two-way communications.

The joystick/MIDI port

A *joystick port* is simply a hole into which you plug a joystick, or "game controller," for your computer. The joystick port is on nearly all PCs now sold, especially those that offer built-in sound; the joystick port and sound options are both used to play computer games (and other stuff too, of course).

The joystick port is also the MIDI port, which can be used to connect your PC to a MIDI musical instrument to help you play or compose digital music.

✔ The joystick port is officially known as the analog-to-digital port (or A-to-D port). The port can be used for a variety of things, most of which are of the science-fair variety: For example, I have one of those twirly wind things (an *anemometer*) that's a home-brew weatherman's kit. It sits on the roof of my office and plugs into my PC's joystick port. That way, I can tell when the wind is blowing without having to look at the trees outside.

✔ If your PC doesn't come with a joystick port, you can add one. You add it most often by installing a sound card in your PC (see Chapter 10); separate joystick-only cards are available, however.

✔ You can use two joysticks on a single computer by purchasing a gizmo known as a *splitter*.

✔ MIDI stands for Musical Instrument Digital Interface. It's a big, round, ugly hole (hey — a port!) you may have seen on any electronic musical instruments you may have lying around your house. The MIDI port is used to connect those instruments to each other and then to a computer. With the proper software, the computer can play the instruments and, lo, you have a symphony on your hands!

✔ You need a special MIDI box to plug into the joystick port, which then enables you to plug in various musical instruments. Oh, and you need software to drive it all. (Remember that software rules the hardware.)

The SCSI port

A SCSI port isn't a port in the true sense of printer, serial, and joystick ports. No, it's more powerful and has much more expensive toys available for it than any of the standard PC ports.

The SCSI port is made available by adding a SCSI expansion card to your PC. This task may already have been done for you automatically; SCSI hard drives and CD-ROM drives are very popular, and many manufacturers install them, along with a SCSI card, in the computer when you buy it.

A SCSI port is essentially a superdooper serial port, one that's fast enough to send information to and from a hard drive. (Normal serial ports are too slow.) Not only that, but you can also add SCSI devices inside or outside your computer — as many as seven or more of them for each SCSI port in your computer; each SCSI device plugs into the other to form a "daisy chain" of gizmos.

Current, popular SCSI devices include hard drives, CD-ROM drives, CD-R drives (recordable CD-ROMs), magneto-optical drives, tape-backup units, scanners, and some devices I probably haven't thought of yet.

- SCSI is pronounced "skuzzy." It stands for Small Computer System Interface, and it's basically a very fast and versatile type of serial port.

- Some computers come with a SCSI port. Others come with one only if you request it.

- If your computer doesn't have SCSI hard drives or a SCSI CD-ROM drive, it probably uses the IDE type of drive. See the discussion about IDE later in this chapter.

- You can always add a SCSI port to your computer — even if you already have IDE hard drives or an IDE CD-ROM drive.

- Differing types of SCSI cards are available: SCSI-2, SCSI-3, SCSI-wide, and SCSI-ultra. These terms describe different ways by which the SCSI card transfers information, how many devices can be connected to the SCSI port, as well as what type of connectors are used on the SCSI cables. Your dealer should configure everything for you. My advice is to get the best possible SCSI port you can afford.

A Full House of Cards

One of the reasons the IBM PC became such a popular computer is because of its open architecture. No, don't think of the Parthenon or any other open-air building. When you're talking computers, *open architecture* means that the computer can be expanded.

It's possible to open your PC's case and find *expansion slots*. Into those slots you can plug special circuit cards to expand your computer's capabilities. The cards are called — surprisingly — *expansion cards*. They enable you to customize and expand your computer beyond what the manufacturer set up.

Lots of expansion cards are available for the PC. In the old days, you added a printer or serial port by using an expansion card. Those items are now built-in. You may still need an expansion card, however, for your PC's graphics, your hard drive, a SCSI expansion card, a network card, an internal modem, a sound card, or any number of interesting devices.

Two pipe-dream ports

The computer industry is addicted to hype. New industry standards are always created, and then Microsoft dreams up newer standards that no one follows. If you follow technology at all, you'll be fooled into believing that some new standard is actually being used. Bunk!

Don't heed a standard until you see it in a computer ad (such as the DVD "standard" discussed in Chapter 7). Two new port standards that may or may not ever take off are FireWire and USB. Here's what I have to say about each:

FireWire port: FireWire (also known as IEEE 1394) is being billed as a super SCSI port, one that can handle as many as 63 devices. Imagine having the ability to expand your PC to 63 hard drives! Alas, this "standard" is not catching on, primarily because it's slow (that and people fear that it will burn down their house).

USB port: Unlike FireWire, USB (or Universal Serial Bus) may actually be a part of a computer you purchase someday. The USB port is one port (or a series of them) that enables you to connect devices such as a printer, keyboard, mouse, or modem to your PC — but nothing fast, like a hard drive. The USB will eventually replace the keyboard, mouse, joystick, printer, and serial ports on all computers. Someday.

Some high-end PCs come with USB ports on them, whether you need them or not. Alas, no USB devices are available. That situation may change, however, so keep an eye open.

✔ Some computers are sold with no expansion slots! This is a crime. These models are typically low priced and labeled "for the home," which is silly: Home users need expansion slots, just like anyone else does.

✔ Computer scientist types refer to the expansion slots as the *bus,* so they use the term PCI bus rather than PCI slot. Same difference.

Slots-a-fun

As with everything else, a PC can't have just one, typical expansion slot. No, thanks to history and bickering standards committees, a PC has several slots. Fortunately, popularity and stubbornness have left computer users with only two types of slots: PCI and ISA.

The most popular type of expansion slot is called the *PCI slot.* This slot connects directly to the microprocessor, which means that the devices plugged into the slot are quicker than those that plug into other slots.

What other slots? The old ISA slots, which date back to the first IBM PC. Only a few expansion cards use the old ISA slots, so when you're shopping for a computer, make sure that it has a majority of PCI slots and only a few ISA slots.

✔ Yes, this PCI and ISA stuff is technical. Your dealer will configure your PC's innards for you. If you ever need to expand your system, however, you'll want a PCI slot, so at least make sure that your system has enough of those.

✔ PCI slots are often home to superfast video adapters, network cards, and SCSI ports.

✔ ISA slots are used for noncrucial PC expansion: sound cards, modems, and other slow-to-pokey things.

✔ PC memory used to plug into expansion cards. Today's PCs are designed, however, so that the memory chips plug directly into the motherboard.

✔ Just in case you're truly bored — or you're working a computer-literate crossword puzzle — the other expansion slot standards available once upon a time in a PC were EISA, MCA, and NuBus. EISA was a successor to ISA that never caught on. MCA was IBM's own solution, which it patented up the ying-yang so that no one else ever used it. NuBus is found primarily on the Macintosh.

A special bus-port thing for laptops

Laptop computers typically don't have expansion slots. If they do, the slots are usually used for something specific, such as a modem or more memory. Laptops never have room, however, for a full PC expansion card. For this reason, the people who make laptops developed a special expansion system that uses tiny, credit-card-size expansion cards. Like most computer standards, this one is an acronym: It's called PCMCIA or PC Card, for short.

PCMCIA stands for Personal Computer Memory Card International Association. It's a group of developers who settled on a hardware standard for credit-card-size deals to plug into PC laptops.

✔ Many different types of PCMCIA cards are available and even different types of PCMCIA slots to plug them into.

✔ Most commonly, PCMCIA cards are used to add a modem, network adapter, or more memory to a laptop.

✔ Some desktop PCs come with the capability to have a PCMCIA port, though this capability is truly useful only if you plan to share PCMCIA cards with a laptop.

✔ It's rumored that PCMCIA stands for People Can't Memorize Computer Industry Acronyms.

Making your PC network-happy

To use your computer on a network, you need a network expansion card inside your PC. (No PCs are now sold with networking capabilities on the motherboard; networking cards must be added.) If so, remember to order a network card when you buy your PC. Sure, you can get one later, but if you buy it with the PC, you spare yourself the pain of having to configure it.

Also, make sure that you get a PCI network card. Refer to your network administrator (the human in charge of your office network) for the type of network connection you have. The dealer needs to know that so that the network card has the proper type of connector on the back (10-base T, thin Ethernet, twisted-pair, and so on).

Stuff to Remember

Here's the list of portly things you should keep in mind when you're buying a PC:

- ✔ Your computer should come with at least

    - One printer port

    - One serial port (it will most likely have two serial ports)

    - One keyboard and one mouse port

    - Maybe also a joystick port, depending on whether it comes with built-in sound

- ✔ You may want to upgrade your PC with a SCSI port, but only if you plan to use SCSI hard drives or peripherals with your system.

- ✔ Ensure that your PC has, internally, enough PCI expansion slots. You don't want to run out! Avoid buying any PC with ISA slots and no PCI slots.

- ✔ If you know what options you want plugged into the slots (such as a SCSI card, network card, sound card — whatever), inform your dealer so that someone there can set that up for you when they build your PC.

Chapter 10

Gizmos Galore

· ·

In This Chapter

▶ A modem for your PC

▶ Internal and external modems

▶ Various modem speeds

▶ PC sound options

▶ The tape backup unit

· ·

*T*he list of things you can add to your computer is impressive. Of the entire pile of stuff, three pieces of hardware are more popular than the rest: a modem, a sound card, and a tape backup unit. Unlike with some of the more specific gizmos, your dealer can typically add these three items to your computer as it's built.

This chapter covers the basic issues that are involved if you want to have a modem, sound card, or tape backup unit in your new PC.

✔ It's best to have your dealer install these devices. Even so, you can add them later, if you like.

✔ As with all hardware, you need software to drive these devices: Internet software for the modem; games or music software for the sound card; and backup software for the tape backup unit.

Modems

Your computer is all alone in the universe — unless you buy it a modem and, through the miracle of the phone company, enable your PC to talk to any other PC also equipped with a modem, which also includes all the computers on the Internet. You can add this capability for fun or for business, depending on which types of computers you allow your PC to dial up.

Modeming opens up an entire world unto itself, full of jargon and mystery. (Indeed, if you think that you're cornering the market on computer terminology, you're in for a surprise when you start to use a modem.) You should look for two things in a modem:

✔ Internal versus external

✔ Speed

Shopping for a modem involves other, more technical aspects. The best advice you can get for buying a modem, in fact, is to talk with someone who uses one. That person probably also has some real-life recommendations — or some worthy warnings — for you.

✔ Modems don't raise your phone bill. Using a modem is like using a telephone. The only difference is that your computer is doing the talking (it's more like horribly screeching) into the phone. Your phone company charges you the same whether you or your computer makes the call, and long-distance charges still apply.

✔ If you're going to buy a modem (and it can be a great deal of fun), my advice is to have a second phone line — one dedicated to the computer — installed in your home or office.

✔ Don't worry about a modem being "Hayes compatible." All modems are now Hayes compatible. It's the same as saying that a modem uses the "AT command set," which is equally no longer important.

✔ Nearly all modems sold today are also capable of sending and receiving faxes. Although the term "fax/modem" formerly described this type of modem, nearly all modems today are fax/modems, so there's no point in using the term. Special software is required to enable your PC to send and receive faxes by using the modem.

Will your modem live inside or outside your PC?

Two types of modems are available: internal and external.

An *internal* modem lives inside your PC, plugged into an expansion slot. This type of modem is the least messy because it has only one cable, the one connecting the modem to the phone jack in the wall.

An *external* modem lives outside your PC, content in its own daybook-size box with blinking lights to impress your friends. An external modem connects to a computer by using a special modem cable to plug into one of your PC's serial ports. It also needs to plug into the wall for electricity, and it connects to the phone jack in your wall with a standard phone cord.

If you get a modem when you buy your computer, the dealer often installs an internal modem. This option works fine. If you buy a modem later, however, my best advice is to get an external model. External modems are easier to install than internal modems.

✔ The advantage of an internal modem is that it doesn't clutter your desktop. External modems require a power cord and a cable to your PC's serial port; internal modems lack these messy items.

✔ The advantage of an external modem is that you can see its pretty lights and tell exactly what it's up to. You can turn it off by flipping its switch or set its volume by using a tiny knob. Also, you can easily move external modems from one computer to another.

✔ My wife likes her external modem because she can turn it off. This feature prevents our two-year-old from dialing up the Internet, which he's prone to do when he's unsupervised.

✔ Pricewise, internal modems are cheaper because they're just a circuit board you plug into your computer. External modems cost more, and they sometimes lack the freebie software that often comes with internal modems.

✔ If you do end up buying an external modem, remember the cable! Modems do not come with cables. Buy yourself a 9-pin to 25-pin modem cable.

✔ Internal modems should be installed in the COM2 port. If you buy a computer with a modem already installed, this port business shouldn't be a problem. If you install a modem later, however, make sure that it's in the COM2 port. (Most modem software assumes that your internal modem is on COM2.)

✔ External modems are typically installed on the COM1 port, though that's not a hard and fast rule.

Going faster and faster

Modems are measured by their speed, which tells you how fast they can send information through the phone lines. The speed is measured in bits per second, or bps. The higher the bps value, the faster the modem.

The standard modem speed is now 28.8K, which means 28,800 bps. Still older, 14.4K modems are available, plus some slower speeds you don't want to mess with.

Emerging standards exist for the 33.6K and 57.6K modem speeds, though these fast modems may be incompatible with other modems. For example, my Internet provider doesn't let me connect by using my 33.6K modem (though this situation will change soon).

✔ Generally speaking, your options are limited when you buy a (dealer-installed) modem with your computer. Try to get the fastest speed possible.

✔ If you know which company you'll be using to connect to the Internet (called an Internet Service Provider, or ISP), phone up someone there to see which type of modems the ISP recommends.

✔ At a speed of 28.8 Kbps, a modem sends or receives about 2,880 characters per second. That translates into 480 words every second.

✔ You may also hear the term *baud rate* used to describe a modem's speed. The more accurate term is *bps;* baud rate is used to describe signal changes in Teletype equipment, which used to apply to early computer modems but is no longer the case.

Sound Options

Sound used to be an added bonus on every PC. Because the original PC lacked sound circuitry on the motherboard, special sound cards were purchased and plugged into an expansion slot to make the PC sing.

Sound cards are now generally included with the purchase price of most PCs. The sound is either integrated on the motherboard or provided on a sound card. Either way, sound is included when you buy the computer.

✔ If you get sound for your PC, also make sure that it comes with speakers and some type of microphone.

✔ Microphones are usually extra, and the ones that come with your PC (if that's an option) tend to be of poor quality.

✔ Better speakers are also available. Some PCs are sold with multimedia options or upgrades that include high-quality stereo speakers and a subwoofer. With this type of setup, annoying the neighbors all night while you play games and kill aliens is entirely possible.

✔ Try to get speakers that plug into an outlet, not battery-operated speakers.

✔ Try to avoid sound cards sold with headphones only.

✔ You don't particularly need the SoundBlaster sound card brand name, although your sound card should be compatible with the SoundBlaster standard.

✔ Nearly all sound cards are capable of synthesizing music. Most can be connected to a MIDI musical instrument.

The very fastest modem

Speed is all relative, especially when it comes to using a modem. For example, the fastest modem you can really get is a cable modem. This type of modem connects to the same cable you use to watch cable TV; however, it's a computer signal you pick up.

The advantage to cable modems is that they're very, *very* fast. The disadvantage is that you need a cable company which provides that service. Other than that, everyone I know who has one raves about it.

Tape Backup Gizmos

Backing up is the art of making safety copies of your stuff. This concept sounds wonderful. Imagine making a backup of all your possessions in case of theft or fire. If anything happens to the originals, the backups are identical copies.

To make backing up as easy as possible, the tape backup drive was invented. It's another hole in the front of your PC (or as an external unit) that records to a tape all the information on your PC's hard drive (or drives) — a safety copy. It works much like a cassette tape does, though because the tape backup stores megabytes of information, it takes much longer to record than your typical 60-minute cassette.

✔ If the stuff on your PC is important to you, be sure to order your PC with a tape backup unit. You can choose from many makes and models.

✔ If you're getting a SCSI port in your PC, try to get a SCSI backup unit. They tend to be faster than the backup units that run off the computer's floppy drive controller.

✔ Try to match the size of the backup tapes to the size of your hard drive. For example, a tape that can store 800MB of data is too small for use as a backup for a 2.1GB hard drive. Although you can swap the tapes (so that the backup continues on two or more tapes), it's much better to keep everything on one tape.

✔ Some backup tapes can store as much as 4GB of data on a single tape.

✔ Some special backup units called DAT (for *d*igital *a*udio*t*ape) can store as much as 10GB of data on a single tape. Although the DAT units are expensive, if you have a large amount of data that's dear to you, it's worth the price.

✔ Yes, you can always add a tape backup drive after you buy your PC.

✔ A tape backup unit doesn't work unless *you* make sure that your hard drive gets backed up regularly. This advice is something you hear about frequently as you use your PC. People who have lost major chunks of work because of hard disk crashes and other mishaps swear by their backup tapes.

Stuff to Remember

You may elect to have three pieces of hardware installed when you first buy your computer: a modem, a sound card, and a tape backup unit. All these items are optional; they only add value to your computer and expand its capabilities. They're nice things to have installed, however, when you first get your system because adding them later is a minor pain.

Here are some key points to remember about modems, sound cards, and tape backup units:

✔ Get an internal modem when you buy your computer. Otherwise, after the purchase, consider buying an external modem, which is easier to set up.

✔ A 28.8 Kbps modem is considered standard. In the future, 33.6K and 57.6K modems will be the standard.

✔ Get a sound card that is SoundBlaster compatible.

✔ Make sure that your sound option includes speakers and maybe a microphone.

✔ Get a tape backup unit! Try to find a model that has tapes with a high enough capacity to back up your entire hard drive.

Chapter 11

All about Printers

In This Chapter

▶ Different types of printers
▶ What printers typically cost
▶ Laser printers
▶ Ink printers
▶ Impact printers
▶ Fax printers

*Y*our new computer will need a printer. It's a necessary part of the purchase — like software, even though few people really consider it before they buy. And, well, honestly, you don't need a printer *right away*, although you need one eventually.

This chapter covers printers in depth. Next to the computer system, choosing the right printer is one of the tougher decisions. Because choosing a printer is important to completing your computer system, you have a great deal of ground to cover. The more you know about it, the better prepared you are.

Different Printers for Different Printing

Several major kinds of computer printers used to be available, although, as they say, the cream has risen to the top, and now you have only a few to choose from, each at a relatively inexpensive price:

- Laser printers
- Ink printers
- Impact printers
- Fax machine printers

All printers, no matter what the type, get the printing job done. Because of the large selection, though, making a decision can be rough.

- ✔ Generally speaking, you'll probably get an ink printer. They're fast, quiet, and relatively inexpensive — and they do color.

- ✔ Laser printers are a must if you're in business.

- ✔ If you want color, go with an ink printer. Nearly all ink printers sold today do color. Some laser printers do color, although their price is quite steep and they're slow.

- ✔ Impact printers aren't as popular as they used to be. The typical dot-matrix printers of yore have given way to laser and ink printers. If you're printing invoices on multipart paper, however, you need an impact printer.

- ✔ Fax machine printers are essentially a combination fax machine and computer printer. They can also serve as a copy machine and, in some cases, be used to scan an image from a sheet of paper, which can be read into the computer.

- ✔ Other printer categories exist: Thermal printers used to be popular for laptop computers (though inexpensive ink printers are used now); daisy-wheel printers used to emulate typewriter output, though that's not really needed anymore (and it was slow); and some businesses may use high-speed line printers, although most everyone gets by with an ink or laser printer.

How much?

Printers range in price from $150 for a cheap model I wouldn't wish on anyone to upward of $4,000 for high-quality color printers. You'll probably pay anywhere from $250 to $600 or more for your printer, depending on what you get.

A typical laser printer ranges in price from $500 up to several thousand dollars for the color laser printers.

Ink printers start out at a couple of hundred dollars and climb up to more than $500 for the high-output color models.

Things that affect a printer's price

What you pay for a printer is based on many factors, primarily quality and speed.

Quality: Print quality is judged by how well the printer produces an image on paper. All that depends on how many tiny dots the printer can squeeze on a square inch of paper. The more dots, the higher the printer's resolution and the better the image.

Early laser printers could print 300 dots horizontally by 300 dots vertically. Today's models can easily manage 600-x-600 dots in a square inch. Some models can manage 1,200 dots per inch (dpi), which is the same resolution as a professional typesetting machine.

Speed: A printer's speed is measured in pages per minute, or ppm. The higher the value, the better. Some laser printers can manage 20 ppm. That's under optimal conditions, of course (usually repeatedly printing the same page of simple text). The more complex the graphics, the slower the printer goes.

Most ink printers manage between 4 and 8 ppm. Color laser printers are very slow, typically dribbling out 4 ppm or fewer. Remember that what they tell you in the ads is an optimal value. The page-per-minute values you experience will doubtless be less.

Other factors determining a printer's price include the printer's memory and how many fonts it knows about.

Memory: Most printers come with about a megabyte of their own RAM, more or less. The more memory you add to a printer, the faster it goes — especially for graphics. In fact, if you plan to print lots of graphics, pay the extra money and load your printer up with RAM.

Fonts: You pay more for printers that know how to use lots of fonts. This capability really isn't important; the operating system sends the printer any font you see on the screen. The fonts the printer knows about (called, remarkably *printer fonts*) print faster and generally look better than other fonts. The more your printer has, the more money you pay for them.

Now, consider the printer's brains:

Brains: Some printers are actually computers, ones that are specifically designed to print on paper (not foul up your phone bill). Cheaper printers? They're cheap because they don't have brains.

For example, you may notice that one color ink printer costs $800 and another model — just as technically good — costs $250. The difference? The $800 model has a brain. The $250 model uses your computer as its brain, which means that it takes that model longer to print *and* your computer slows down while the printer is printing.

Other stuff: Oh, and other factors determine a printer's price: whether it has an optional serial port, PostScript capabilities, networking options, and other details too technical to bore you with here.

Printers do not come with cables (or paper)!

Before diving in to the fast and exciting world of printer types, it's important to note one little-known axiom of the computer-buying world: Printers do not come with cables. Gasp!

Unlike a stereo or VCR, which comes with all the required cables, a computer printer doesn't come with everything you need to hook it up to your computer. The reason is vague: Not all printers are hooked up to a PC-type computer. Although that fact was important 20 years ago, now it's not. Still, printers don't come with cables, and you have to deal with that.

It almost goes without saying that your printer needs paper. Laser printers eat regular copy-machine paper, or you can pay more to get special high-quality paper. Ink printers can print on any paper, though special plastic or photo-quality papers are available that hold the image better than typical cotton paper types.

If you're getting an impact printer, you probably need fanfold paper (the kind with the sheets connected to each other). The paper has little holes on the sides (called "tractor food" because the "tractor feed" mechanism uses the holes) that help guide the paper through the printer. The tractor food is perforated so that it can be removed after printing to make the paper normal size.

✔ The printer cable can't be more than 20 feet long, which is kind of common sense because the best place for your printer should be within arm's reach — or did you know that? Well, now you do.

✔ Always buy the proper paper for your printer. Look in the documentation that came with your printer. Sometimes printer manufacturers recommend the kind of paper that is best for your printer.

✔ Stock up on paper! Nothing is worse than running out of paper and not having any backup. Go to a discount paper warehouse place, if one is near you, and buy a whole box.

TECHNICAL STUFF

Blah PostScript printers blah blah

A special type of laser printer is the PostScript printer. Essentially another type of computer, this one is dedicated to producing high-quality images. The PostScript printer does all the thinking on its own. Your software merely says "Do this," and the printer does the rest, freeing up the computer to do other things.

PostScript printers originally appeared for the Macintosh computer. Although you can get one for your PC as well, you have two pills to swallow. The first is that PostScript printers are expensive. All them thar PostScript brains cost money. The second pill to swallow is that PostScript printers work best with software that produces PostScript output, including primarily graphics applications, though you can look on the side of any software box to see whether it's PostScript happy.

Laser Printers Go "Fwoom Pkt Shhh!"

Laser printers are similar to the desktop copying machine, and they work on the same principle. The difference is that a laser printer receives its information from the computer instead of using a reflected image, as does the copy machine. A laser beam is used to draw the image.

The printed result from a laser printer is impressive. Laser printers produce what's called near-typeset-quality printing. For example, most typesetting equipment is capable of printing characters at a resolution of 1,200 lines per inch. An affordable laser printer can produce characters at a resolution of 400 to 600 lines per inch. Pay a little more, and you can get a number close to the 1,200 lines per inch that a real typesetting machine can achieve (all in the privacy of your own home, office, or underground revolutionary headquarters).

Laser printers are whisper quiet. Odds are that the fan in your computer is louder than a laser printer will ever be. Feeding paper into the printer is as easy as putting a sheaf of paper into a tray and sliding the sheaf into a slot — just like in a copy machine. Envelopes stick into their own slot. You can even print on your own letterhead by simply substituting that paper. (Sadly, with a laser printer, you can't "Xerox" your face, hands, or other body parts.)

Ink Printers Go "Thwip, Sft-Sft-Sft, Clunk!"

First, what you fear: Ink printers work by spewing ink all over paper, similar to the way a three-year-old spits water on his little brother in the bathtub.

Now, the truth: An *ink printer* works by lobbing a tiny ball of ink precisely at the paper, forming a teensy-tiny dot on the page. The ink dries instantly, and the resulting piece of paper does not smudge. In many cases, the paper looks *exactly* like it came from a spendy laser printer.

Another truth: Ink can be any color. Most of the newer, swankier ink printers actually lob four different colors of ink at the page: black, red, yellow, and blue. These colors combine to make outstanding — almost photographic — output.

Truly, an ink printer is ideal for most situations. Although it's not as fast or spiffy as a laser printer, its output is impressive — especially when you print on top-quality ink printer paper. Ink printers are also the least expensive way to print color, which is perfect for the home or small business.

- ✔ Odds are pretty good that you'll get an ink printer for your first PC purchase. It's a good way to go.

- ✔ If you can afford it, get a four-color ink printer. That's one black ink source, plus a three-color ink source (cyan, yellow, and magenta).

- ✔ Because no mechanical movement is involved, ink printers are quiet. Sometimes the brand name implies something about the printer's silence: Quietwriter, Whisperwriter, and Gaspingforairwriter, for example.

- ✔ Ink-jet printers keep their ink in a reservoir rather than on a ribbon. Some brands have a number of reservoirs, each with a different color. When you buy the printer, make sure to buy some spare ink cartridges.

- ✔ That special photographic paper is expensive. I just bought a box of eight sheets for $15. (Call me dumb, but it's what I do for a living.) The output on that paper, however, is almost the same as an 8-x-10 photograph.

Impact Printers Go "Rrrrrrrrttttteeee!"

Impact printers, also known as dot-matrix printers, are reliable, inexpensive and robust devices for getting that all-important hard copy. These printers are ideal for the home, or any place where speed and quality are not an issue, like the bowels of any major government bureaucracy.

Dot-matrix printers work by firing a series of pins, arranged vertically in a column. These pins stab at the printer's ribbon, forming a dot on the paper. As the print head (the device that contains the pins) moves back and forth, the pins create a pattern, a matrix of dots, in which characters are formed.

Over the years, the quality of impact printers has improved substantially. You may remember the classic (and ugly) computer printout of early dot-matrix printers. Today's models are more refined and occasionally have output that rivals ink printers.

- ✔ Unlike laser or ink printers, impact printers are slow and noisy.

- ✔ Always keep a supply of ribbons handy for your impact printer. Never use the printer with an old or frayed ribbon.

- ✔ Impact printer speed is measured in cps, or characters per second. The average impact printer should clip along at about 180 to 200 cps.

- ✔ One more thing! Dot-matrix printers generally do not come with a paper-feeding mechanism. This device guides the paper through the printer. Three types of paper-feeding mechanisms are available: friction feed, tractor feed, and pin feed (the latter two are the best).

- ✔ During the time I've been researching this book, I've yet to find a dot-matrix printer for sale in any major computer store. I assume that they're still available. Ask your dealer about a special order if you really want one.

- ✔ The only true advantage an impact printer has over the laser and ink models is when you're printing multipart forms. This printer is the only type that can "press hard" enough to get duplicate or triplicate copies.

Fax Printers Go "Slowly"

The newest, coolest thing to come from the world of printing is the fax printer. It's a fax. It's a printer. Some can even be used as copy machines, although they can't slice, dice, or shoot salad around the room.

A fax printer is essentially a fax machine that can be plugged into your PC and used as a printer. This machine is ideal for a small office on a budget that needs a "real" fax machine in addition to a computer printer.

As with any jack-of-all-trades, having a fax machine as a printer has some drawbacks. The biggest are speed and quality; a fax printer cannot compete with a similarly priced ink printer in the areas of output quality and printing speed. Yet it remains an option for those who need it.

- ✔ Fax printers cost between $400 and $600 — steep!

- ✔ I wouldn't use a fax printer as your only printer. They are really rather slow.

- ✔ If you don't get a fax printer, you can still send faxes from your computer by using a modem (see Chapter 10).

Stuff to Remember

Every computer needs a printer. Keep the following information in mind when you choose your PC's printer:

- ✔ Printers are judged by the quality of their output, speed, and price. Output is measured by dot resolution, horizontal by vertical. A 600-x-600 resolution is considered good, with higher values considered better. Speed is measured in ppm (pages per minute), and more is better. Price is measured in the local currency.

- ✔ If you can afford it, buy a nice laser printer.

- ✔ Ink printers are nice and inexpensive and also the best way to get color output, if that's what you're after.

- ✔ Try to avoid buying an unknown printer brand.

- ✔ Your printer will end up costing between $300 and $1,200 or higher, depending on what your needs are.

- ✔ Your printer does *not* come with a cable! Buy yourself a printer cable! And some paper!

Chapter 12

Put It in a Box

In This Chapter
▶ Types of PC boxes
▶ Small and teensy-tiny computers
▶ Laptop computers

*A*ll the early PCs looked like the original IBM PC*. They didn't have to. You could, if you wanted, put all the PC's innards into a blender and (as long as everything fit), use that as your computer box, or *console*. For some reason, all PCs tended to look alike in the early 1980s. I suppose that the manufacturers figured that some sort of good mojo existed in having all computers look alike.

Today, fortunately, not all computers look alike. They're not all even white anymore, with different colors (black is popular) available. This chapter lightly touches on the various PC models you can get and why you would care about them, one way or the other.

Computers for Every Mood

Not every dealer gives you a choice for which type of PC you want. Generally, most of them sell you what's called a *desktop model*. Other models, the *tower* and *minitower,* are generally more expensive. Whatever the case, remember that your PC's box — the console — doesn't have to look like the original IBM PC.

✔ All computers sold today are modeled after the IBM PC AT, introduced in 1984.

✔ Generally, the smaller the console, the fewer expansion options the PC has.

*I was in a junk store last month and thought that I spied an original IBM PC sitting on the shelf. Alas, it was an Eagle computer, an early clone (or imitation) of the first IBM model.

✔ Some PCs aren't really computers. They're really *dumb terminals,* which means that they have some brains but lack the sophistication of standard PCs. For example, some large business may buy a Network PC (NPC), which can't do anything unless it's shackled to a computer network.

The standard desktop model

The majority of PCs fit into the desktop-model type. The console is about the size of a fat, squat VCR, about 18 inches square and 5 inches tall. Figure 12-1 shows a typical model with a floppy drive, CD-ROM drive, three buttons, and some breathing slits.

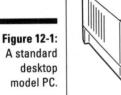

Figure 12-1:
A standard desktop model PC.

Advantages: Everything you need is right up front on a desktop model, with all the buttons and access to the disk drives. Plenty of internal room is available for expansion, plus a few extra "bays" for additional disk drives. Also, because this model is the most common, it tends to be less expensive than the tower and minitower designs.

Disadvantages: The standard desktop model PC has been successful for a number of reasons, one of which is that it has no true disadvantages. On some models, adding more expansion cards is difficult, which is why most power users go with a tower-model PC. Also, because a monitor typically sits atop the desktop model, accessing the desktop's innards isn't easy, which, again, makes power users shy away from this model. If you're not a power user, the desktop model has no real disadvantages.

The small-footprint PC

PCs don't have feet. Well, in a way, they do: The amount of desk space a PC occupies is referred to as a *footprint.* A small-footprint PC is typically a smaller, thinner version of the standard desktop PC. Figure 12-2 shows what one may look like.

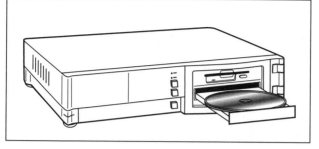

Small-footprint PCs were created to save desk space. C'mon, though, let's get real: No matter how large your desk is, it will be cluttered with stuff. Buying a small-footprint PC probably won't save you any space.

Advantages: A small-footprint PC takes up less space and is generally the least expensive type of PC you can buy. That doesn't mean that it's contents are cheap; it just means that by saving space, its manufacturer is passing along savings to you.

Disadvantages: Many. Primarily, small-footprint PCs lack internal expansion. Although some have one or two expansion slots, most have none. True, the PC may have everything you need; cutting off your expansion options, however — especially in an office situation — is dumb. Also, if you put the keyboard up to the console, it generally blocks access to your disk drives. Then you have to move your keyboard every time you want to access a disk. Again, that's dumb.

- Small-footprint PCs are also known as *home* models. For example, the Compaq Presario series generally consists of small-footprint PCs.

- Not all small footprint PCs are home systems. The first Pentium computer I bought was a small-footprint model. I quickly filled up its three expansion slots and was very disappointed when I found out that I couldn't add another internal hard drive.

The tower

The original IBM PC AT consoles (and their clones) were monsters, often twice as big as today's console units (sometimes two feet square!). To save desk space, users discovered that you could turn the behemoth consoles on their sides and set them on the floor, under a desk. Thus, the tower model PC was born, as shown in Figure 12-3.

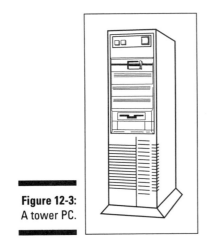

Figure 12-3:
A tower PC.

All tower PCs are now constructed in an up–down orientation. (You can turn any PC over on its side, but the tower PC is designed to sit that way.) The tower model sits on the floor, under your desk and monitor, and its keyboard and mouse sit on top of the desk, where you work.

Advantages: A tower PC has lots of room in it. Heck, it's the largest model. Tower PCs have more expansion slots, more drive bays, and more everything.

Disadvantages: Like a tower downtown in the city, a tower PC is expensive. You pay for all those expansion options. Also, a tower PC doesn't really reduce desk space because your keyboard and monitor still occupy the same space as a desktop PC would. Finally, tower PCs — even though they're geared toward internal expansion — are the most difficult of any type of PC to open to be able to access the inside.

 ✔ Today's tower PCs are constructed to live in a vertical orientation. Even though the idea was to turn the original PC AT on its side, all the disk drives and buttons on a tower PC are oriented level to the floor.

 ✔ No, if you live by the airport, you don't need to put blinking red lights on top of your tower PC.

 ✔ The movie *The Towering Inferno* was based on two books: *The Glass Inferno* and *The Tower*. It was O.J. Simpson's first movie role.

The minitower

I saved the best for last: My favorite type of PC box is the minitower. It's like a tower PC, except that it's squat. The minitower fits nicely on your desktop, giving you easy access to all its disk drives and buttons. Figure 12-4 shows you what one kind of looks like.

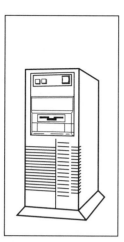

Figure 12-4:
A mini-
tower PC.

Advantages: The minitower has the expansion of a tower PC, but not the bulk; it has lots of expansion slots and disk drive bays for potential up-grades. It gives you easy access either right on top of your desk or under-neath it.

Disadvantages: A minitower PC is more expensive than the standard desktop console. A minitower also takes up more desktop space because the monitor and keyboard must sit alongside the minitower.

Not Really PCs

Some things that are called computers really aren't. Although normally I wouldn't mention these types of things, my publisher has urged me to cover them anyway. I'll do so briefly.

Too small to see or type on

Some PCs can fit in the palm of your hand, and a tiny minority of the PC-using world actually uses these devices. Sure, technology lets you stuff all a PC's essence into something the size of an eyeglass case, but is it *really* a computer?

Some handheld computers really are computers, complete with a version of Windows and common desktop software. Plug in enough external goodies (which kind of ruins the whole "portable" concept, but work with me here), and the result has the same capabilities as a desktop PC.

These cute little devices can be handy. I don't recommend them as your first computer purchase, however. What I can recommend, in fact, is to go to a store where these goodies are on display and play with them. See whether they offer anything you need. If so, buy it.

- Handheld computers are called *palmtops*.

- Another type of handheld computer is the PDA, or *personal digital assistant*. Unlike a real computer, a PDA comes with built-in software and offers little expandability. Still, for most handheld uses, it's fine.

- The limiting factor in making anything too tiny is, obviously, the size of your fingers. Can you type on a Barbie-size keyboard? The display for these teensy computers is always wacky; the screen is either too small or all scrunched up, which makes reading difficult.

- Most people who buy a palmtop or PDA generally know exactly what they want, which makes them a different type of crowd from the folks who would read this book, which is why I'm being vague in this section.

- If you do get a palmtop or PDA, make sure that it has some method to communicate with your desktop PC: in the form of a cable or infrared hookup, plus the software for your desktop PC.

Laptops and notebooks

Unlike palmtops or PDAs, a *laptop* is a genuine computer. It's a portable, battery-powered model you can take with you just about anywhere you go. With a docking station, in fact, you can use it as a "real" desktop computer and then unplug it to take it on the road. More about that subject in a bit.

When you buy a laptop, you should look for everything you would look for in a desktop model: microprocessor, memory, disk storage, modems, and the like.

Because the monitor is built into the laptop, you have no real decision there. Laptop monitors are all the same size as the laptop's lid, which makes them small compared to a desktop's screen.

You should look for three specific features in any laptop PC: low weight, long battery life, and a docking station.

Weight: Sure, 15 pounds isn't that heavy. You could move a 15-pound sack of sugar from one counter to the other in your kitchen and not suffer any major injuries. Try lugging a 15-pound computer around O'Hare Airport, though. Nope. Don't buy any laptop that weighs more than 9 pounds. The lighter they are, the more expensive.

Another thing: Keep in mind that it's not just the laptop that makes up the total weight you tote. You also have to consider the laptop's power brick, which plugs into the wall, an optional portable printer, and any other items you may lug along in your laptop case.

Battery life: Here's one truth about all advertised laptop battery ratings: They lie. Oh, they lie, they lie, they lie. Although it may say eight hours on the box, count on maybe a solid two-hour session with your laptop. Why? Because they lie.

They don't really lie; it's more like they *mislead.* The advertised battery life is a rating based on some oddball manufacturer's specs. They power-down the laptop and don't use the modem or the hard drive or the floppy drive, and then they can squeeze maybe six hours use from an eight-hour battery. In real life, plan on maybe three hours of battery life.

A three-hour battery life isn't bad (unless you think that you were getting the full eight hours promised on the box). Do read the section in the laptop's manual, however, about how to get the most from the battery. Definitely stay away from anything that advertises less than two hours of battery life.

The docking station: The best situation for a laptop is to have it both on the road and as your desktop system. To make that happen, you get a docking station. This doohickey enables you to plug in your laptop to a standard-size keyboard and monitor, which makes it work just like a desktop PC. When you go on the road, you undock your laptop and take all your work with you.

If you want a docking station, check to see whether your laptop comes with one. Some do, most don't. Either way, you still have to buy a monitor and keyboard to run with your laptop while it's docked.

- ✔ Laptops are not cheap. They are specific devices for specific uses. Because they need to be light and just sip at the power, they have specialty components that are very expensive.

- ✔ If you're lucky, your employer may assign you a laptop as part of your outside-the-office duties.

- ✔ I do not recommend a laptop PC as a first-time computer purchase. Only if you're out on the road all the time should you consider one (and even then, your employer may provide you with one or make a recommendation).

- ✔ All laptops should have a case. Although the laptop generally comes with some sort of case, that may not be enough. You may have to buy your own laptop tote to carry everything you need.

- ✔ Some airlines have power sockets that enable you to plug in your laptop while you're flying hither to thither. You may get a charge [sic] for this service. Ask your travel agent.

Portable PC history you can skip

The computer industry has tried to make PCs portable since the first days of the IBM PC. In fact, the early Compaq PC clone was a portable PC — called a "luggable." The first Compaq looked like a piece of large Samsonite luggage. It had a tiny screen and two floppy drives, and Compaq sold a mountain of them. Like all early portable PCs, it was merely a desktop model with a handle.

The laptop computer emerged in the mid-1980s looking something like a construction worker's lunch bucket. It weighed anywhere from 15 to 25 pounds and could run from a battery for 20 to 40 minutes. Most of these lunch-bucket PCs had to be plugged in, though.

The modern laptop computer debuted in 1988 as the NEC Ultralite PC. It weighed less than 8 pounds but lacked disk drives. Since then, all 8-pound and lighter laptops were called *notebook* PCs because they're about the size of a notebook. The terms are now interchangeable, though most in the industry prefer *notebook* over *laptop*.

✔ Some PDAs and palmtop PCs have a battery life of 24 hours or more! The reason is that they lack the moving parts a real laptop has that consume more juice.

Stuff to Remember

Just as no typical automobile exists, no typical computer chassis exists. You can choose from the desktop (sedan), small footprint (economy), tower (pickup truck), and minitower (sports utility vehicle) models, each with its pluses and minuses.

✔ If you need internal expansion in your PC, steer clear of the small-footprint models.

✔ Most people opt for the desktop or minitower type of PC console.

✔ Small, handheld computers are cute. Consider one only if it's really all you need.

✔ Laptops are special computers in their own right, ideally suited for people who need to take their machines with them.

Part III
Software Overview

"WELL'P — THERE GOES THE AMBIANCE."

In this part . . .

Without any software to control your computer, you essentially have a very expensive paperweight on your desk. Just go ahead and ask around; you'll find lots of computer owners with various *boat anchors* in their closets or used as doorstops. Although these machines were impressive, they lacked the proper software to harness their hardware horsepower.

Fortunately, you won't own a boat anchor computer. You have the foresight to see how much a lack of software can hurt a computer — no matter how impressive the hardware. Software is really the key. That's the subject of the chapters in this part of the book: what to look for to find the software you need to run your new computer.

Chapter 13

Your Computer's Operating System

In This Chapter

▶ Understanding all about operating systems

▶ Picking an operating system

▶ Searching for a large software base

▶ Looking at the issue of user-friendly versus user-hostile

▶ Picking a version of Windows (NT or 98)

▶ Lunching at the operating system smorgasbord

Central to all software in your computer is the main piece of software. That one program controls all the others and just about everything in your computer. It's the first program that's run in the morning, the program other programs defer to, the head program in charge, the boss, the czar, *el queso grande,* the king o' everything. It's called the operating system.

Choosing your computer's main control program is important. But is it hard? Na-a-a-h. Thanks to the dominance of Microsoft, you'll probably use the Windows operating system on your computer. True, others are out there. In a "fair" world, you could have fun making a decision. But real life is Windows, which this chapter pretends is an option (so play along).

Understanding Operating Systems

An *operating system* is a program that controls your computer, specifically, the main chip in your computer, or the *microprocessor*. Together, the microprocessor and the operating system are at the heart of the computer: They go hand in hand.

The operating system is the brains of the operation. The microprocessor is the brawn. This setup fools many people.

If you've read Part II, you know that the microprocessor sits on your computer's throne. Although some say that the microprocessor is the computer's "brain," it holds no hideous intelligence and is really only good at carrying out orders. The computer's operating system (software) tells the microprocessor how to control the computer system. The operating system is the brain. Without instructions from the operating system, the microprocessor chip may as well be a potato chip.

After controlling the microprocessor, and therefore the rest of the computer's hardware, the operating system has a second job: It controls all the other software on your computer.

Suppose that you use a word processor to write the next *Gone With The Wind*. That word processor is *software* — a computer program. It must work with your computer's operating system to be completely happy.

When you choose software for your new computer, you select it for which operating system it runs on (or is compatible with) more than you select it for a particular computer. This situation wasn't always the case. In the early days, software stores were organized by computer brand. The brand doesn't matter anymore — it's the operating system.

In the chore of buying a computer, software comes first, and the first software you choose is the computer's operating system. Without the operating system, the hardware and all your software programs are useless.

 ✔ The operating system is the main program running your computer.

 ✔ The operating system controls the microprocessor. In fact, operating systems are written for specific microprocessors.

 ✔ Operating systems also have a hoard of software that runs "under" them. For example, the Jove editor runs under the UNIX operating system, and the 1-2-3 spreadsheet runs under the DOS operating system.

 ✔ Another chore for the operating system is to work with you. Different operating systems offer different degrees of friendliness when it comes to working with humans. (Windows is very friendly.)

Choosing an Operating System

In the old days, you chose the computer first. Now you choose an operating system first. The reason is that the operating system "owns" all the software. You pick the right operating system, and its software base follows. Only then do you look for the hardware to make everything run.

Microsoft. Windows. Monopoly?

Why is Windows the only choice you have for an operating system? Lots of reasons exist. The foremost is that Microsoft sells Windows and sells it hard.

Windows is a successor to the old DOS operating system, which was the most popular operating system in its day. Although DOS was popular, it wasn't dear to anyone. DOS was ugly and had limitations. Windows was the Microsoft answer to those problems.

For an operating system to be successful, it must have a large software base. People were drawn to that. Hardware was geared toward it. After all, every program wants to be compatible with the most popular operating system. Sure, competition existed. Because

Windows had the lead, however, it just eventually took over — thanks to that large software base. This takeover would have happened to any operating system; eventually only one would dominate all PCs.

The problem isn't a Microsoft "monopoly." The problem is really a stifling of creativity. Without serious competition, Windows loses innovation. The Microsoft updates to its operating system software are cosmetic and weak. The advantage to you, of course, is that you don't have to make a decision when it comes to selecting an operating system. The lack of innovation on the part of Microsoft, however, means that everyone suffers. That's the true tragedy.

Let me be honest: The operating system you will use is Windows, probably Windows 98 or some other version. Eighty-five percent of the computers in the world run that operating system. About the same percentage of software that's available runs on Windows 98. *You see, it's really not a decision to make!*

Please bear with me as I go through the motions in the following sections. Just pretend for a moment that you can choose from operating systems other than Windows.

Check that software base!

If you were *really* shopping for an operating system, the first thing you would check is the amount of software available for it. That's easy to do: Visit any computer store, and see how many aisles of software it has for each operating system.

I just visited my local Computer City, for example, and found two long aisles full of software. All except two "stacks" were for Windows. The two remaining stacks were for the Macintosh. The largest software base, and therefore the most selection, belongs to Windows.

Another way to check the software base is to review computer magazines. You have to check a few because magazines are typically geared to one operating system or another. Even so, you get an idea of the software base available by the number of related software ads.

- ✔ Sometimes the software base isn't a good clue. For example, most of the best graphics and design software is still available primarily for the Macintosh. Although Windows versions exist, they're usually not as good as the Mac originals.

- ✔ If you're using proprietary software, such as an inventory system written specifically for your company, you need whichever operating system that software requires. This example is one of the rare instances in which the software base doesn't matter.

- ✔ As an example of proprietary software, a majority of the software used by Internet Service Providers (ISPs) operates under the UNIX operating system. If you were setting up your own ISP shop, you would probably buy computers that run UNIX to take advantage of that software.

How friendly is it?

An operating system can be cute and easy — maybe even fun. Or an operating system can be like an SAT exam. This statement may lead you to believe that fun operating systems are best. It all depends, however, on how much control you want over the computer.

The more terse the operating system, generally the more power you have over the computer. Tough operating systems, such as UNIX and DOS, give you more control over the computer — direct access, in many cases — in comparison with fun and easy operating systems, such as Windows and the Macintosh.

Fun and easy operating systems, on the other hand, are easier to figure out how to use. Honestly, who really wants to set internal timing options or use the ANSI.SYS device driver?

- ✔ On the friendliness scale, Windows is about as friendly as you can get. Although Windows can be confusing at times, all computers are bewildering until you get to know them.

- ✔ The Macintosh operating system is perhaps the easiest and most intuitive to use. In fact, Windows is the Macintosh's ugly cousin.

- ✔ UNIX is the least friendly operating system. It is not only terse but also allows you to do dangerous things quite easily.

✔ Unfriendly operating systems, like UNIX and DOS, have special programs you can run that make using the operating system easier. These programs are called *shells*. Like a seashell protects soft and tasty creatures from other creatures who want to eat them, an operating system shell protects you, the user, from terrible programs that would make you blanche.

✔ Yes, DOS was quite popular despite its ugly mood. In fact, Windows started its life as a DOS shell.

✔ Friendly operating systems generally sport friendly software. The programs on a Macintosh, for example, are intuitive after you know the feel of the operating system. On the other hand, programs in UNIX are all twisted and ugly as scrap metal and about as friendly.

Windows 98 versus Windows NT

You should look at *two* flavors of Windows: Windows 98 and Windows NT. Both are similar in look and feel, and Microsoft makes both. Each is targeted, however, to a different crowd.

Windows NT: Considered the "high end" operating system, Windows NT requires quite a bit of hardware horsepower to run. It's designed primarily for business applications or for use on a computer network.

Windows 98: Though this operating system is considered "low end," it's not by any means cheap. It still has the largest software base of any operating system and is still more popular than Windows NT. Odds are really good that this operating system is the one you'll use.

✔ Do you plan to play games on your PC? Then you need Windows 98. That operating system is still the most compatible of the two Windows versions; it runs all the older Windows and DOS programs as well as some programs written for Windows NT.

✔ Consider Windows NT only if you're exclusively running 32-bit applications. The software box tells you whether an application is 32 bits and whether it runs better under Windows NT.

✔ Windows NT comes in two flavors: workstation and server. The server is designed to be a central office computer on a network. The workstation flavor can be used on a network or individually.

Operating systems other than Windows

Fear not — you can buy operating systems other than Windows. You can even have a computer geek set up your PC so that it can use any of these operating systems, switching between them like the changing of records in a jukebox (well, except for the Macintosh operating system, for which you need a Macintosh computer).

DOS: Yeah, DOS is dead. IBM still makes a version of it, though, called PC-DOS. Lots of DOS programs are still out there, many of them available for free (because the developers don't stand a chance of making money any other way!). A free version of DOS, called Caldera DOS, is also available from the Internet. It's quite popular with the anti-Windows crowd.

(As the author of *DOS For Dummies,* which is published by IDG Books Worldwide, Inc., I look back fondly on DOS. Although it may have been ugly, it was fast, and its programs were tiny and lite. I don't remember my DOS stuff crashing as much as Windows does. And I don't remember having to mess as much with the computer for its own sake. Then again, I'm a DOS romantic.)

OS/2: Before Windows, OS/2 was to be the successor to DOS. Ha! Never happened. IBM still makes OS/2 available, though. No software is available, or at least nothing worth looking at. And if it has no software, then the thing really has no point to it, eh?

UNIX/Linux: UNIX is really the operating system for programmers and hobbyists. A home-brew version of UNIX, called Linux, is now all the rage (even a version of the popular game DOOM is available for it). Alas, UNIX/Linux is really rather technical; although an outside chance exists that it may be a contender someday, the software base isn't quite there yet.

Macintosh: The only true alternative to Windows is to get a Macintosh. Although the Mac now captures about 7 percent of the total computer market, it's a robust 7 percent. Just about any major application available for the PC has a Mac counterpart (which is often better).

Rumors abound that the Mac may be dying, and its percentage has, in fact, slipped from a high of 20 percent of all PCs sold to a dismal 7 percent. Even so, I don't think that it's a boat anchor yet. Although Mac hardware is a little more pricey than the hardware for its PC counterpart, the Mac is widely supported by a hoard of overenthusiastic fanatics.

Though Linux is "free," it's typically available on a CD-ROM disk in the back of a Linux book you pay money for. Don't bother with it if you're not the least bit technically inclined.

Stuff to Remember

When it comes to buying a computer, software is more important than hardware. The most important of the software is the operating system, your PC's main control program. Keep the following points in mind as you hunt for an operating system that's just right for you:

- ✔ The operating system must work with both you and the computer hardware to give you a useful computer system.

- ✔ The success of an operating system is directly related to the number of software applications available.

- ✔ Operating systems can be user-friendly or user-hostile.

- ✔ Get Windows. In a few instances, you may seek out a Macintosh, primarily if your work is in one of the creative fields.

- ✔ Consider Windows NT only if you plan to use all 32-bit software and not run any older Windows or DOS applications (or any games).

Chapter 14

Everything You Wanted to Know about Software (But Were Afraid to Ask)

● ●

In This Chapter

▶ Understanding software

▶ Word-processing programs

▶ Desktop publishing

▶ Spreadsheet software

▶ Database applications

▶ Graphics programs

▶ All about bundled software

▶ Communications and the Internet

▶ Games and learning software

▶ Utility programs

▶ Writing your own programs

▶ Free and almost free software

● ●

*Y*our computer needs software like an orchestra needs a conductor, like a car needs a driver, like an actor needs a script — you get the idea. Whatever it is that a computer does, it does it because of software. And a great deal of software is out there to choose from.

Even though you may have heard the terms tossed around, the information in this chapter properly describes the more popular categories of software and what each one does. Odds are good that you'll pick one or more of the following types of software, depending on your needs, likes, and whims.

Applications, Categories, and Programs

Just as hardware consists of different parts, software consists of different parts. You can have a program or an application. All of it is software.

Overall, software is divided into categories — just like the grocery store has a cereal aisle. Those categories are called *applications:* for example, word processors, spreadsheets, and databases. All those are applications.

A *program* is an individual application. For example, WordPerfect is a word-processing program. Microsoft Excel is a spreadsheet program.

Why all the terms? Because the people who create the applications have to make it all sound attractive when it's sold to you. Most people say "word processor," not "word-processing application software." In fact, many people just say "WordPerfect," which is synonymous with word processing.

- ✔ The next few sections in this chapter cover various applications — major software categories.

- ✔ A program is any individual piece of software. WordPerfect, for example, is a program.

- ✔ All this stuff costs money, and software isn't cheap. Although most users don't realize it, you can expect to spend almost as much on software as on your computer purchase. Maybe not all at one time, but eventually.

Word Processors

The most popular type of application on any computer is the word processor, as shown in Figure 14-1. As an office tool, the computer first replaced the typewriter. Word processors have come a long way, of course, from being just a better typewriter. Modern word processors can correct grammar and spelling, and they now allow you to include pictures and format your text in various and sundry ways.

At one time, several "levels" of word processor existed: one for beginners, one for writers, one for lawyers, and so on. However, most of the major programs have combined all these tools; you pay for them whether you need them or not. That situation makes word processors full featured yet expensive.

Figure 14-1:
A word
processor.

✔ The most popular word processor is Microsoft Word. It's one big program to chew, so make sure that you buy a copy of *Word 97 For Windows For Dummies,* written by yours truly (and published by IDG Books Worldwide, Inc.) or whichever book is appropriate for the version you use.

✔ The second most popular word processor is WordPerfect. It used to be number one, but the WordPerfect people were too late in making the transition from DOS to Windows, so Microsoft took over.

✔ The original, arcane word processor for all personal computers was called WordStar.

✔ If you're into writing plays or movies, some special word-processing software has been developed especially for you. This type of software is advertised in the back of both movie and computer magazines.

✔ A good entry-level word processor is the WordPad program, included with Windows 98. Although it lacks a real word processor's powerful features (like spell checking) and some of the fancier formatting commands, it works well.

✔ A basic type of word processor is the *text editor.* It's a program that lets you just write text — no formatting or any fancy stuff. Though you may not think that you need it, every operating system comes with a text editor, and you'll probably use one sooner or later.

✔ Not all word processors save information in the same way. For example, if you use WordPerfect at home and Microsoft Word at the office, you have two different document formats. For that reason, it's best to stick with one brand of word processor if you plan to work between two different computers.

Desktop Publishing

An offshoot of word processing is *desktop publishing,* in which you combine words and pictures and create a "layout" of your finished page — for example, to create a pamphlet, a church bulletin, or even a novel.

Many word processors incorporate desktop publishing features as part of their design. You can mix different type styles on the screen so that you can see in advance exactly what will be printed. This style of word processor is called *WYSIWYG* ("wizzy wig"), which stands for What You See Is What You Get. You can even add graphics to your text to spice things up.

For desktop publishing in particular, you usually need separate word-processing and graphics software. If you're into this area, make sure that the desktop publishing package recognizes your word-processing and graphics software.

✔ Desktop publishing is abbreviated DTP.

✔ The most popular desktop publishing program is PageMaker.

✔ Although some word processors approach desktop publishing in their sophistication, buying a separate desktop publishing application is always a better idea (the right tool for the right job, and all that).

Spreadsheets

The second thing the computer replaced in the office was the adding machine, or calculator. To work with numbers, you use spreadsheet software. It enables you to plug numbers into a grid, with each "cell" in the grid calculated by using values from other cells. Using a spreadsheet, you can manipulate, examine, and change numeric values and their relationships to other values, but it's really not that boring.

Used primarily for business applications, spreadsheets enable you to design an electronic balance sheet or general ledger for your company. You can also manipulate various figures and instantly see how other figures are affected. You can see, for example, how it's possible to embezzle funds without anyone's noticing!

✔ Spreadsheets are not just for numbers. They can produce graphs, charts, and organizational charts and work with any type of lists (see Figure 14-2). If your information appears in any type of grid, working with it in a spreadsheet is a breeze.

✔ The most popular spreadsheet is Microsoft Excel. The most popular program used to be Lotus 1-2-3 (Lotus was the name of the company, and 1-2-3 was the name of the program). Like other programs, however, Lotus was too slow to make the transition from DOS to Windows, so Microsoft took over.

✔ The original, prototype spreadsheet was called VisiCalc. It stood for *visi*ble *calc*ulator.

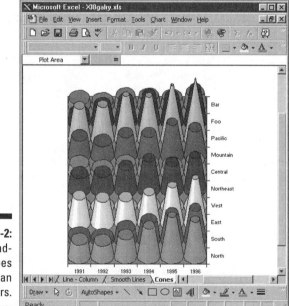

Figure 14-2: A spreadsheet does more than numbers.

Databases

A *database* program is used to manipulate information, such as a listing of your record collection or a tally of unruly employees. The database software stores the information and then helps you sort it, sift it, print it, retrieve it, or mangle it in any number of interesting ways.

You may not believe it, but more database programs are out there than anything else — even word processors. The major packages are more like programming languages: They let you create your own database and write a teeny program that somehow controls it. These programs are for diehards.

Home budgeting software

Although spreadsheets are fine for home use, what you probably need is some type of home budgeting software. These programs can do more than just balance your checkbook or print your checks (with the proper check-like paper). They can track investments and loans and even make forecasts.

Several popular home budgeting and checking packages are available, and you can quickly figure out how to use any of them. The most popular are Quicken and Microsoft Money.

Be careful when you're ordering computer-printed checks for your home budgeting software: You don't have to order them from the company that makes the software. Inquire at your bank to see whether it offers computer-printed checks. They're often cheaper than the ones the software company offers.

If you're looking for a home database or you want something easier than the programming language database, consider a customized database program. For example, you may find an address program for keeping track of your friends and contacts that can also print mailing labels.

Another popular example is personal organizer software, which includes an address list, appointment calendar, and other goodies. These programs vary from simple phone lists to advanced tickler systems that keep details about customers or vendors or overseas secret agents.

- Tons of popular databases are out there, although Microsoft Access is the most common. The reason is not that it's the best; it's that Access is included with the popular Microsoft Office program.

- The original database program for personal computers was called Vulcan — after Mr. Spock, from *Star Trek*! It was later renamed dBASE (short for database), which was for years the most popular PC database program.

Graphics

Graphics software falls into two categories: drawing and painting programs. These programs enable you to create and manipulate a graphical image on the screen. Each one uses a different technique to create the image.

Drawing programs (also known as *CAD*, or *computer-assisted design* programs) are much more precise than painting programs. CAD deals with "objects" rather than dots on the screen.

Painting programs are more recreational and not as accurate as CAD. They enable you to paint more realistic images, as shown in Figure 14-3, although the process of manipulating an image after it's created isn't as precise as in a drawing program.

Figure 14-3:
A painting
program.

✔ If you're an engineer or architect, you probably will spend some serious bucks for a decent graphics system. The advantage is that changing a design is easy because the thing is stored in a computer.

✔ Almost every aspect of graphic arts is now done by using a computer. Most of the best stuff is available on the Macintosh, with some applications also available on Windows.

✔ The most popular CAD program is AutoCAD. It's very, *very* expensive and requires special computer hardware to make it work.

✔ A popular drawing program is CorelDraw for Windows. For the Mac crowd, it's Adobe Illustrator. (I used Illustrator to create many of the images you see in this book.)

✔ A popular painting program is Fractal Design Painter. It comes in a paint can rather than in a box! I've seen some artists do absolutely amazing things with it.

Bundled Software Packages

Chances are that you'll probably need a buncha software when you first start out computing. This fact surprised me when I first bought a computer, in 1982. I took it home and turned it on only to find that it didn't really do anything, so I drove back to the store and bought some software. I hope that you don't make the same mistake.

Because software developers know that you will buy a stack of stuff to get started, they've created special bundled software packages. These packages come in several different types and flavors, each of which is designed to get you started with just what you need.

Meanwhile, the back-at-the-office type of integrated program

A popular tactic of major software vendors is to distribute the "office" integrated package of software. For example, Microsoft Office and Corel Office (which includes WordPerfect) are two popular packages that are sold. These office packages include a real word processor, database, and spread-sheet. They aren't cheapie versions either; the companies have just combined all their top-selling stuff and sell it for a lower price in a bundle.

Buying your software bundled in an office package has many advantages, and low cost is the most obvious. Buying one office package is often cheaper than buying everything a piece at a time. Even if you use only two of the applications in the office package, you come out ahead.

The disadvantage to integrated software is that some of it isn't integrated. For example, the package may consist of two or three unrelated programs that can't share information between them.

Another major disadvantage lies in upgrading the software. After six months to a year, most software developers produce a newer, better version of their programs. The cost of upgrading each one, especially when you have an "office," can be outrageous. Refer to Chapter 21 for more information about upgrading and how to deal with it.

Bundled software

Another type of bundled software is stuff that comes with the computer "for free," especially with laptops. I haven't bought a laptop in the past six years that didn't come with megabytes of crap I really didn't want or need. Some of the stuff is useful, of course, but what's the point of it's being "for free" if you have to uninstall it?

If possible, remember to ask which types of programs come bundled with a computer when you buy it. In a common practice among many of the major computer makers, they offer a variety of "for free" packages, from business to home to entertainment.

In addition to seeing what's available, ask whether you can easily remove any of the add-ons. For example, does the program that lets you use your modem to hail a taxi from any phone booth in Manhattan come with an "uninstall" program? (I have no idea why anyone would ever need that type of program anyway.)

> ✔ Obviously, bundled software isn't a bonus if you don't plan to use it.
>
> ✔ If you don't need any bundled software, see whether the dealer can knock some money off the purchase price. (A discount rarely happens, because a dealer generally pays up front for the bundled stuff.)

Communications and Internet Software

Communications software enables your computer to take advantage of a modem and the phone system to talk with other computers. It does so in two ways: through the Internet or by directly phoning up another computer with a modem.

Doing the Internet

The Internet can be informative and fun and a tremendous waste of time. Take your pick. The computer industry is now all a-spaz about the Internet. Personally, I could take it or leave it. Why not see for yourself, though? To do that, you need software to access the Internet.

The primary means for storing information on the Internet is the World Wide Web. To see that information, you need a piece of software called a Web browser. Although Netscape is the most popular, as shown in Figure 14-4, Microsoft Internet Explorer (which is given away with Windows) is gaining ground (and I wonder why?).

You also need, more importantly than software, a way of accessing the Internet. That process doesn't require software. Instead, you must hunt for an Internet Service Provider (ISP). An *ISP* connects you to the Internet, often offering free software and classes to help you get the job done.

In addition to your Web browser, you need e-mail software. This type of software is required if you want to send and receive e-mail messages from others on the Internet. Netscape comes with its own e-mail program, though you can get others. Although Windows has its own e-mail program, it's as frustrating as being stuck in traffic with a car full of screaming 2-year-olds.

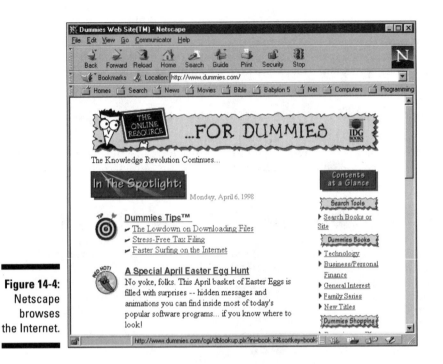

Figure 14-4:
Netscape
browses
the Internet.

✔ Your computer needs a modem in order to connect to the Internet (refer to Chapter 9).

✔ To connect to the Internet, you need a dialer program. Windows comes with one, as does the Mac operating system, OS8.

✔ Personally, I recommend the Netscape browser. It's more of a complete package than what Microsoft offers. Also, I get a great deal of e-mail from people who can't figure out the Microsoft e-mail program, Outlook. I get no mail from Netscape e-mail users.

✔ Another popular e-mail program is Eudora. It has more features than what either Netscape or Microsoft offers.

✔ There's much to do on the Internet, and it can be overwhelming. My advice is to find a good book about the subject if you want to dive in. (Get the book *after* you buy your computer.)

Regular old telecommunications

Beyond the Internet is a whole world of computers and modems. Before the World Wide Web, in fact, most computers and modems called up electronic bulletin-board systems (BBSs) where people could exchange programs and information and discuss topics of interest — like gun control (over and over).

Also available to anyone with a computer and modem are the national online services. Although quite a few used to be available, the only big and noticeable one now is America Online (AOL) — which also provides its users with Internet access.

To use your computer and modem to call a BBS or a national online service like AOL, you need a modem and special communications software. AOL provides its own software (which it sends to you for free in the mail from now until forever). Local BBSs and other systems require telecommunications software. Fortunately, it comes with Windows, so you really have nothing to buy. (Oh, software is available, but why bother paying money when you already have it?)

- ✔ Modeming is fun.

- ✔ Sadly, this area of computer communications is dwindling as the popularity of the Internet increases. When I was the editor of a local computer magazine in San Diego, we had a list of almost 300 local BBSs, and even more existed that we didn't list. That number has now dwindled, partly because of the Internet.

Recreation and Education

Though few admit it, computers can be used to play games. Oh, and don't forget education — although with a computer, a thin line exists between education and entertainment; both are rather fun.

Games

This whole personal computer craze really started with the home arcade games of the early 1980s. Although the arcade games are going strong, it's hard to compare those machines that only play games well with a computer that plays games well *and* does other things, like process words and browse the Internet.

- ✔ Your PC needs sound and a CD-ROM drive to play most games.

- ✔ Most games require that you have a joystick. Although they do make gameplay better, most games run fine without a joystick. (You can play some games just as well with a keyboard and a mouse.)

- ✔ Some fancy joysticks are out there. Check the side of the game software box to see whether it supports any of the swanky joysticks.

✔ Many different types of computers games are available: arcade-style shoot-'em-ups; classics, such as Chess, Go, and Othello; adventure games; "little man" games a là PacMan; and simulation games: flight simulators, war simulators, and business simulators. The creativity well never runs dry with computer games.

Education

If computers are magnets, then kids are tiny balls of steel. They love computers. They're bold. And there's a reason for that. Nope, it's not that kids today are smarter than we were. It's that kids have no fear. In fact, I recommend that you get your kids their own computer. Data loss means little to them.

Some great educational programs are out there, from stuff to teach toddlers their colors and numbers to encyclopedias and SAT exam simulators. Thankfully, much of it is really good. Although some bad programs are out there, just ask around at a PTO meeting, and you'll quickly find out what's good and what stinks.

✔ Generally speaking, all the Microsoft reference titles tend to be very good.

✔ For small kids, I can recommend the Jumpstart series of programs. Also, my kids love the *Sesame Street* and Dr. Seuss programs.

Utility Programs

A special category of software is the *utility* program. These programs differ from applications in that they aren't used for productivity. A utility program doesn't do your work on the computer; it works on the computer itself. A utility program typically does one of three things: improve performance, diagnose a problem (see Figure 14-5), or repair something that's wrong.

Utilities come in bundles of several dozen programs. For example, one program may recover files you deleted, another may rescue a damaged hard drive, and another may optimize the way your PC uses memory. Other utility-like programs include calculators, appointment books, and little word processors (called *text editors*).

✔ Utilities are also referred to as *tools*.

✔ Your computer's operating system comes with a host of utilities for doing various computer chores.

✔ About the oldest and most venerated set of utility programs is the Norton Utilities.

Figure 14-5:
The
ScanDisk
utility
checks your
hard drive.

▸ One of the best utilities to own is a virus scanner. This type of program ensures that your computer is not infected with a nasty program (a *virus*) that can really foul things up. The most popular antivirus program is the one McAfee makes.

▸ If you ever find yourself saying, "I wish I had just one little program that could. . . ." or "I keep repeating these same steps over and over. Can't the computer do that for me?" — you need a utility. Chances are that something is available which does that specific job. If not, you can write your own computer program, as covered in the next section.

Programming

Programming languages enable you to write and run your own computer software. Check out the instructions in Figure 14-6. Many programming languages are available, some easy to get a grasp on and some hard. You don't have to be good at math to understand a programming language. Just having a healthy curiosity about computers helps.

Nowadays, no one using a computer has to know how to program the thing. In the olden days, that's all you could do with one. Fortunately, however, enough people do program the things and have created all the other types of programs covered in this chapter. Still, if you're curious or you just want to have ultimate control over the thing, you can program.

▸ Don't be fooled: It takes a long time to write a program, even a simple one. Still, you can do it. No one will stop you. It's one of the more charming things about a computer.

▸ To program, you must know a programming language, which is a dialogue you use to tell a computer to do certain things.

✔ The most popular programming language is C++. Unfortunately, it's not the easiest to start using.

✔ Two popular versions of the C/C++ language are available, one from Borland and the other from Microsoft. I prefer the Borland stuff.

✔ The easiest programming language to use is BASIC. The most popular version is Microsoft Visual Basic. In a way, it lets you create a Windows program as easily as cut-and-paste.

✔ Other languages are available, each with its own army of followers and individual charms and detractions.

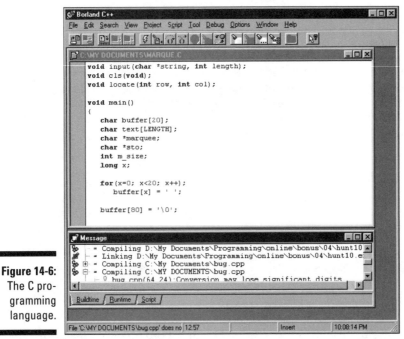

Figure 14-6:
The C programming language.

Software for Free and Almost Free

Believe it or not, not all software costs money. A good number of programs, in fact, are available for free or almost free. Some software may come "free" with your computer; some may be available from nice people who write software and give it away because they're eccentric geniuses and expect their rewards in the hereafter.

Please keep in mind that, though software is available for nothing or next to nothing, not all software is free. Don't accept from a well-meaning friend who's giving it away any software that you know can be purchased from a store. This practice constitutes theft. Only if the software states that it's free (or it's a "demo") can you legally use it without paying.

- You can find these free and almost free software programs all over the place. Computer stores sometimes have bins full of disks of free stuff (though you pay for the disk it's copied on). You can also get software from the Internet.

- These freebie programs are often a source of computer viruses. It's not that all free stuff is tainted; however, a few unscrupulous individuals pass off supposedly free software that is in fact plagued with a virus. The best way to be sure is to get your free stuff from a reputable source or buy a virus-scanning utility.

Public-domain software

Software that costs nothing is known as *public-domain* software. These software packages are written by little men in small rooms who stay up all night and think philanthropic thoughts. They program their brains out and then give away the software. Not all the programs are crap, either; some really nice applications occasionally rise up from the swamp.

- Public-domain software says so, either in the program or in the documentation. Never assume that something is public domain just because someone else tells you that it is.

- Do not sell public-domain software, nor should you buy it from anyone. It's free!

Freeware

Freeware is the term used for software that has no cost and is not in the public domain. The primary difference is ownership. Because public-domain software has no owner, anyone could, theoretically, modify it and resell it. With freeware, the author gives the stuff away but may, at some later point, decide to sell it instead.

Shareware

A popular form of free software is referred to as *shareware*. It's distributed for free, just like public-domain software and freeware. The exception is that if you use and enjoy the program, the author requests that you contribute a donation.

✔ I've used many shareware programs and pay for those I continue to use.

✔ The fee for buying shareware is really cheap, often $10 or less.

✔ Unlike real software, which you cannot give away, shareware authors encourage you to give their programs away.

Demo software

Another category of free software is the *demo* program. These programs are special versions of major applications you can try before you buy. Sometimes, they're the real thing and lack only a few features. Other times, the demo software "self-destructs" after a few weeks (the demo is over).

Stuff to Remember

Your computer needs software, and, fortunately, plenty of it is out there. For just about anything you do, an application is bound to be available to carry out that task. If not, you can write your own!

✔ Plan to spend as much for your software as you do for your hardware.

✔ You don't have to purchase all your software immediately. Just start with those few programs you plan to use right way. Find out how to use them, and then buy other applications.

Part IV
The Buying Process

"COMPATIBILITY? NO PROBLEM! THIS BABY COMES IN OVER A DOZEN DESIGNER COLORS."

In this part . . .

If buying groceries were as complex as buying a computer, we would all starve. Food is easy to eat. I'll even bet that the first caveperson to eat an avocado wasn't thinking about whether it was a fruit or vegetable or how much fat was in it or which vitamins it supplied or what other kinds of food would go well with it. Nope, he was thinking, "Big pit."

The first step of your computer search is discovering what you want the computer to do for you. Hopefully, you know that by now. The other four steps are covered in the chapters in this part of the book, including shopping for software, finding hardware to match the software, searching for service and support, and, finally, buying the computer.

Oh, and an avocado is a fruit. So is a tomato. (For political reasons, the United States government legally declared that a tomato is *really* a vegetable. Go figure.)

Chapter 15

Shopping for Software

. . . .

In This Chapter

▶ Test-driving software

▶ Looking for help

▶ Checking for developer support

▶ Reading the software box

▶ Filling in the software worksheet

. . . .

See computer. See computer go. Go, computer go!

And how does the computer go? Software! To make your computer do things you need done, you need the proper software. By now, you should know what you want a computer to do. After reading Part III of this book, you should have a general idea of the software you need to get that done. Now you're ready to go out and find that software, which this chapter helps you do.

How to Buy Software

Before heading off to the Mr. Software store, you should know what it is that you're about to do. I don't want you to walk around and pick up various software boxes because they're pretty or look impressively large. No, you need a plan of attack. Here 'tis:

- ✔ Take a test-drive.
- ✔ Check for support.
- ✔ Obtain product information.
- ✔ Fill in this book's software worksheet.

Before you buy anything, you have to take a test-drive — that is, use the software before you buy it. Then you see what kind of support a developer provides for its software. After that, look on the side of the software box, and jot down that information on your software worksheets — the worksheets that help you pick out the hardware to run your software.

- Don't buy anything just yet! You're shopping, not buying.

- A fad among software developers in the late 1980s involved making software boxes *very large*. For a time, the large boxes were full of manuals and disks and stuff you needed. Then, they started putting the manual *on* the disk electronically — but kept the box the same size! They sold a lot of air in those days. . . .

- Another trivial point: All software boxes are a certain size because that's the size that looks good on the shelf at the software store. The box isn't designed to hold the disks and manuals!

- I have a theory that developers make their software packages large so as to literally push the competition off the shelves!

- More pointless trivia: For a while, the product name on the software box appeared one-third of the way from the top. The reason was that the shelves at Egghead Software were tilted in such a way that you couldn't see the top third of the box.

Taking a test-drive

Buying software is a matter of taste. Like discovering new food, you should sit down at a computer and try out any software you plan to buy. Any store that sells software should let you do so. All you have to do is ask, "Can I try out the Crunchy Spreadsheet?" As a buyer, you're entitled to take a test-drive.

What should you look for? Look for things you like. If the program is a word processor, how easy is it for you to start typing? Do the various things on the screen look obvious to you? Is it cryptic? Does it feel slow or awkward? Make a note of these things, and, if the word processor isn't to your liking, try another. You should apply this technique to all the software you test-drive.

- Most decent computer stores have machines set up on which you can test-drive the software. Some of the large "office"-type stores may not let you do that, however.

- Don't feel guilty about asking to test-drive! If the stores have computers available for it, then they should let you. Otherwise, go somewhere else.

- Please, please don't have a salesperson demo the software; they're often too familiar with it to do you any good. It's up to you to fiddle with it.

- When you find something you like, fill out a software worksheet for it (see the worksheet at the end of this chapter).

Other sources for test-driving

Not everyone lives near the dream Software-o-Rama that carries everything and lets you test-drive *and* has truly knowledgeable and trustworthy employees. If you're one of those folks, you can consider some other test-driving sources:

Your guru: Having a computer-knowledgeable friend can be a boost to picking out some good software. Let your friend show you some of his or her favorite software packages. That's how I got started, a dozen or so years ago; I basically used everything my "computer guru" was using on his computer. Although it wasn't what I ended up using, it was a good start.

Computer groups: Most areas have coffee groups that meet to discuss computers and hear guest speakers. These groups are listed in the newspaper. Stop by and visit one to find out what people use and what their opinions are.

Magazines: Computer magazines offer reviews of major software brands all the time. You may have to pick up a few to get an idea of what you need or order back issues.

Buy what's popular: Another tactic some people use is to look at what's popular. If you live out in the boonies (like I do), call up a mail-order place and ask what sells best (for example, "What's the best-selling database for a philatelist like me?"). Then have the person you're talking to read the requirements from the side of the box for you. That person may also be able to fax you information, if you have access to a fax machine.

Use school or the office: An easy way to instantly decide which software is best for you is to go with what you know. If you use WordPerfect at work, why not buy it for home? Likewise, find out what kind of software you child uses in school and buy that to use at home.

Please make sure that you don't "borrow" software from work or school. Though it seems an easy and thoughtless thing to do, it's really theft. Always buy every software package you use or own unless it states right up front that it's free or in the public domain.

Helpful Hints

Most software developers have given up on "user-friendly." Thank goodness. Whenever a developer tried to make something user-friendly, it usually wound up being inane or boring. Rather than look for software that's friendly, you should examine the various ways the developer has to offer you help.

You should find two kinds of help in any software package you plan to buy: help in the form of online help (while the program is running) and help from the software developer.

- ✔ User-friendly software never works, because the programmer and development staff are way too intimate with the product to understand the needs of someone new. It all makes sense to them, after all!

- ✔ Whenever the computer industry attempts to make something user-friendly, it usually winds up making something dopey or stupid.

- ✔ If you can't get help in using your software, you probably bought the wrong thing in the first place (which is what this chapter tries to prevent).

- ✔ Because many places don't let you return computer software after you open it, make sure that you're looking at the right thing in the first place.

Types of help you find in software

Programs that are nice enough to offer help come in two varieties: online help and contextual help.

Online help: Wherever you are in the program, you can press a special key and see a list of commands or a copy of the manual. This technique is good for looking up topics or seeing how things are done.

Contextual help: It's the same kind of help as online help, except that the helpful information you see pertains to whatever you're doing in the program. If you're about to print, for example, the helpful information is about printing. If you're about to save something to a disk, the helpful information is about saving.

All Windows programs use the same type of help, which is a combination of both online and contextual. The *content* of the help you receive, however, varies widely. I've used programs that tell you *exactly* what the problem is, and I've used other programs that merely explain a term and don't explain what it is or how it works.

Don't forget support!

Some software manufacturers offer telephone support for when you really get stuck. With phone support, you can call up the company and directly ask questions about the software. Strange but true. In fact, one of the reasons WordPerfect shot to the top of the charts in the late 1980s was because of its toll-free phone support.

Ah! The stinking manual!

Nothing is more delightful than poking fun at the traditional computer manual. They were bad! They were confusing! They were next to useless!

I'm happy to tell you that computer manuals are better now than they've ever been. Why? Because they're no longer included with the software! That's right — to save weight and production costs, few developers bother with manuals anymore. That's good and bad news.

The good news is that you no longer have to fuddle with a manual. The bad news is that the same manual you no longer have to fuddle with is now on the same disk the product came with. If you can't get the product to work, however, you can't access the manual on disk. It must be a mixed blessing.

Fortunately, whether the manual is put on paper or on a disk, you have a decent alternative: Buy a good computer book instead.

Not all software phone support is created equal. It comes in what I call the four flavors: vanilla, chocolate, carob, and fudge. These are my flavors, by the way — not an industry standard (well, maybe in the ice cream industry).

Vanilla: With this type of phone support, you pay not only for the phone call but also for the support. When the software developer answers the phone, you're usually greeted with, "Hi! What's your credit card number?" These software houses charge upward of $60 per hour just so that you can ask questions about their product. (Customer service, rest in peace.) For fancier, user-hostile packages, however, this price may be agreeable.

Chocolate: With this type of support, which is better than the vanilla type, you pay only for the phone call. After you get connected, you simply wait on hold until someone happens by to answer your question. The *answer* is free; it's just that most of these places tend to involve long-distance calls.

Carob: This type of support is like chocolate, but not as good. It starts out like chocolate: You get free support but must pay for the phone call. After 90 days (or so), you pay for everything — the phone call *and* the support.

Fudge: Fudge phone support is the best. With this kind of support, you get an 800 number to call — a free phone call for free support. The only drawback is that these numbers are busy — all the time.

> ✔ Take note of the kind of support offered by the developer of the software you've chosen. If the type of support isn't listed on the box, ask a salesperson what type of support is available.

✔ The computer industry is geared toward selling hundreds of software packages at a time to major corporations and big business. Its support polices are designed mostly to please those customers. People like you and me (and small businesses), who are intrepid enough to buy our own computer, are often left out in the cold.

After You Find What You Want . . .

When you feel that you've found a software package that will get your work done much easier, don't buy it! Instead, make a note of it. Fill out the form at the end of this chapter or one of its duplicates in the back of this book. Describe the software you've found to get the job done.

✔ This section helps you fill in the form at the end of this chapter.

✔ After you've found your software, wait. Buying time isn't here yet. Your next step is to find the hardware to match the software you've selected. For now, keep your software worksheets handy.

✔ Write down information about *all* the software packages you're interested in. If you can't decide between two packages, fill out a worksheet for both. You can decide which one you want to buy later, when you buy a computer.

Stuff you find on the software box

Software comes in a box. Inside the box are the disks, the infamous manual, and other goodies, such as registration cards, keyboard templates, bumper stickers, buttons, and more sheets of paper than you ever find in a Publisher's Clearing House giveaway.

On the side of the box are the software program's "nutritional requirements." You should find a list of the equipment the software requires. You typically find one or more of these informational tidbits:

✔ Which computer is required

✔ Which operating system is required, and which version of that operating system is necessary

✔ Which microprocessor is required

✔ How much memory (RAM) it needs

✔ How much hard drive space it needs

✔ Which type of graphics is required

✔ Whether it has any special hardware requirements (mouse or joystick, for example)

✔ Whether any sound equipment or multimedia support is offered

✔ What kind of printers are supported

✔ Which kind of support is offered

You may see even more information about even more confusing issues. Don't let that boggle you now! (If you need to, review Part II of this book to reacquaint yourself with PC hardware.)

✔ Information on the side of the software package tells you which type of computer runs the software best. If you eventually buy computer hardware that matches or exceeds those requirements, you're doing okay.

✔ Never buy any software without first reading its box! I'm serious. Even a pro (well, myself!) should read the box before buying. I've had to return a few software packages because they were for the wrong PC or incompatible with my equipment. Reading the box would have saved me — uh, I mean "those people" — sometimes.

Things to look out for in software descriptions

Before getting all excited, you should bear in mind a few warnings when you're reading the information on the side of a software box.

If the word *recommended* is used, beware! The box may say, for example, that it requires 3MB (megabytes) of RAM and that 10MB are recommended. This recommendation usually means that you *need* 10MB, or else the product won't perform to your expectation.

If you don't have a CD-ROM drive, don't buy the CD-ROM version of the software. Software sometimes comes in two boxes — one with a CD-ROM disk and the other with standard $3^1/_2$-inch floppy disks. Buy the proper one for your PC.

Beware of the "upgrade" version. Sometimes software is sold as an *upgrade,* which means that its manufacturer assumes that you have the old or original version already on your computer. If you don't, the upgrade may not install properly, and you'll be out of luck and money. (Because upgrade versions are generally cheaper, don't think that you've found a bargain or are saving money by getting one when you don't have the original version already.)

Filling in the form example #1

Figure 15-1 shows the information on the side of a software box, just like you find in a store. It's from a painting (graphics) program called Fractal Design Painter.

Minimum system requirements

- Any PC compatible with 486 or Pentium processor

- Hard drive and color or grayscale monitor

- 8MB of total computer RAM (12MB for Windows 95)

- Windows 3.1 or Windows 95

- Floating point unit (FPU) required for some effects

Figure 15-1:
Software re-
quirements
on the side
of the box.

Assume that the product costs $490. Also, after asking a salesperson, suppose that you find out that the manufacturer offers chocolate support. In addition to that information, here is a distillation of what the software tells you about itself:

✔ You need a PC with a 486 or Pentium microprocessor. You had better get the Pentium because it's faster and better and all that.

✔ That computer you get needs a hard drive and a color monitor. (It doesn't say how much hard drive space you need; most packages list this information.) The gray-scale monitor is rare; you want color.

✔ You need at least 8MB of RAM, or 12MB if you're running Windows 95. Go with 12MB.

✔ The box refers to either Windows 3.1 or Windows 95. That means that it will work on Windows 98 as well, but circle Windows 95 as the latest and best operating system listed.

✔ You need a math coprocessor, called an FPU on this box (just to be confusing). Because all Pentiums come with a math co-processor, you'll be okay.

You would fill in the software worksheet according to the information specified in this list. If you don't know how to fill in one of the items, leave it blank (or ask a salesperson for more information). Figure 15-2 shows how you would fill out the worksheet.

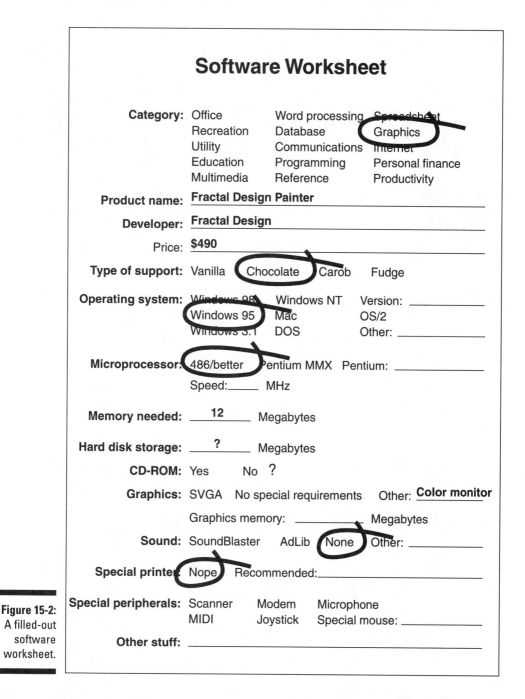

Software Worksheet

Category: Office   Word processing   ~~Spreadsheet~~
Recreation   Database   (Graphics)
Utility   Communications   Internet
Education   Programming   Personal finance
Multimedia   Reference   Productivity

Product name: **Fractal Design Painter**

Developer: **Fractal Design**

Price: **$490**

Type of support: Vanilla   (Chocolate)   Carob   Fudge

Operating system: ~~Windows 98~~   Windows NT   Version: _____
(Windows 95)   Mac   OS/2
~~Windows 3.1~~   DOS   Other: _____

Microprocessor: (486/better)   Pentium MMX   Pentium: _____
Speed:____ MHz

Memory needed: ___12___ Megabytes

Hard disk storage: ___?___ Megabytes

CD-ROM: Yes   No   ?

Graphics: SVGA   No special requirements   Other: **Color monitor**
Graphics memory: _____ Megabytes

Sound: SoundBlaster   AdLib   (None)   Other: _____

Special printer: (Nope)   Recommended:_____

Special peripherals: Scanner   Modem   Microphone
MIDI   Joystick   Special mouse: _____

Other stuff: _____

Figure 15-2:
A filled-out software worksheet.

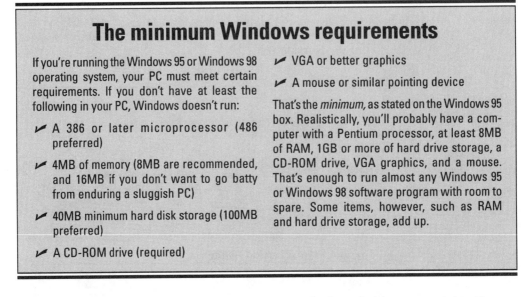

The minimum Windows requirements

If you're running the Windows 95 or Windows 98 operating system, your PC must meet certain requirements. If you don't have at least the following in your PC, Windows doesn't run:

- ✔ A 386 or later microprocessor (486 preferred)

- ✔ 4MB of memory (8MB are recommended, and 16MB if you don't want to go batty from enduring a sluggish PC)

- ✔ 40MB minimum hard disk storage (100MB preferred)

- ✔ A CD-ROM drive (required)

- ✔ VGA or better graphics

- ✔ A mouse or similar pointing device

That's the *minimum,* as stated on the Windows 95 box. Realistically, you'll probably have a computer with a Pentium processor, at least 8MB of RAM, 1GB or more of hard drive storage, a CD-ROM drive, VGA graphics, and a mouse. That's enough to run almost any Windows 95 or Windows 98 software program with room to spare. Some items, however, such as RAM and hard drive storage, add up.

Generally, if some information isn't listed, it's probably not crucial to the operation of the software. Don't worry about it.

Filling in the form example #2

Microsoft is anything but brief. Its description for the requirement to run Microsoft Office 97 isn't exactly an example of brevity, as shown in Figure 15-3. What's there can be deciphered, though. Assume that this package costs $350 and that Microsoft is famous for its carob level of support:

- ✔ You need a 486 or later microprocessor. The "or later" part is your clue that you would be better off with a Pentium.

- ✔ You need either Windows 95 (or later) or the Windows NT Workstation, Service Pack 5 edition. (Remember, as Chapter 13 explains, that you need Windows NT only if you plan to run 32-bit software — like Office — and no games or old DOS programs.)

- ✔ How much RAM is enough? The package is rather vague. Because it lists the 16MB figure, I would go with that amount — or more. Even though that's only for Windows NT, you don't want to cut yourself short.

- ✔ An amount of 121MB of disk space is the highest figure listed, so go with that.

- ✔ You need a CD-ROM drive.

- ✔ You need SuperVGA or better graphics.

- ✔ Because the IntelliMouse is listed, it means that this software can take advantage of its features (the wheel button). Better jot that down.

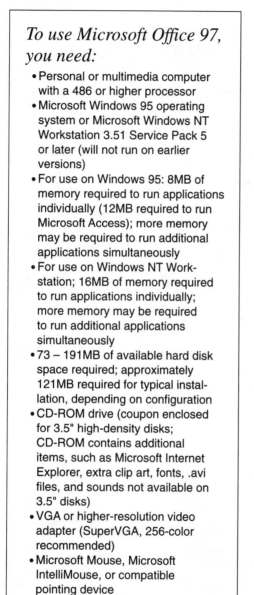

To use Microsoft Office 97, you need:

- Personal or multimedia computer with a 486 or higher processor
- Microsoft Windows 95 operating system or Microsoft Windows NT Workstation 3.51 Service Pack 5 or later (will not run on earlier versions)
- For use on Windows 95: 8MB of memory required to run applications individually (12MB required to run Microsoft Access); more memory may be required to run additional applications simultaneously
- For use on Windows NT Workstation; 16MB of memory required to run applications individually; more memory may be required to run additional applications simultaneously
- 73 – 191MB of available hard disk space required; approximately 121MB required for typical installation, depending on configuration
- CD-ROM drive (coupon enclosed for 3.5" high-density disks; CD-ROM contains additional items, such as Microsoft Internet Explorer, extra clip art, fonts, .avi files, and sounds not available on 3.5" disks)
- VGA or higher-resolution video adapter (SuperVGA, 256-color recommended)
- Microsoft Mouse, Microsoft IntelliMouse, or compatible pointing device

Figure 15-3:
Software re-
quirements
(really!).

Figure 15-4 shows how the software worksheet could be filled in for Microsoft Office 97.

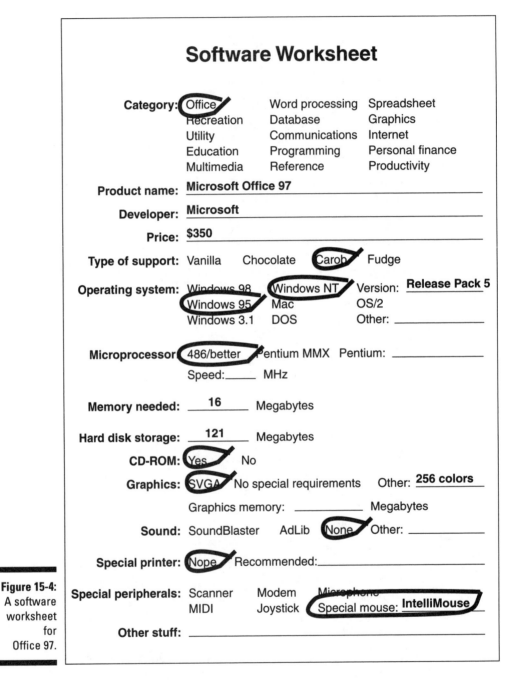

Software Worksheet

Category: ~~Office~~   Word processing   Spreadsheet
Recreation   Database   Graphics
Utility   Communications   Internet
Education   Programming   Personal finance
Multimedia   Reference   Productivity

Product name: **Microsoft Office 97**

Developer: **Microsoft**

Price: $350

Type of support: Vanilla   Chocolate   ~~Carob~~   Fudge

Operating system: ~~Windows 98~~   ~~Windows NT~~   Version: **Release Pack 5**
~~Windows 95~~   Mac   OS/2
Windows 3.1   DOS   Other: _____

Microprocessor ~~486/better~~   Pentium MMX   Pentium: _____
Speed: _____ MHz

Memory needed: _____ **16** _____ Megabytes

Hard disk storage: _____ **121** _____ Megabytes

CD-ROM: ~~Yes~~   No

Graphics: ~~SVGA~~   No special requirements   Other: **256 colors**
Graphics memory: _____ Megabytes

Sound: SoundBlaster   AdLib   ~~None~~   Other: _____

Special printer: ~~Nope~~   Recommended: _____

Special peripherals: Scanner   Modem   ~~Microphone~~
MIDI   Joystick   ~~Special mouse: **IntelliMouse**~~

Other stuff: _____

Figure 15-4:
A software
worksheet
for
Office 97.

At last: The software worksheet

Figure 15-5 shows the software worksheet before it has been filled out. You
can use this sheet or make one of your own based on it or use the spares in

the back of this book. Take 'em to the software store when you shop. Fill 'em out. Then get ready to move on to the next step in the buying process.

Software Worksheet

Category: Office   Word processing   Spreadsheet
Recreation   Database   Graphics
Utility   Communications   Internet
Education   Programming   Personal finance
Multimedia   Reference   Productivity

Product name: _____

Developer: _____

Price: _____

Type of support: Vanilla   Chocolate   Carob   Fudge

Operating system: Windows 98   Windows NT   Version: _____
Windows 95   Mac   OS/2
Windows 3.1   DOS   Other: _____

Microprocessor: .486/better   Pentium MMX   Pentium: _____

Speed:_____ MHz

Memory needed: _____ Megabytes

Hard disk storage: _____ Megabytes

CD-ROM: Yes   No

Graphics: SVGA   No special requirements   Other: _____

Graphics memory: _____ Megabytes

Sound: SoundBlaster   AdLib   None   Other: _____

Special printer: Nope   Recommended:_____

Special peripherals: Scanner   Modem   Microphone
MIDI   Joystick   Special mouse: _____

Other stuff: _____

Figure 15-5:
The ...*For Dummies* software worksheet.

Stuff to Remember

Shopping for software is not the same as buying software. The idea is to find stuff you need to get your work done, specifically those programs that work well with you. Then you fill out the software worksheet, and you're on your way.

- Test-drive the software! Try it before you buy it. Or get advice from a friend or computer users' group.

- Check the level of help the software program offers.

- Check the kind of support the software developer offers.

- Write down all the important information about each software package you're interested in. Save those worksheets for the next step in the buying process.

Chapter 16

Matching Hardware
to Your Software

In This Chapter

▶ Using the hardware worksheet

▶ Filling in the worksheet

▶ Examining a sample worksheet

*N*o, you're still not shopping. It's time to figure out just how much hardware you need, though. That can happen only after you've chosen your computer software (refer to Chapter 15). Now you're ready to see just what type of computer your software desires.

This brief chapter covers the steps you have to fill out on the ... *For Dummies* hardware worksheet. After you've done that, you'll have the ideal picture of the perfect PC for you. (Notice that I'm still not telling you any brand names; that doesn't happen for two more steps!)

The . . .For Dummies Hardware Worksheet

Your software will get the job done for you, but only if you find the hardware horsepower to make the software happy. Welcome to the second-biggest mistake people make when they're buying a computer: not getting enough hardware. Fortunately, that mistake won't happen to you.

Figure 16-1 shows the hardware worksheet. When you fill out this worksheet properly, it tells you exactly which type of computer you need. It doesn't tell you a brand name, and it doesn't recommend a store. That stuff comes later.

Hardware Worksheet

Operating system: Windows 98   Windows NT
OS/2   Mac   Other: _____

Microprocessor: Pentium _____   Speed:_____ MHz

Memory: _____ Megabytes

Hard drive storage: _____ Gigabytes

SCSI: Yes   No

Floppy drive(s): Drive A   3½-inch   1.44MB
Drive B   5¼-inch   1.2MB

Removable: Zip drive   Jaz drive   MO drive

Tape backup: Capacity: _____   DAT

CD-ROM: Speed:____ X   Tray   Cartridge

Graphics: SVGA   Other: _____
Graphics memory: _____ Megabytes

Monitor: Diagonal: _____ inches   Dot pitch: _____ mm
Multiscanning

Modem: Internal   External
Speed:_____ bits per second

Mouse: Standard mouse   Trackball   Other: _____
"Wheel" mouse

Sound: SoundBlaster   AdLib   Other: _____
External speakers   Subwoofer

Ports: Serial: COM1 COM2 COM3 COM4
Parallel: LPT1 LPT2
USB   FireWire
Joystick   MIDI

Other options: _____

Printer: IBM/Lexmark   Hewlett-Packard   Epson   Canon
Other: _____
Laser   Ink   Dot matrix
Color

Figure 16-1:
The *...For
Dummies*
hardware
worksheet.

Properly fill out the worksheet, and you'll be able to walk into any computer store in the known universe and find the computer that's perfect for you.

✔ Not buying enough hardware (or "just enough" hardware) is the second biggest mistake in buying a computer.

✔ Not looking for proper service and support is the biggest mistake.

Filling In the Worksheet (Step-by-Step)

Gather up all your software worksheets, and get ready to make some tallies. A calculator may help if, like me, you think that 2 x 3 is 5.

Choose an operating system

Look over all your software worksheets, and locate the most advanced operating system listed. That's the operating system you need on your new PC.

Okay, that's how it *may* work. In today's world, however, your operating system will be Windows. You have two choices.

If you have Windows NT — and only Windows NT — listed, go with that. You probably want the workstation version.

If you have Windows NT listed and also have some older Windows or even DOS applications, you need Windows 98.

Write down your operating system selection.

✔ Review Chapter 13 for more information about operating systems.

✔ Although Windows NT requires more computing horsepower than Windows 98, it runs the 32-bit applications better than normal Windows.

✔ You want the Windows NT workstation version.

✔ I've listed other operating systems on the hardware worksheet. The chance exists that all your stuff may be Macintosh or even OS/2. If so, that's the way you need to go. Note that only a few manufacturers make Macintosh computers; IBM itself offers OS/2 computers directly from the factory.

Pick a microprocessor

You want the latest and fastest microprocessor you can afford. For the sake of filling out this worksheet, however, write down the latest microprocessor your software specified.

For example, you may get these results:

- 486 or better
- Pentium
- Pentium II
- Pentium MMX

The latest, greatest system in that bunch is a Pentium II with MMX. (All Pentium II systems come with MMX built-in.)

For the processor speed, write down the fastest rating specified by any software package. For example, if some game program says that it needs at least a 90 MHz Pentium, write down that value.

Yes, yes: You'll probably get something much faster and maybe fancier than the minimum requirements you're writing on the hardware worksheet. Be patient.

Calculate your memory needs

Memory is a maximum value. To find out how much memory your computer should have, just look for the *highest* value specified on your software worksheets.

Suppose that the memory requirements from various software packages are 12MB, 8MB, 24MB, and 16MB. You pick the highest value, which is 24MB. That's the *minimum* amount of memory your PC should have. After that, you should round up to the nearest value listed here:

16MB

32MB

48MB

64MB

128MB

In this example, that value is 32MB.

Again, as with the microprocessor, if you can afford it, you'll probably get even more memory. The value you calculate here merely tells you a good minimum amount of memory you should have. Calculate that value, and enter it on your hardware worksheet.

- ✔ The amount of memory the software needs should be less than the total amount of memory in your computer. You never want to cut this value short.

- ✔ If a memory size is recommended, always go with it. The minimum memory size is put there by marketing types who want the package to have the widest appeal. The engineers who design the software specify the "recommended" value.

- ✔ You have to round up the memory size because PCs come configured with specific amounts of memory.

- ✔ You don't have to add together all the memory requirements. Although that would make sense at first, you rarely use several programs at one time. Even if you do, the operating system handles any memory over-head. All you need is one value, the highest amount of memory any of your programs uses.

Calculate your hard drive storage

Unlike computer memory, hard disk storage is a cumulative thing. It adds up. And you will, eventually, run out of hard drive storage. The idea is to put that day off as far in the future as possible.

Add together the hard disk storage requirements from all your software worksheets. If the package doesn't list the storage requirements, use the value 10MB. Total 'em all up.

Suppose that you have the following storage requirements: 131MB, 10MB, 10MB, 26MB, 65MB, 20MB. (The two for 10MB are from two packages that didn't list hard drive storage requirements.) The total of those values is 262MB.

After you add the values, double the result. In this example, the amount is 524MB. If you're using a database or graphics program, double the number again. The result is approximately the *minimum* amount of disk space you need in order to use your computer.

Now round up the value to the nearest gigabyte. In most cases, it's probably only 1GB. That's fine because most hard drives are 2GB or more. You have room to spare — which is the point of this exercise.

- ✔ Of all applications, the ones whose documents hog the most disk space are graphics programs. A typical graphics file can use anywhere from a few kilobytes of disk storage to several megabytes.

- ✔ Computer animation files also tend to be huge.

- ✔ Databases also take up a huge amount of memory. Maybe not at first, but after a few years any database should grow to be several times larger than you originally thought.

- ✔ Disk storage is different from memory storage. A program uses memory only when it runs. Every program, however, as well as the files and documents the program creates, have to be stored on disk.

Do you need SCSI?

If you plan to use a number of SCSI peripherals (tape backup units, external hard drives, external removable drives, extra CD-ROM and CD-R drives, scanners, and the whole lot), you should get SCSI. Mark that down on the worksheet, and remember to tell your dealer that you want a SCSI hard drive.

If you don't need SCSI, you'll be happy with whatever the dealer gives you for a hard drive interface. Ain't no big deal.

More storage decisions

Chances are that your software will not require any specific type of disk drive. If it does, jot down that information. Otherwise, you probably can get by with one or more of the following:

Floppy drive A: Your computer comes with one 1.44MB $3^1/_2$-inch floppy drive. Mark that down as drive A.

Floppy drive B? All computers can have a floppy drive B. If you have an old PC that sports $5^1/_4$-inch disks, you should consider getting a $5^1/_4$-inch drive so that you can move your old files to your new computer. Otherwise, you don't need a drive B.

Zip drives and Jaz drives: Many manufacturers are now including Zip or Jaz removable drives with their PCs. These drives are good to have, not only for backups but also for moving large files between two PCs. For example, my wife and I created a brochure for our local community theater, put it on a Zip disk, and handed it over to the local InstyPrint, which printed it all up. Very convenient.

Zip drives store 100MB on a disk. Jaz drives store 1GB or 2GB on a disk.

MO drive: If you're working with graphics, you may consider buying a magneto-optical drive. It stores more than a Zip drive and is commonly used in many graphics production houses. They're quickly being replaced, however, by the beefier Jaz drives.

Tape backup drive: If you love your data (and we all should), you need a tape backup drive — plus tapes — on which to store safety copies. The capacity of your tape backup drive should be equal to or greater than the capacity of your hard drive; for example, a 4GB backup tape for a 3.1GB hard drive.

Special high-capacity tape backup drives use the DAT (digital audiotape) format, which is expensive but very reliable. Specify DAT if you have demanding hard drive storage needs.

You can also back up your data to Zip or Jaz drives.

CD-ROM: Write down the fastest rating listed on your software worksheets. If one program requires a 12X CD-ROM, for example, write down that value. Otherwise, you can leave this item blank; whatever the dealer gives you should be fast enough.

If you can, try to specify the "tray" type of CD-ROM. Personally, I find that method of sticking CDs into the drive easier than using the cartridge. If this issue doesn't matter to you now, leave it blank on the worksheet.

Various stuff

After your memory and storage requirements, the rest of a computer system tends to fall into place without many heavy decisions on your part. Here's a rundown of almost everything left in your computer system:

Graphics: Write down any specific graphics requirements your software lists; for example, "256 color display" or "4MB video memory recommended." You must make sure that whatever graphics adapter you buy is capable of those feats, at least at minimum.

Monitor: A monitor is a personal-preference item. For me, a 17-inch monitor is a great size, though my wife loves her 19-inch monster (and all computer users drool over the 21-inch size). Bigger monitors are more expensive, though.

Make sure that you get a multiscanning, non-interlaced monitor. If you can't afford it, that's okay. I recommend it, though. Also make sure that the dot pitch is at least .28 mm or *smaller*.

Modem: Your computer doesn't need a modem. Only if you plan to dial up another computer should you bother, and then you can always add an external modem. If you need one now, however, buy an internal model, the fastest speed you can afford that's at least 28.8 Kbps.

Mouse: You can have many fancy mice, so make sure that you visit a computer store to see what's available. The dealer will probably give you a choice. Remember to get a fancy mouse, such as the "wheel" mouse, only if your software knows what to do with it.

Sound: Most sound cards sold with PCs are generally compatible with all the games out there. Only if your software requests a specific sound card should you write it down on the worksheet.

Be sure that your PC comes with external speakers. Any PC with sound should have them. For extra money, you can get the subwoofer option, which beefs up your computer's sound. All this equipment is extra and not truly required. If your money is tight, you should spend it elsewhere.

Ports: Your PC should have at least two COM (serial) ports and one LPT1 (printer) port. Any extra ports you get depend on your needs. Get the USB or FireWire ports only if you plan to use USB or FireWire devices. The joystick port generally is provided on any PC with sound, though you should always inquire about it.

Other options: Specify any other items your PC may need: a scanner, backup power supply, graphics tablet, or whatever else your software programs may specify.

Pick a printer

Your final duty is to select a printer for your computer. This task can be optional; it's okay to choose a printer later. Whenever you do it, fill in your hardware worksheet so that you get the proper make and model.

A brand name means something only if your software requests it. If your computer graphics package recommends the Epson color printer, for example, you'll probably get more from it. Otherwise, brand names mean little. The ones listed on the sheet, however (IBM/Lexmark, Hewlett-Packard [HP], Epson, and Canon), are the major brands.

Choose whether you want a laser printer, ink, or dot-matrix model. One big deciding factor is whether you want color output. If so, you'll probably go with an ink printer. If you need fast output (but no color) for the office, a laser printer is the best choice.

A Sample for You to Review

Figure 16-2 shows how a sample worksheet could be filled in. The first thing to notice is that not every item is required. Remember that you're configuring a *minimal* computer. The model you probably get will have more stuff in it. According to the software requirements written on the box, though, Figure 16-2 shows which type of computer is needed.

Stuff to Remember

Matching hardware to your software is the second most important part of buying a computer. As long as your hardware meets with your software's appetite, you never have to worry about not having bought enough computer.

- ✔ Fill in the hardware worksheet based on the requirements listed on your software worksheets.

- ✔ Find the largest amount of RAM required.

- ✔ Total all the hard disk space required, and then double that value (and maybe even double it again).

- ✔ Choose peripherals based on your software program's requirements.

- ✔ The tally is a minimum hardware configuration. Your final computer choice will contain more than what is specified on the sheet.

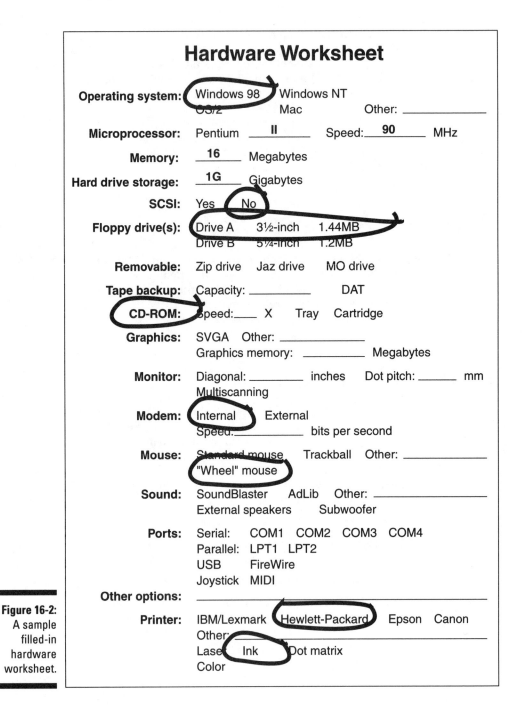

Hardware Worksheet

Operating system: (Windows 98) Windows NT
OS/2 Mac Other: _____

Microprocessor: Pentium __II__ Speed: __90__ MHz

Memory: __16__ Megabytes

Hard drive storage: __1G__ Gigabytes

SCSI: Yes (No)

Floppy drive(s): Drive A 3½-inch 1.44MB
Drive B 5¼-inch 1.2MB

Removable: Zip drive Jaz drive MO drive

Tape backup: Capacity: _____ DAT

CD-ROM: Speed:___ X Tray Cartridge

Graphics: SVGA Other: _____
Graphics memory: _____ Megabytes

Monitor: Diagonal: _____ inches Dot pitch: _____ mm
Multiscanning

Modem: (Internal) External
Speed: _____ bits per second

Mouse: Standard mouse Trackball Other: _____
"Wheel" mouse

Sound: SoundBlaster AdLib Other: _____
External speakers Subwoofer

Ports: Serial: COM1 COM2 COM3 COM4
Parallel: LPT1 LPT2
USB FireWire
Joystick MIDI

Other options: _____

Printer: IBM/Lexmark (Hewlett-Packard) Epson Canon
Other: _____
Laser (Ink) Dot matrix
Color

Figure 16-2:
A sample
filled-in
hardware
worksheet.

Chapter 17

Where to Buy?

In This Chapter

▶ Reading a computer ad

▶ Avoiding advertising tricks

▶ A shopping Q&A

▶ Visiting your local computer store

▶ Visiting a megastore

▶ Ordering mail-order PCs

*F*inding a place to buy a computer is easy. They sell computers every-where. A computer is like a toaster, really. "Two slurpies, a lotto ticket, and one of those Pentium IIs, please." Of course, you don't want to walk into just anywhere to buy your computer.

Lots and lots of places sell computers. Some are dedicated computer stores, some are mom-and-pop places, some do mail order, some sell directly from the factory, and some places even sell washers and dryers. This chapter describes each place and gives you an idea of what to expect when you walk in.

Where do you start? Probably by picking up the paper and reading the computer ads. Heck, you've probably been doing that already. Now find out what it all really means.

Reading a Computer Ad

The first step in buying that computer is to look at computer ads. Although this process can be boring, it's definitely not as boring as browsing in a warehouse-size computer store. After all, you're going to show up knowing exactly what you need; you don't have to be sold anything. Computer stores aren't really set up for that kind of customer (just look around the next time you visit one).

Finding computer advertisements

You can find computer ads in computer magazines, your local newspaper, and freebie computer fliers.

First, look in your newspaper, in the sports section on Saturday (don't ask me why). That's usually where you find some computer-related ads from some local stores. You may also want to check the business section throughout the week. Some newspapers even have computer-specific inserts. (As soon as newspaper editors realize that a computer-literate buying public is out there, more will come.)

Second, visit a magazine rack and look for computer magazines. It doesn't matter how technical they are. Just grab some thick magazines to help you with your research.

Finally, several cities across the land have supplemental computer "magazines" published locally. These freebie publications are crammed full of ads from local vendors. If you can plug your nose long enough to get by their editorial articles, you may find some local dealers with some prices — plus service and support — that meet your needs.

Dissecting an ad

Figure 17-1 shows a typical computer ad, something I mocked up myself this morning. It shows various "systems" along with their hardware contents and prices.

First, realize that the systems displayed in ads are set up primarily for price comparison with competitors. You can assemble any PC you want with any microprocessor, amount of memory, hard drive size — whatever your needs are. Don't be put off by a place because it may not have your personal computer right there in the ad.

Second, notice that the ads use lots of abbreviations. Although I'm sure that some fondness for computer jargon is responsible, space restrictions are the most likely reason that the ads say *RAM* rather than *memory* and *MB* or *M* rather than *megabytes*. You may even see *HDD* used in place of *hard disk drive*. *VRAM* means *video RAM* or *video memory*. You often find customized products, such as the "clackity" keyboard or maybe some special type of mouse.

One important abbreviation you often see is $CALL. It means that the advertiser wants you to phone up to see what price it offers. You can interpret $CALL in several ways: The price is too ridiculously cheap to advertise (which happens), the price changes frequently (that happens too), or someone there just wants to talk to someone on the phone (not often).

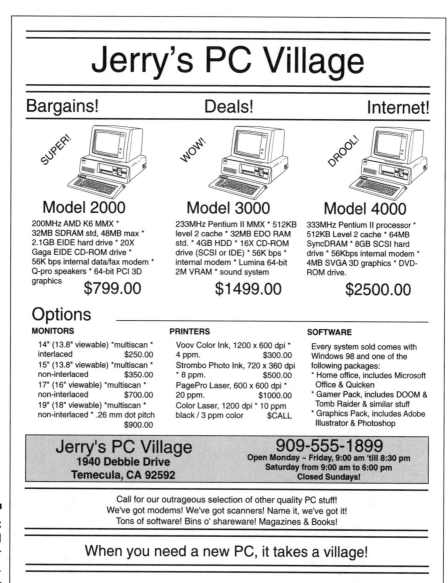

Figure 17-1:
A typical
computer
ad.

Third, some items are missing from the computers' descriptions. Most importantly, *where is the monitor?* Those prices may look cheap, but all PCs need a monitor. Also, should you assume that the computer has a serial port and printer port? I would ask.

Fourth — a good thing — the phone number *and* address are listed. Although just about any place lists its phone number (and its fax number and maybe its Internet address), you know that a dealer is legit if it has an address. (Some fly-by-night operations never give addresses.)

Finally, don't forget service and support! The ad may not say anything about what's offered, so be sure to phone or visit the store before you make a decision.

Looking at a buying grid

Your PC can be configured any way you want. True, some of the preconfigured models, such as the ones Jerry's PC Village offers (refer to Figure 17-1), are cheaper. Why? Because they're preconfigured! A customized PC may cost you a little more.

A common practice of manufacturers that offer different configurations is the price grid; a sample is shown in Figure 17-2. After you find your microprocessor, memory requirements, hard drive, and CD-ROM, you get a good idea of what you'll pay.

- ✔ Buying grids usually accompany some standard configuration, including graphics card, ports, floppy drive, and whatnot.
- ✔ Some manufacturers may even "part out" the entire PC piece by piece, letting you know how much each item costs if you want to "roll your own" PC.
- ✔ Use the grids only for a price comparison (what I personally need is rarely shown in the grid).

Recognizing common tricks used to make an advertised price look really cheap

Because the competition out there is fierce, computer dealers go to great lengths to make their systems look cheaper than the other guys'. Here are some common tricks you may want to look for or inquire about when you find a ridiculous price:

- ✔ Not including any memory in the computer. Look for 0K RAM or 0MB RAM in the ads, or see whether maybe the memory value is missing altogether.
- ✔ Not including the price of the keyboard.
- ✔ Not including the price of the monitor or video adapter card (the most common trick).

Desktop Model	Processor	RAM	HDD	CD-ROM	Price
D150	Pentium Pro 150 MHz	16MB	2.1GB		$1,000.00
D150-16	Pentium Pro 150 MHz	16MB	2.1GB	16X	$1,200.00
D200-16	Pentium II 200 MHz	16MB	2.1GB	16X	$1,300.00
D233-16	Pentium II 233 MHz	16MB	2.1GB	16X	$1,400.00
D233-32	Pentium II 233 MHz	32MB	2.1GB	24X	$1,550.00
D233-32	Pentium II 233 MHz	32MB	3.8GB	24X	$1,650.00
D233-64	Pentium II 233 MHz	64MB	4.1GB	24X	$1,800.00
D266-32	Pentium II 266 MHz	32MB	4.1GB	16X	$1,550.00
D266-32x	Pentium II 266 MHz	32MB	4.1GB	24X	$1,600.00
D266-64	Pentium II 266 MHz	64MB	4.1GB	24X	$1,850.00
D266-64x	Pentium II 266 MHz	64MB	6.4GB	24X	$1,950.00
D300-32	Pentium II 300 MHz	32MB	4.1GB	24X	$1,700.00
D300-32x	Pentium II 300 MHz	32MB	6.4GB	24X	$1,850.00
D300-64	Pentium II 300 MHz	64MB	4.1GB	24X	$2,100.00
D300-64x	Pentium II 300 MHz	64MB	6.4GB	24X	$2,350.00
Mini-tower					
T150	Pentium Pro 150 MHz	16MB	2.1GB		$1,250.00
T150-16	Pentium Pro 150 MHz	16MB	2.1GB	16X	$1,450.00
T200-16	Pentium II 200 MHz	16MB	2.1GB	16X	$1,550.00
T233-16	Pentium II 233 MHz	16MB	2.1GB	16X	$1,650.00
T233-32	Pentium II 233 MHz	32MB	2.1GB	24X	$1,800.00
T233-32	Pentium II 233 MHz	32MB	3.8GB	24X	$1,900.00
T233-64	Pentium II 233 MHz	64MB	4.1GB	24X	$2,050.00
T266-32	Pentium II 266 MHz	32MB	4.1GB	16X	$1,800.00
T266-32x	Pentium II 266 MHz	32MB	4.1GB	24X	$1,850.00
T266-64	Pentium II 266 MHz	64MB	4.1GB	24X	$2,100.00
T266-64x	Pentium II 266 MHz	64MB	6.4GB	24X	$2,200.00
T300-32	Pentium II 300 MHz	32MB	4.1GB	24X	$1,950.00
T300-32x	Pentium II 300 MHz	32MB	6.4GB	24X	$2,100.00
T300-64	Pentium II 300 MHz	64MB	4.1GB	24X	$2,350.00
T300-64x	Pentium II 300 MHz	64MB	6.4GB	24X	$2,600.00

Figure 17-2:
A price grid.

- Not including the price of the microprocessor (although this practice sounds ridiculous, it happens).

- Not including the price of the operating system. Technically, this item should be "thrown in," but the dealer may be saving a few bucks by not including it.

- Omitting support or service!

- Showing an unrelated illustration. Watch out for "Model 400 shown" or "Optional monitor shown" written in tiny print below the illustration.

Some Q&A before You Rush Out to Buy

You probably have some questions right about now. Hopefully, the one you want to ask is among the following:

"Should I get a quote?"

Most stores offer a "meet or beat" way to price a computer. They claim to meet or beat any advertised price on similar or the same equipment. If you like to shop this way, get several quotes from different sources before you buy.

When you're comparing prices, don't forget to factor in a few dollars for service and support. How much? Anywhere from $50 to $300, depending on the kind of support that's added. A lack of support will cost you from $50 to $300 to maybe much, much more if you're not careful.

Although some hole-in-the-wall place always wants your business when you buy, will it want to see you again when you have a question or need help?

"Can I haggle?"

The days of haggling over buying a computer are long gone. It used to be that computers were marked up so much that only a complete nebbish would pay the list price. You could typically count on a 20 to 50 percent discount in swankier stores.

Now the competition between stores is too great to allow for any haggling. The price you see advertised is usually what it sells for. Computers still have a manufacturer's suggested retail price (MSRP), and you may see that ridiculous value listed above the store's "discount." Whatever. Don't expect to get any more breaks than that.

"Should I get a discount off the manufacturer's suggested retail price?"

Yes. Especially on software. The "street price" of all computer whatnots is always less than the manufacturer's price — a weird holdover from the days of haggling.

"Isn't there any way to get a deal on a computer?"

About the only way left to get a lower price on a new computer is to buy two or more at a time. This technique works just about anywhere and with anything: Buy two or more cars, and the car dealer will cut you some slack. Be forewarned, however, that some computer stores don't start to cut deals until the 10th or 100th computer you buy!

You probably don't need two or more computers for your first PC purchase. Does that leave you out? Nope! Just find an associate or willing relative who is also on the verge of buying. Sometimes you can receive substantial discounts for purchasing two computers at the same time, often without losing valued service and support.

"Is it better to buy from a noncommissioned salesperson?"

I've been buying computers for more than 17 years and have yet to find a commissioned salesperson. Because most stores are either discount or locally owned, there is no commission to be made. I would guess that only the manufacturer's direct sales reps who sell to major accounts get commissions, although I doubt that even that's the case anymore.

If commissioned salespeople bug you, you can always consider going elsewhere.

"What about buying a used computer?"

A used computer is a bad idea for a first-time buyer. Why? Because you're cutting off your service and support. You get no guarantees or warranties with used equipment. For a second purchase, sure, but not when you're just starting out.

"What about refurbished stuff?"

I've purchased a few refurbished PCs, but only because they came with a manufacturer's warranty. The equipment was older, but because it served the purpose I had in mind, it was fine for me. And it was cheap!

"You didn't say anything about the swap meet"

The reason I don't mention swap meets — even computer swap meets — is that no service and support are available. True, if you find a local dealer that is simply making its presence known at the swap meet, that's okay — as long as the dealer has local service and classes or some kind of support.

Swap meets are havens for fly-by-night outfits and jerks who sell stolen or substandard crap from the back of pickup trucks. I don't mean that everyone there is shifty; some reputable dealers do show up. If you do business with a jerk, though, don't expect him to be there the next weekend.

Where to Buy

Looking over the ads gives you an idea of what's out there. Eventually, however, you have to pick a few places to phone or visit and get a more lasting impression. You don't want to shop by price alone. A store's reputation is based on service and support, which you can't determine over the phone.

When it comes time to narrow your choices, you can buy your computer from several types of places:

- ✔ A local computer store
- ✔ National chains
- ✔ A megastore
- ✔ Mail order

Any of these is fine by me for buying a first-time computer. Even mail-order places offer service and support, though the support takes place over the phone rather than in a classroom.

Your locally owned and operated computer store

If you're one to support your local economy, a locally owned store is probably your first choice for buying a PC. These places may look tacky. Although they may have stuff on Price Club tables and boxes stacked in back, they may also have fair prices and owners who offer more personal support than their Big Brother competitors.

The most serious issue about a local store is how long it has been in business. Any store that has been around for three years or more probably has an excellent reputation (or at least a reputation you can verify). Give new places a chance, but consider hanging out in the lobby or checking the service counter to see whether it has any disgruntled customers. You may also ask for a list of satisfied customers to confirm its reputation.

✔ I often go to local stores to pick up something quick: a keyboard, modem, or some piece of software that they have in stock.

✔ Some smaller stores may have to order your PC or assemble it. Although this process takes time, you're getting a custom PC. Larger stores tend to sell more things off the rack.

✔ Another type of local store is a university bookstore, but don't think that it's cheaper! It used to be that some computer manufacturers offered decent discounts to students who bought computers at the school store. That may not be the case anymore. Never assume that the school bookstore is cheaper than a local store.

National chains

National computer stores aren't what they used to be. Those upscale, haughty computer stores of the late 1980s suffered when smart shoppers realized that local and discount stores carried the same stuff and that the national stores charged a premium and offered little in return.

National computer chains have been replaced by computer megastores (see the next section). However, some national stores that are not necessarily computer stores do carry PCs: Sears, Radio Shack, K-Mart, Costco, Sam's Club, and other places sell PCs right next to stereos and videotape.

The big benefit of buying a computer at a national chain is that they're everywhere. Unlike with local dealers, you never have to worry about finding a Radio Shack or Sears, because they're all over the place.

The big drawback to national chains is that they're not geared specifically toward helping people buy computers. Although some places are exceptions, it's hard to expect sincere support from the guy who sells you a computer, a hair dryer, and a country-and-western compact disc. They don't have a classroom to teach you about DOS or Windows, and don't expect to get far when you phone up to ask a question about formatting a disk.

The megastore

Megastores are those super computer stores, some bigger than a grocery store, that have everything and anything to do with a computer. You can browse, check out new hardware, ask questions, take classes, and spend money until you have to take out a third mortgage.

Megastores are quickly replacing the mom-and-pop local dealers and national chains as the place to go for computers. Megastores offer substantial discounts and usually have on-site service and support, and everything is in stock.

One downfall of these stores is that their sales staff turns over too quickly. Just as I start a relationship with someone, he's off to somewhere else. This quibble is a minor one as long as the new clerk is just as knowledgeable as the guy he's replacing.

Before you commit to one of these megastores, be sure to check on its warranties and return policies, and double-check on its service and support. Also find out *who* fixes the stuff. Is it fixed there, or does the store just ship broken PCs to some factory in another state?

Mail-order brand names

Welcome to the 1990s, where you can have just about anything mailed to your house — including a computer! You typically order from a catalog or magazine article, someone quotes you a price, and a few days or weeks later your computer shows up, ready to go.

(Okay, the computer shows up in a box, and you have to set it up. Don't worry — this book shows you how!)

Mail-order computers offer the same things as your local dealer or megastore. The only difference is that it's sent to your home or office rather than to a loading dock. The price is often cheaper because you aren't charged an in-store markup, and often you can dodge your state's sales tax (though I'm not recommending that you do so).

Many people are concerned about mail-order computers showing up dead or damaged. Before you order, make sure that you get a no-questions-asked return policy and that the manufacturer pays (or reimburses you) for shipping. Most places have these types of polices, and, even so, rarely does equipment arrive damaged.

What about building your own computer?

Do you want to build your own computer from scratch? It certainly is possible. Many places sell the pieces' parts, and everything plugs in or is screwed in to one thing or another. Buy a book about making your own PC, use a knowledgeable friend's help, or do it on your own. It's possible. Unfortunately, it's not a task I recommend for anyone starting out.

The main problem with rolling your own PC is that you get no service or support. Even if you're gutsy enough to try, you have no one to turn to when something doesn't work right. Individual parts may be covered by a warranty, but not the complete unit.

Some may argue that building your own computer is cheaper, which may or may not be true. However, I would seriously factor into the bottom line the support you're not getting. Never build your first computer. Your second or third, okay — but not the first.

About the only downside to mail-order computers is that its support takes place over the phone. Most places offer an 800 number you can call at just about any time to ask a question. If you're more comfortable with in-person support, however, consider a local dealer or megastore.

One other perk to look for is free on-site service. This service is especially important if you live or work in the boonies, as I do. Make sure that this service is offered even after the warranty period expires, and double-check that your city and state are included in the deal.

Mail-order pieces' parts

There is a difference between a mail-order brand-name computer and what I call "mail-order pieces' parts." That is, no one should buy a mail-order pieces' parts computer as a first computer. Instead, if you take the mail-order route, buy a brand name you know: Apple, Compaq, Dell, Gateway, IBM, Micron, and a host of others I don't have time to list.

The main way you can recognize a pieces' parts mail-order outfit is that it sells pieces' parts in addition to complete computer systems. Right along with its main Pentium and 486 systems, you see a list of hard drives, memory, video cards, modems, printers, and other stock, ready to roll. Sure, those prices look good, but if the outfit doesn't offer the kind of service and support you need, why bother?

Buying on the World Wide Web

Another place to buy your computer is on the Internet, specifically the World Wide Web. You can browse computer manufacturers and computer stores right there from your own comfy chair — if you already have a computer. Or, maybe you're in a library or shopping from your desk at work (when you really should be working and not shopping). Anyway, it can be done.

Honestly, I don't recommend buying your first computer from the Internet — even if you have one at the office or are getting good with the one at the library, cybercafé, or university. Why? Because you're utterly cutting out service and support. It's hard enough to find those things when you're shopping locally; imagine trying to find them on the Internet!

For people who are already bathed in the computer experience, buying online has some real advantages. As an example, if you know *exactly* what you want, it's easy to find it online as opposed to searching through a catalog or wasting time on the phone or in a computer warehouse. Because you're not paying for that overhead, the price is cheaper too. I buy monitors, printers, and pieces' parts this way all the time — but I *know* what I want and wouldn't recommend this method to someone who's starting out.

Oh, and watch out! Buying online isn't foolproof. So far, I've found one company on the Internet I would never do business with: It charges your credit card *before* shipping even if it's out of stock. (It's not a computer company; it sells sheet music.) Another company I've dealt with on the Internet (again, not a computer company) has no customer support. Letters written to its e-mail address are returned or left unanswered. That's not the kind of experience you want for your first PC purchase or your 20th.

- ✔ The same tips and warnings about local and national computer stores apply to places that sell PCs online: Stick with major brands, avoid places that sell things piecemeal, don't buy used computers, check the return policy — all that stuff.

- ✔ Always pay with a credit card when you buy online. This method is entirely safe, especially if the vendor offers a "secure sockets" type of server. Even if it doesn't, the odds of a credit card number being stolen online are much less than when you hand your credit card to a waiter in a restaurant, for example.

- ✔ Don't use your credit card number as a password. Avoid places that require your credit card number *before* you've selected anything to buy.

- ✔ Make sure that the vendor has a phone number and street address. You don't want to get stuck online and have to fumble with e-mail to get satisfaction. It's just doesn't work.

✔ Always have your order shipped by a shipping company, not by the post office. Shipping companies (like UPS, Federal Express, and Airborne) keep track of each parcel they ship. Since the post office doesn't do that, when your computer is lost in the mail, it's lost for good.

✔ Obtain the tracking number from the online vendor. Most vendors offer this information automatically when they confirm that your order has been shipped. With that number, you can visit one of the following Web sites to track your order as it's shipped across the country:

- **UPS:** `http://www.ups.com/tracking/tracking.html`

- **Federal Express:** `http://www.fedex.com/`

- **Airborne Express:** `http://www.airborne.com/trace/`

✔ You can find a full list of online computer stores at Yahoo! Visit `http://computers.yahoo.com/computers/shopping/online_stores/`.

Stuff to Remember

With your hardware worksheet in hand, it's time to go out and find some dealers. Remember these key points when you're looking for a computer dealer:

✔ Beware computer ads! Although they can be used for comparison, they're not always complete, nor do they tell you about service and support.

✔ Local computer stores are a good place to pick up a PC, as long as they have a good reputation in the community.

✔ Although megastores offer lots of selection and low prices, ensure that they have adequate service and support.

✔ Buying your PC by mail order is fine, as long as you don't mind getting support over the phone.

Chapter 18

Shopping for Service and Support

● ●

In This Chapter

▶ Some important service questions to ask

▶ Some important support questions to ask

● ●

A common mistake new computer buyers make is spending all their time worrying about the brand name of a computer or the size of its monitor. You cannot overlook one extremely important factor: the service and support you need after you set up your computer.

Step four in the buying process is to shop for service and support, which is covered in this chapter. If you know anyone who has had a bad computer-buying episode, that person probably forgot this step.

How to Find Service and Support

In this section, I make some enemies: Large warehouse stores and department stores are the worst places to buy a computer. Sure, the price may be nice, but after you buy your computer, you're on your own, and that's a mighty lonely place to be if you have a computer question with nowhere to go to get help. It's almost sad, really. My eyes are welling up now, just thinking about it (sniff, sniff).

The moral to this sad and pathetic story is that shopping for service and computer support is just as important as shopping for the computer itself — more so if you're buying your first PC and don't want to feel lost.

To help you, use the following list of questions to drill your prospective computer salesperson. If the salesperson answers most of the questions to your satisfaction, you've found your service and support. If not, you buy somewhere else.

✔ Price is not the most important part of buying a computer. You need
     service and support more than you need a deal.

   ✔ Not all warehouse or department stores have awful-to-no service and
     support. It helps to ask, though, so that you don't become one of the
     legions who discover a lack of it later.

Service Questions

Service means "Where does my computer get fixed?" and also "Who pays for
it?" Consider asking the following questions.

"How long is your warranty?"

A typical computer warranty is only about half a page long, but that's not
important. What is important is the length of *time* the warranty covers your
computer.

All major computer manufacturers offer some type of warranty, from a few
months to several years. Does the dealer support that warranty and offer
additional coverage? Consider it a plus.

"Do you fix the computers here?"

If the place that sells your computer fixes them too, great. If it has to send
your computer to Japan to have it fixed, buy it somewhere else.

"Do you fix the computer at my home or at the office?"

Because I live in a remote part of northern Idaho, I always insist that any
computer I buy comes with an on-site service policy. When one of my PCs
did break awhile back, a representative from the company came to my home
office and fixed the PC right there on my kitchen table. And, the service rep
had a great view of the lake while fixing my computer.

Extended-service policies? Don't bother

I don't recommend that anyone purchase an extended-service policy for a computer. The reason is simple: Computers are electronics. If it's going to break, it will break during the first few weeks of use. If your computer can survive that long, then it will be around for its full lifetime, which should be anywhere from three to four years — longer if you take good care of your equipment.

The first things to break on any computer are its moving parts: the disk drives, hard drive, power supply, and CD-ROM drive. When those things do go, the odds are high that you can buy a replacement part that's cheaper, that works better, and that is much faster than the original. Not only that, but the replacement part also probably costs less than any extended-service policy a dealer will try to sell you.

For years, I've followed this rule of never buying an extended-service policy and have never had any problems. When I do, the something that breaks is usually covered by the warranty. In fact, the only time I ever buy any type of extended-service policy is for my car because I trust my private mechanic more than I trust any car dealer's service department (but that's another story).

Support Questions

Support is help after the sale. It's not help in fixing the computer; it's help for you as a computer user.

For your software, you use the developer's phone support — or buy a good book. For some hardware, you may have to call the hardware manufacturer directly; for what you buy from your dealer, however, you should be able to call them. (Some super nice dealers even help you with your software questions.)

"Can I phone someone to ask questions?"

This question is very important. Will the dealer have someone available to help you? Many super-discount places lack the proper support staff to deal with your after-sale troubles. Nothing is more frustrating than to plunk down Big Bucks for a PC and have the dealer ignore you when you come back for help 24 hours later.

✔ *Hint:* Any place that also sells TV sets and Levi's next to its computers probably won't give you much after-sale service and support.

A sample support question to ask

If you're unsure about whether a dealer truly allows you to ask questions after the sale, phone up before you buy and ask this question:

"I am installing a game, and it says that I need to 'swap diskettes.' What does that mean?"

The answer to this question is something along the lines of "Take one diskette out of the disk drive and put the next diskette into the disk drive." It works just like changing cassettes in your car radio. If the dealer makes it sound easy on the phone, you've found good support. If the person sounds annoyed by the question or tells you to call the game developer, buy your computer somewhere else.

✔ Your salesperson may not be the person you end up calling for support. Salespeople sell. Support people answer questions. (Although sometimes your salesperson may help, don't count on it.)

✔ Test the dealer! See the nearby sidebar, "A sample support question to ask," just to make sure that the sales rep is being honest about phone support.

"Do you offer classes?"

All the better computer dealers have a classroom with a real live, human teacher right there, ready to help you do something bizarre, such as run Windows. A major plus. Some dealers have classes in conjunction with local universities or high schools. Great.

✔ Expect to pay perhaps a little more for the support, handholding, and general warm-fuzzy feeling you want. The price more than offsets any after-sale anxiety, however.

✔ I first went out to buy a computer with $1,500 in my pocket. I waited and waited in the showroom and eventually grabbed a salesman by the arm and said, "What can you tell me about this Apple computer?" He said, "Why don't you just go out and buy a book on it?" Needless to say, I bought my first computer elsewhere.

Stuff to Remember

You need service and support, which is more important than the purchase price of your new computer. Don't think that a dealer is being rude by not offering service and support; different levels of support are available for different types of PC owners. Eventually, you may not need much support and can cut that factor from the buying process. Until then, don't discount it!

- ✔ Service means "Where do they fix it?" The best answer is "Right here, in our store!"

- ✔ All computers should come with a warranty, typically 30 to 90 days or more. That's all you need.

- ✔ Support means "help!" Can you call the dealer on the phone? Does it offer classes?

Chapter 19

Buying Your Computer — Go for It!

· ·

In This Chapter

▶ A quick review of the buying process

▶ Spending your "extra" money

▶ Taking the plunge and making the purchase

▶ Remembering some last-minute buying tips

· ·

*F*ind someone whose fingernails have been chewed to the nubs, and she has probably been looking for a computer. Simply mention "buying a computer" to anyone, especially someone who is now looking, and he'll probably faint; maybe even die.

Fortunately, you've read this book and are more than ready to buy a computer. Waiting for this chapter, in fact, was probably the only thing keeping you in your chair.

A Review

Welcome to Step 5. By now, you should have completed these steps:

  ✔ Identify your computer needs.

  ✔ Find the software to meet those needs, and fill out the software worksheets.

  ✔ Find the hardware to run your software, and fill out the hardware worksheet.

  ✔ Locate a place you can do business with — some outfit with both the service and support you need.

Now you're ready to buy your computer.

What to Spend "Extra" Money On

Buying anything above and beyond what you have written down on your worksheets depends on how much you can afford. So the real question is "Where should I spend my money first?"

Without a doubt, spend any "extra" money you may have on the following items, in this order:

- ✔ Microprocessor
- ✔ Hard drive
- ✔ Memory
- ✔ Monitor

Buy a faster microprocessor. First and foremost, buy yourself a faster microprocessor if you can afford it. This item is a must. If your software craves only a simple Pentium, then go for a Pentium II. If you can afford the fastest Pentium II, spend your money there. You won't regret it.

Get a bigger hard drive. Second, buy a higher-capacity hard drive. If you've followed the hard drive size calculation from Chapter 16 and can afford a large hard drive, buy it.

More memory! Third, get more memory. If your software can get by with 16MB, then 32MB is even better. If you can afford it, get 64MB with 128MB around the corner.

Jumbo-size your monitor. True, a 17-inch monitor is plenty big enough, but 19 inches impresses. And those 21-inch monitors — if you have the money — are wonderful.

The idea is to spend more money on the things that are the hardest to upgrade later. Everything on a PC can be swapped out for something faster and better, although some things are more easily swapped than others.

The most difficult upgrade is the microprocessor, so that gets first priority. Then comes the hard drive and the memory. Most PCs can sport a second hard drive, and memory is easy to upgrade. Doing so first, however, saves you the trouble later (especially if you have the money now!). Finally, monitors can be upgraded at any time.

"When Do I Get My PC?"

It's extremely rare to go to buy a computer and walk out of the store with it that day. Some preconfigured PCs are sold off the shelf. If you have a special configuration, however, it may take longer.

Most of the time, plan on waiting anywhere from a couple of hours to several days for your computer, depending on how busy the dealer is and whether it runs tests on your computer before giving it to you. (Read more about that in the next chapter.)

Mail-order computers may arrive right away, or they may take anywhere from a week to three weeks to arrive. The amount of time depends on how busy the dealer is and whether the parts you need are in stock. Always ask! Never assume that the Federal Express driver is sitting there with his engine idling and waiting for someone to load up your PC.

Don't Ever Put a "Deposit" on a Computer!

When someone asks you for a deposit up front for your computer, run like the wind! Up-front deposits are one surefire way to find a shady computer dealer. You should never put down a deposit on a computer. The best way to be sure is to always pay by credit card.

Not everyone is out to rip you off. Most of the classic computer-store scams, however, involve a "rob Peter to pay Paul" scheme. Writing a check for your computer at this type of place usually means that you lose your money.

Paying with a credit card is the best option because you can always cancel your order. Most dealers don't charge your card until you get the computer. If you don't receive it and the charge shows up on your bill, call the dealer and ask what's up. If their answers or attitude don't sit well with you, immediately phone your credit card company and place the charge "in dispute." The credit card company will tell you what to do from there.

Don't fret over having to put a deposit down to hold a special on-order item. For example, you may need some special piece of equipment that's not in stock. If so, a 5 to 20 percent deposit is okay to ask for to hold it for you. Again, use the dealer's reputation as the deciding factor and pay by credit card.

Hey, Bud! You're Ready to Buy

It's time to take the plunge. Jump in with both feet, and get that computer. As always, you need to take into consideration and remember some things when you're buying your dream computer:

✔ Some places are so busy that it may take anywhere from several days to a week for them to assemble your computer and have it ready.

✔ If you're buying by mail order, expect a two- to three-week delay before you get your PC.

✔ Ask your dealer about *burn-in,* a period of time before you buy a computer when the dealer puts it through its paces, just to ensure that everything is working properly.

✔ Don't forget software! You need software to make your computer hardware go. Software is expensive; you'll eventually spend as much on software as you spend on your computer.

✔ If your dealer offers classes, now would be a good time to sign up for one. Give yourself a week or so alone with your computer before you show up (with your yellow pad full of questions).

A few last-minute buying tips

Computer ads are riddled with cryptograms and small words that may earn you big points in Scrabble but confuse the heck out of any first-time computer buyer. Check any unfamiliar terms with *The Illustrated Computer Dictionary For Dummies,* 3rd Edition, which my wife and I wrote (and IDG Books Worldwide, Inc., published). Also look in that book's index to find a more detailed definition or explanation.

Most mail-order places don't bill your credit card until your computer ships. The same should hold true for walk-in dealers. Some places do take a few days to assemble your PC. If it's taking several weeks to build your PC, however, it's probably a scam.

Never pay for a computer with a check; use a credit card when you can.

Try not to buy your computer on a Saturday. This advice has nothing to do with the zodiac. It's just that Saturday tends to be the busiest day for buying a computer. Also, most computer stores close on Sunday, so if you get stuck, you have no one to call.

The final step is to . . .

Go for it! When you're finally ready to buy, take a deep breath and buy your computer!

✔ See Chapter 24 for some stuff you may consider picking up when you buy your PC.

✔ The next part of this book covers setting up your PC and getting acquainted with it.

Stuff to Remember

It's time to buy, so off to the dealer you go:

✔ Knowing exactly what you want makes the trip to the dealer much more enjoyable.

✔ Pay by credit card, if you can.

✔ Expect a wait for your PC, especially if it's specially configured.

✔ Don't forget your software!

Part V
You and Your
New PC

"WE FIGURE THE EQUIPMENT MUST HAVE SCARED HER AWAY. A FEW DAYS AFTER
SETTING UP, LITTLE 'SNOWBALL' JUST DISAPPEARED."

In this part . . .

Wouldn't it be great if your computer came fully assembled? Or, better still, if expedient and cheery young people in white lab coats brought it in and set it up for you, making everything just so? O! But those are mere dreams, the stuff of television commercials in which dancing mops and dustpans clean everything while the cat watches in amazement and you're out of the room.

The whole ordeal of buying a computer doesn't stop after you sign the credit card slip. No, next come the boxes, unpacking, assembling, and trying to work with things. That's the subject of this part of the book, along with some good advice about how to maintain your computer for years to come.

Chapter 20

Setting Up Your New PC

• •

In This Chapter

▶ Finding a spot for your new PC

▶ Unpacking and assembling

▶ Plugging things in

▶ Turning your computer on and off

▶ Breaking in your new PC

▶ Understanding how to use your system

• •

*T*he five buying steps may be over, and you probably have a new computer sitting in front of you. Congratulations — you won't be disappointed. First, you have to make sure that everything works. Now you start to put to the test some of the service and support from your dealer. Hopefully, nothing will go wrong, and most of the time that's the case.

If you haven't yet put your computer together, this chapter offers some helpful hints and strategies. If your computer is fully assembled and up and running, skim to the section "Breaking It In: The "Burn-In" Test," later in this chapter, for some helpful hints for putting your computer's wee li'l rubber feet to the fire.

Setting Up Your PC

Unless the nice person you bought your computer from sets it up right there on your desk, you have to do it yourself. It's much easier than it was in the early days. The first Apple computer (which cost $666 in 1977, by the way) came as a bag of diodes and electronic parts. You had to solder the whole thing together from scratch! Assembling a PC is now more of a plug-and-go operation. You may not even need a screwdriver because almost everything has thumb-tighteners now.

- ✔ Computers come in boxes, probably two big ones: one for the computer's monitor and another for the computer box.
- ✔ You may have other boxes too, depending on your computer's manufacturer and how many peripherals you bought.
- ✔ If one box screams "Open me first!" open it first. It probably contains instructions. Otherwise, open the biggest box first, and look for the instructions.

Finding all the pieces' parts

After you find the instructions, locate the sheet that lists all the parts that came with your computer. The sheet may also be on your invoice or packing list. Try to find all the parts to make sure that you have everything. Nothing is more distressing than discovering on Saturday that you're missing a part and having to wait until late in the day on Monday to use your PC.

Also, don't panic if you can't find some small computer part (like the keyboard) when you're unpacking your computer. These beasts come in lots of boxes and in boxes within boxes. Look everywhere before calling your dealer and accusing him of omitting something.

If you bought any expansion options — extra memory or a network card, for example — the dealer will have installed them. You don't have to plug them in on your own.

"Do I have to read the manuals?"

Nope. I recommend looking over all the manuals, though, just to see what you have. You may get a humorous tutorial or guide for assembling your PC. Keep all the manuals together in one spot so that you can read them later — if you dare!

Finding a Place for Mr. PC

Before you start putting together all those odds and ends called a computer, you have to find a place to put the darn thing. The obvious place to set it is on a well-supported computer desk. You can set the computer's monitor on top of the computer box or set it to the side.

- ✔ Avoid putting your computer in a spot where it can't breathe. Closed cupboards, cabinets, and closets make lousy computer homes. They need air to keep cool and must be kept in a cool, relatively dry environment.

WARNING!

Really truly awful places to set up your computer

On the beach: Talk about sun glare!

In the kids' room: Ever try to get a peanut butter and jelly sandwich out of your CD-ROM drive?

In the closet: You'll have no air, cramped quarters, and no one to walk by and keep you company.

On a wobbly table, which will eventually fall down anyway: When it does, make sure that it doesn't have $1,000 of computer equipment on it.

On a table in the middle of the room: Why? Someone can easily trip over all the extension cords. At best, your PC gets unplugged; at worst, the thing gets yanked from the table to the floor.

✔ Try not to set your computer in direct sunlight. Setting a computer in front of a window is a bad idea, in fact, because that's how most of them get stolen (using the old "smash-and-grab").

✔ Try to position the computer so that no lights shine directly into the monitor. Your eyes can get really frazzled from the glare of the lights or the sun. My eye doctor tells me that monitor glare is, in fact, the biggest cause of eye fatigue from using a computer.

Putting the PC Together

Now that you know where the computer goes and you have everything situated for optimal computer usage, go ahead and put it together. How? Although each computer is different, you put everything together in some standard ways.

Preparing to plug things in

Just about everything on a computer has a plug that plugs into the wall socket. Your monitor, computer box, printer, and anything else that's peripheral (such as a modem) has to plug into a wall socket. Find that wall socket now!

Before plugging anything else in, make sure that the computer is turned off! You don't want to plug something into the computer when it's turned on, or else you may damage its electronic components. Double-check to make sure that you have everything switched off. (For switches with a l and an O, the l means On.)

✔ I recommend buying one of those *power strips* that lets you plug four or six or more items into one receptacle.

✔ An even better deal is to get a *surge suppressor* or a *UPS* (short for Uninterruptible Power Supply).

Plugging things in

First, the monitor plugs into the back of the computer box. You should see a hole, called a *port,* labeled Monitor or VGA or Display or something similar. Plug your monitor's cable into that hole.

Second, the keyboard plugs into the computer box somewhere. Because the keyboard sits in front of the computer box, you may assume that the connection is on the front. Don't expect this process to be that logical, though. Most keyboard connectors are on your computer's rump (which doesn't mean that that's where the keyboard goes).

Third, if you bought a mouse, plug it into the proper port on the back of your computer box. The mouse sits in front of your computer, next to the keyboard, with its cable, or tail, pointing away from you. Southpaws like the mouse on the left; otherwise, put it on the right.

Fourth, if you bought a printer, plug its printer cable into its back. Then plug the other end of the cable into the back of your computer box. Notice that the cable has different funny ends, only one of which plugs into the printer or computer box.

Fifth, anything else you bought also has to be plugged into the computer box. For example, an *external* modem (one that lives outside your computer), has a cable that connects the modem to your computer. The modem also has a cable that connects to a phone jack in the wall, plus a place for you to plug your desktop phone into the modem. (Yes, this process is complex, but if it weren't, it wouldn't be a computer!)

Finally, plug all the power cords into the wall socket. Ensure that everything is switched off, and then plug it all in.

Turning it on for the first time

To use your computer, turn everything on! One school of thought says, "Turn the monitor on first, then the computer, and then anything else, such as the printer." A different school of thought (this one's on the east coast), says, "Turn the computer box on last, no matter what." What gives?

Properly plugging things into a UPS

If you have a UPS, or an Uninterruptible Power Supply, you've done much to make sure that you and your computer aren't startled by any power outages. Don't let thoughts of glory enter your head, though: You won't be the envy of your block during a blackout, when you're the only one working on a computer while everyone else is eating cold beanie weenies by candlelight!

A UPS should be used to power, at most, only two things: The computer and the monitor. Everything else, especially the laser printer, can plug into the wall. The reason is that those extra loads quickly draw down power from the UPS. The PC and the monitor can live off the UPS for maybe five minutes (this length of time seems to apply no matter how long the manufacturer claims). The idea is that — whew! — you were saved from a blackout. Immediately save your files and documents, and then turn off your computer. There, your stuff is safe, even though you're waiting with your neighbors for the power to be turned back on. Laser printing can wait. Modeming can wait. Go have a cold latté.

The truth is that it doesn't matter what you turn on first. If you've invested in a power strip, in fact, just turn everything on and plug it into the strip. Then you can shut everything off with one switch. (You can even use your toe — if you're that dexterous.)

- ✔ I used to have a monitor that would scream like it had been scalded whenever I turned it on after turning on my computer. Strange. When I turned the monitor on first, however, it didn't scream. If you experience an oddity like that, feel free to change the way you start up your computer.

- ✔ Actually, the *order* in which you turn things on isn't as important as your *timing*. If you turn on a modem or an external disk drive too long after turning on the computer, the PC may not recognize that you've done so. Make sure that you turn everything on at one time or at least one after the other.

Turning it off

To turn off your computer, you just flip its various switches. If your computer has a power switch, just turn off the switch to shut everything down. Although that action sounds easy, remember this warning:

Thoughts on leaving your PC turned on all the time

It has been said that every time you turn your PC off and on again, you subtract one day from its life. Although no one will ever know whether this belief is accurate, the fact remains that it's bad to keep turning a computer on and off, especially more than once a day. For this reason, I recommend leaving your computer turned on all the time (except for the burn-in period, described later in this chapter).

The reason that it's bad to turn a computer on and off varies. Some claim that the sudden *rush* of electricity startles a computer to life. More likely, the reason is the changing temperature inside a PC: When a PC is turned on, it's hot inside it. When you turn it off, it cools. This heating and cooling can loosen the solder joints inside the computer, which eventually leads to damage.

Some energy-conscious users urge you to shut off your computer to save on your electrical bill. This reason is bogus. I run four computers in my office 24 hours a day, and the electrical bill (minus heating) for my office is never more than $14 per month. A typical computer uses the same energy, in fact, as a 100-watt lightbulb.

Most computers sold now are *Energy Star compliant:* They wind down by themselves after a given period. The hard drive stops, and the monitor goes blank. Rather than burn 120 watts, the computer just sips a few watts to keep it aware (and to save your data). When you press any key, the computer comes back to life.

So when should you really turn off Mr. Computer? Whenever you'll be away from your computer for more than a day, it's okay to turn it off. If I'm leaving on business for a few days, for example, I turn everything off. Otherwise, tell everyone that you have my permission to leave your computer on all the time.

Never turn off your computer when a program is running!

This advice means that you should always properly quit or exit your programs before you turn off the computer. On a PC, turn it off only when the screen says, "It's okay to turn off your computer" (or something similar).

The reason for this caution is that some computer programs leave pieces of themselves all over your hard drive if you just switch off the power without quitting first. Because those pieces slow down your computer's performance and lead to trouble later, obey the rules and quit your programs before turning off the computer!

Breaking It In: The "Burn-In" Test

One way to ensure that your new equipment is up to snuff is to put it through a special test — the *burn-in test*. The object of this test is to break in your new computer during its warranty period. If something is amiss, you want to know about it before the warranty expires.

When you take your new computer home, follow these two instructions:

- ✔ Keep your computer turned on 24 hours a day for two weeks.
- ✔ Once a day, turn the machine off, wait a minute, and then turn it back on.

Because of the way electronic components are designed, faulty chips usually go bad within their first 48 hours of use. By testing your computer this way, you're certain to find any faults immediately. Turning the power supply off and on each day helps to ensure that it's tough enough to stand the load.

After the two-week test, you can obey whatever on–off habits you've deemed proper for your computer. At that point, in fact, it will probably behave itself for years!

Understanding Your System

Give yourself time to read about your system, time to play, and time to relax and have fun with your computer. Believe it or not, the best way to understand how to use a computer system is to play around with it. Poke around. Test things. Try weird options, and see what they do. As long as you're not rushed to start your serious work, you have time to easily grow with the system. After the workload comes, you'll feel good about the system, and, lo, that expected and much-rumored frustration won't be there.

- ✔ After you've used your software for about a month, go back and reread the manual; you'll be surprised at how much clearer it seems. It actually makes sense! (People who write manuals are overly familiar with the product and forget what it's like to be a novice.)
- ✔ By reading the manual a second time, you pick up a few more tips and some shortcuts. This trick is just another one the experts use to become experts.
- ✔ As a kind word of advice, give yourself about a week to find out about your software before you start doing any serious work with it.

✔ The more time you have to play with and figure out how to use your software, the more productive you become.

✔ Give yourself three weeks (if you have it) to become used to your new computer system. Then, when you're ready to get to work, you'll know some tricks, and you should proceed smoothly. Heck, you'll be a computer wizard by then!

Chapter 21

When to Buy, When to Sell, When to Upgrade

● ●

In This Chapter

▶ Knowing when your PC is a geezer

▶ Deciding whether to upgrade your old stuff

▶ Determining whether to upgrade the microprocessor

▶ Upgrading your software

▶ Upgrading your operating system

▶ Selling your PC

▶ Considering used computers

● ●

*N*othing lasts forever. Well, except for taxes and death. Diamonds, maybe. The things we use have a life span. Rubber spatulas, for example, seem to last about three months before they get all melted and cracked. Cars? Maybe five or seven years (just in time to pay off the loan). Computers? They have life spans too.

Expect your computer to last at least four years. Although a computer can last longer, technology advances so much and software demands that new technology so strongly that, after four years, your new PC is seriously dated. What should you do? Should you sell it? Should you upgrade it? Should you buy a new one? This chapter helps you make those decisions.

Unlike Wine, PCs Don't Age Well

Your computer is dated the second it rolls off the assembly line. Because those guys in white lab coats are always creating tomorrow's technology today, right now, in a lab somewhere, they have the next-generation microprocessor ready and a smaller, faster, high-capacity hard drive and more memory. The stuff isn't ready to ship just yet, though.

Nothing is more disappointing than reading a computer ad six months after you buy a computer and discovering that you could have had, for the same money, a much better computer. Don't get discouraged! This situation happens *all the time,* which is why I say "Buy!" when you're ready to buy. You have your computer. You're using it. That's much better than waiting.

When exactly does your PC become a true geezer? Generally, after four years of service. After four years, two things generally happen: The hardware becomes much better and cheaper, and the software starts craving that hardware.

A third thing also happens: Your PC starts to go south. The hard drive may start making a louder noise, especially when the system first starts up. It's a sign that the bearings are starting to go. (It's not an emergency; the drive may still have years of life left.) Anything mechanical generally starts to reach its prime after four years.

Your monitor may also show signs of age. You probably won't notice it — until you look at a newer monitor. Older monitors get fuzzy. The text blurs. The colors bleed. It adds excess eyestrain, which is the perfect clue that it's time for a new monitor — or a whole new computer.

Should You Upgrade?

One of the joys of owning a computer is that you can upgrade or replace any of its components at any time — as long as the computer is turned off when you do so.

Upgrading is an easy alternative to tossing out a fairly good PC and spending more money on a new one. Upgrades are inexpensive. And often all you need is a simple upgrade: more memory, another monitor, another hard drive. A few twists of the screwdriver later, and you have an almost new computer again.

- ✔ Upgrading should come from some serious need: Software demands more memory, you run out of disk storage, or something breaks.

- ✔ Yes, owning a computer has its joys, too. Ask anyone who has ever successfully configured her own network.

Which hardware to upgrade first

What you upgrade first depends on your needs. Does your software need more memory? Upgrade it. Is your monitor shot? Buy another one. Is your modem just too slow? Get another.

Memory. As long as your PC is properly configured for memory (refer to Chapter 6), plugging in another 8MB or 16MB or even 32MB of RAM is relatively easy. This upgrade often solves a number of problems you may have with a sluggish PC. Windows is a memory hog. The more memory you have, the happier Windows is.

Hard drive. Although plugging in another hard drive is easy, getting it going can be a pain. Hard drives must be formatted, and it's hard to find where it's written down exactly how that's done. Better leave this upgrade to your dealer.

The best part about upgrading a hard drive is that you can add a second one of immense size. If you miscalculate and find that 4GB of storage isn't enough, for example, buy an 8GB hard drive! You can install it right inside the console.

Upgrading the hard drive is more expensive than upgrading memory. Because humans tend to collect things, however, you'll enjoy the extra space right away.

Monitor. Buying another monitor is cinchy: Buy it! Turn your computer off, unplug the old monitor, and plug in the new one. Done!

If you're money mad, you can actually use *two* monitors on the same PC. Windows 98 lets you do it, although you have to buy a second, compatible video adapter to make it happen. Although I've never seen it done, it sounds like fun.

Old monitors don't keep their value. You cannot sell them, and you shouldn't toss them out in the trash. Instead, refer to your locality's disposal people for the proper method of tossing out an old PC monitor.

Modem. Quite a few computer experts don't even know that you can upgrade your modem. To find out how, contact its manufacturer. Tell them your modem model number and ask how it can be upgraded. Sometimes, it can be done through software, and sometimes you may have to plug in a new chip. You rarely have to buy a new modem, though.

Other stuff. Just about everything in your PC can be upgraded. You can upgrade, in addition to the preceding items, your CD-ROM player, a floppy drive, a video adapter, or virtually any component in your PC.

Watch your upgrade costs! Sure, it may be fun to buy your computer a present in the form of an upgrade. Tally what you spend, though. If you're not careful, you may wind up spending more on your old PC than it would cost to buy a new one.

My $.02 on upgrading your microprocessor

Another hardware upgrade touted in the computer magazines is the micro-processor upgrade. It's not hard to do: The microprocessor slides or clips into a socket. Most motherboards are designed that way. I don't recommend it, though, for several reasons:

- ✔ **Cost:** When your dealer buys microprocessors to plug into his comput-ers, he buys them by the truckload. He gets a discount; you don't. You pay top dollar for a new microprocessor, which can be several hundred dollars for the current top-of-the-line model. Spending your money on a memory upgrade may give you better results anyway.

- ✔ **Compatibility:** Although the new microprocessor may plug into the old one's slot, is all your computer's circuitry geared to work with it? Motherboards are designed around microprocessors. Although the new one may function, it may be crippled or inhibited by the older circuitry on the motherboard. What's the point of having a faster microproces-sor when it has to slow down to access your PC's old memory, for example?

- ✔ **The whole motherboard upgrade:** This upgrade involves another microprocessor upgrade, which directly addresses the issue of compat-ibility but not price! New motherboards are spendy. If you go that route, you may as well buy a new case and a new hard drive and hey! — you have a new computer! You have the old one too, gutted out and not good for anything.

Upgrading software

You'll often be bombarded, more so than with hardware upgrades, with developers' propaganda for upgrading their software. Hurry! Version 4.02 is available! It's only $69 because you're a registered user and *we like you!*

When should you upgrade your software? As with everything else, the answer is "according to your needs." Do you *need* the new features the software offers? Does the new version fix the bugs that annoyed you? If so, buy it.

It's possible and quite common to skip software upgrades. I do it all the time. For example, I had Version 3.0 of a word processor. Version 3.1 was released, but because it didn't impress me, I skipped it. Then came Versions 3.2 and 3.3 and, for some reason, the manufacturer skipped up to Version 3.5. I passed them all by. When Version 4.0 was released, however, I upgraded. I saved money by not upgrading step-by-step (or version-by-version), and I still got the latest version of the product.

✔ If you're using the same software at home as you are at work, upgrade when your office does. If you don't, your older software at home may not be capable of reading the documents the newer software at work produces.

✔ A good argument to eventually upgrade any application, in fact, is that the documents it creates will eventually be incompatible with any new versions.

Upgrading your operating system

Like all software, your operating system eventually will have a new version. In days of yore, this situation caused a real debate: Everything worked fine with the current operating system, so why upgrade? Even if the new version had exciting features, the upgrade may not be compatible. It was a puzzle.

Fortunately, I have the answer. Because Windows took over and because Microsoft is consistent, I can give you this advice:

Never upgrade your operating system.

Don't do it. The only true way to get the next version of Windows is to wait until you need to buy a new computer. The new version comes installed on that computer. Otherwise, you risk a great deal by upgrading your current operating system. (I'm not slamming Microsoft here; it's just the documented truth that upgrading Windows leads to many, many problems.)

You may eventually encounter new software that requires the newest operating system. Traditionally, however, that doesn't really happen until the new operating system is about two years old. Why? The answer is that because software developers don't want to lose you as a customer, they don't write a specific version of their applications until *everyone* has upgraded. So don't panic.

Should You Sell Your Beloved PC?

I remember when friends of mine in the mid-1980s tried to sell their computers. They had sold cars, so they tried to figure the price of their used PCs in the same way.

The stuff never sold.

Used PCs have no value. If you wait four years, the new stuff will be so much better that you'll never be able to recover any value from your original purchase. I have my accountant rapid-depreciate my computers, in fact, because they just don't hold any value.

If you do try to sell your PC, ask only $200 to $300 for it. The best buyer is someone who already has that type of computer and wants to buy another one.

Sell everything when you sell. Make the computer as complete as you can. You can throw in software too, although that doesn't add to the price of the computer. (Old software has no value.)

Ask for either cash (because it won't be that much) or a cashier's check for your old PC. The last insult you want is to sell something you paid $2,000 for to a guy who writes you a rubber check.

A better thing to do with your old PCs is to donate them to charities or schools. Give them as much PC as you can, including a printer. Give them your software manuals and disks. And, ask for a receipt. You get more from the computer that way, as a tax deduction, and you give something back to your community.

Please give away your *entire* computer, and make sure that the thing works! An accountant "donated" her old computers to our local community theatre, but none of them had keyboards or monitors *and* she wanted the hard drives back. That's not a donation — it's a joke. If you want to give away your old PCs, do so. Don't be cheap.

Buying a Used Computer

Many reasons exist for buying an old computer. The most common is that you have a computer just like it and want another as a spare. Or maybe your software just runs better with an older microprocessor. Some companies that do data entry need no more than a 386 PC. Buying a used one saves them hundreds of dollars over buying a state-of-the-art system whose power just isn't needed.

Test-drive a used computer before you buy it. Take some software with you, and load it up. Make sure that it runs. Save something to disk. Print something. If it works, then the used PC is worthy.

Used computers, unless they've been used less than a year, are worth only a couple hundred dollars — max. Don't overpay! Check the classified ads to see what's being asked for used equipment. Then check the prices of new equipment and compare. Obviously, paying $400 for an old 386 computer makes no sense when a new Pentium PC sells for $800.

Software adds no value to a computer. Someone may tell you, "Oh, but you also get $2,000 worth of software for only $200!" Just laugh at the person. "Ha-ha!" Old software has no value. Sure, the guy may have paid $2,000 for it originally, but it's worth nothing now.

Do insist that the seller include all the boxes (if they're available), original software, and documentation.

Used computers do not come with a warranty. Don't expect service or support from the person who sells it to you. That's one reason they're so cheap!

Part VI
The Part of Tens

The 5th Wave

By Rich Tennant

©RICHTENNANT

COMPUTERS AND OFFICE SUPPLIES

ALL ITEMS REDUCED!

PRINTERS

PC'S

In this part

People always have last-minute lists that need to be checked off. When you travel by air, for example, the pilots in the plane check off dozens of tiny items to ensure that the trip is a safe one, that they'll have enough coffee, and that they can actually see out of both eyes. The same types of lists have to be completed when you buy a computer.

The chapters in this part of the book contain lists of ten items (sometimes more, sometimes less) that you should review at various stages in the buying process. It's all good advice. Read it and heed it.

Chapter 22

Ten Common Mistakes First-Time Computer Buyers Make

● ●

In This Chapter

▶ Not knowing what it is you want the computer to do

▶ Buying hardware rather than software

▶ Shopping for the cheapest system

▶ Being unprepared for the sale

▶ Forgetting the "extras"

▶ Paying by check or cash

▶ Not reading the setup manuals

▶ Forgetting that software is expensive

▶ Not looking for a printer

▶ Buying too much

▶ Not counting learning time

● ●

*I*f you've followed this book from beginning to end, you (hopefully) won't fall into the trap of making one of the following ever-so-common mistakes. It's worth putting them in a list, just as a reminder.

Not Knowing What It Is That You Want the Computer to Do

Computers are capable of many things — nearly as many things as there are people who own them. Don't make the mistake of buying a computer just because "everyone else is doing it" or because you "want to do word processing." You must have a solid reason for buying a computer or know how a computer can help you in some way.

Buying Hardware Rather Than Software

Software controls the hardware, by telling it what to do. Don't be tempted by marvelous hardware features. Don't be lured into buying one brand or the other by some advertising campaign. Without software support, the hardware is next to useless.

Shopping for the Cheapest Computer System in Town

When you buy a *bargain system,* you will probably wind up with a competent and functional computer. When things go wrong, you'll want the dealer to provide service to get your system fixed. That bargain price often doesn't include service, however. Look for a dealer you can grow friendly with. The dealer's reputation, which is more important than his prices, is how he stays in business.

Being Unprepared for the Sale

Computers have a different jargon (in case you haven't noticed). Don't expect a computer salesperson to be able to explain to you all the subtleties of things like VRAM, MMX, scan rate, MPEG, and SCSI-3. Some disreputable salespeople might even dupe you into paying more money for obsolete and unnecessary technology.

Forgetting Some Extra Items

The ad says $700, and you have just a hair over that — enough to pay the sales tax. Alas, you didn't read the fine print: That $700 computer doesn't come with a monitor. Oops!

Ensure that you buy a complete computer system! Double- and triple-check the ads for any missing pieces. You need a monitor, a keyboard, memory, and a hard drive to make a computer system.

Not Paying By Credit Card

Never pay for a computer with a check. Never pay cash. Always pay with a credit card. Why? Because credit charges can be put into dispute if anything nasty happens between you and the dealer. Credit card companies support their clients. If someone sells you junk, the credit card company won't force you to pay for it (as long as you've taken legitimate steps to resolve the problem).

Most banks don't let you reverse the charges on a check. If you pay cash to a shady dealer, your money is gone forever. Computer dealer scams aren't as popular as they used to be, but look out for them anyway.

Not Reading the Setup Manuals

As a general rule of advice from a self-proclaimed computer guru: Read things over before trying them. If you make a mistake or something doesn't happen right, read the instructions again and try a second time. Consider it a last resort to make that phone call to your dealer. Don't substitute the phone for not reading the manual.

Forgetting That Software Is Expensive

Contrary to what you may think, computer hardware is only half your cost. The computer software your computer needs will probably cost the same amount as what you paid for your computer (over time, of course). Piece by piece, package by package, software is expensive.

Not Looking for a Printer

Buying a computer "system" implies buying a computer printer too. Several years ago, printers were too expensive to buy at the same time as a computer system. Today, they're relatively cheap. So don't forget one!

Buying Too Much

Start simple. If you buy too much stuff too quickly, you may go overboard and never find out all about your system. My recipe for becoming a computer guru, in fact, involves starting with a minimal system. After you have that mastered, upgrade slowly and learn as you go.

Not Counting Learning Time

If you've just figured out that you need a computer "yesterday," you're too late. I advise everyone (businesspersons, students, or just the idle curious) to give themselves at least three weeks to use and become comfortable with their computer system before the real work starts.

Chapter 23
Ten Warning Signs

In This Chapter
- ▶ Industry standards versus ads
- ▶ Out-of-date stock
- ▶ Money down required
- ▶ Missing pieces
- ▶ No address in mail orders
- ▶ Salespeople too busy
- ▶ You're ignored
- ▶ No classroom
- ▶ No software documentation

*I*f all people were good, wholesome folks with high morals, standards, and a strong sense of customer support, I wouldn't have to write this chapter. Because this chapter is here, though, I suppose that you'll have a better understanding of human nature.

Because the computer industry is full of terms and standards that only real computer geeks have a knowledge or understanding of, it's rather easy to pull the wool over your eyes. I don't want that to happen. The best thing I can do is educate you on what to be aware of. Consider this chapter a computer-buying self-defense class.

Hi-yah!

Industry "Standards" versus the Ads

Beware of computer hype! You may read about "groundbreaking" technology, but, honestly, unless you see such a technology available in a computer ad, forget it. A case in point is the current rage over the DVD disk. Sure, it may one day replace the CD-ROM drive, but where are those DVD drives in the computer ads? More importantly, where are the DVD disks in the software stores?

Any new hardware technology takes time to become accepted. Wait until something "fabulously new" is available on most new computer systems before you decide whether to buy one. ***Remember:*** Software controls the hardware. You need software in order to use the new hardware regardless of whether every PC has one.

Out-of-Date Stock

Computer dealers like to sell stuff they don't have to fix. No one — neither you nor the dealer — likes to see you come back with your computer in the box because it doesn't work. I don't mean, however, that shady dealers won't try to sell you old stuff just to get rid of it.

Do your research (like reading this book) before you walk into a store. Be aware of what is appropriate for your needs and what the computer industry suggests as standard (which you determine by reading the ads). You don't want a pushy salesperson convincing you that a 14,400 bps modem is a pretty darn fast modem because she has three dozen stacked up in the storage room and the boss told her to get rid of them.

(I worked *one day* at a computer store. During my only sales meeting, we were told to "unload" an ailing computer, to steer customers to it first regardless of what their true needs were. Like I said, I worked there only one day.)

Money Down Required

For what possible reason would anyone need money down on a computer? It's just not necessary. Don't believe them if they pull this bit: "We need the down payment to ensure that you are committed to buying this computer." Computers are selling like hotcakes, so it's not like they would build a computer and be stuck with it forever if you didn't take it. Someone else will buy it.

Never put money down, especially cash, on a computer. Always pay for your purchase with a credit card. Sure, sometimes putting a $50 or $100 deposit on a new system is considered normal. But money down? Never!

Missing Pieces

If you open the box and everything isn't there, take it back immediately! Chances are good that you were sold a computer someone else returned and everything wasn't put back properly. Tell the people at the computer store that you want another computer. Don't accept their giving you the missing parts. Unless someone there told you that you were buying a refurbished computer, he cannot legally sell it to you. Check the laws in your state about selling refurbished equipment.

No Address in the Mail-Order Ad

In some cases of fraud committed in the 1980s, fly-by-night outfits bilked hundreds of people out of money on computers the shysters never planned to build or sell. Reputable dealers post their addresses in their ads and not only their 800 numbers but also their direct lines.

Salespeople Too Busy to Help or Answer Questions

My theory has always been that if people are too busy to take my money, I don't want to give it to them anyway. Go someplace else, to wherever you find someone who's willing to answer your questions and take the time to fully explain what they have to offer you.

Salespeople in the Store Ignore You

If the salespeople in the store are ignoring you, one of two things is going on: Either no one knows enough to walk up and help you, or no one gives a hoot whether you buy a computer. Apathy and ignorance are two qualities you don't ever want to do business with, regardless of whether you're buying a computer, a car, or some shoes.

(I was ready to plunk down $800 for a new hard drive in a local store, and *everyone* in the store ignored me. The salesperson didn't know what a SCSI drive was. The techie only commented on the SCSI drive, not telling me whether it was in stock or available for sale. It was a nice store, too; it had a classroom in back and competitive prices. Because the people in there were jerks, though, I bought my $800 hard drive by mail order.)

Also, be wary of any salesperson who refers to you behind your back as a "mark" — unless, of course, your name is Mark.

No Classroom

If a store doesn't offer some kind of computer class to help you with your new purchase, the folks there really aren't concerned with giving you complete customer service. They're more concerned with making a sale.

If you are a first-time computer buyer, taking a class gives you a better sense of confidence to go exploring with your computer, and your frustration level will be much lower.

No Software Documentation Is Sold with the Computer

All software comes with some kind of documentation: installation instructions, how to play or work the software, and maybe even some technical notes. This stuff is all-important. If the software documentation doesn't come with the computer, chances are that the software is stolen. Don't leave the store without seeing that documentation. If someone makes any of the following comments, leave the store!

  ✔ "The software doesn't come with any documentation."

  ✔ "Oh, you'll be able to figure it out."

  ✔ "The program tells you what to do as you go along."

All software must be sold with documentation!

Chapter 24
Ten Other Things You Should Buy

● ●

In This Chapter

▶ Mousepad and wristpad

▶ Power strip and surge protector

▶ Uninterruptible Power Supply

▶ Printer cable

▶ Printer paper

▶ Toner or ribbons

▶ Modem cable

▶ Floppy disks

▶ Backup tapes

▶ Roll of paper towels

● ●

*T*his chapter is dedicated to the ten additional things, whatnots, and items you need to buy that will help with your whole computer-using experience. Buying these things is not optional. You really need them. They may not be as important as the monitor or the keyboard, but, hey, they're pretty darn important.

Mousepad and Wristpad

Ever try to use a mouse with a dirty ball? No, really, I'm being serious. The mouse has a ball it rolls on, and if that ball becomes dirty, it doesn't roll smoothly and you have a heck of a time trying to get it to point, drag, or do anything.

A *mousepad* is a screen-size piece of foam rubber that sits on your desk and that the mighty mouse rolls on. A mousepad makes the mouse roll more smoothly and keeps that mouse ball clean (as long as you don't drop cookie crumbs all over it).

You get the best performance from your mouse if you buy a mousepad that is slightly textured. Smooth pads don't work as well.

Buying a wristpad is more of a health measure than a technical one. Lazy keyboarders drop their wrists to an unnatural position, which eventually causes stress on their wrists and the infamous carpal tunnel. This condition, of course, can be painful.

The purpose of a wristpad is to keep your arms and hands in a normal, healthy position. It fits right below your keyboard, and your wrists gently lie on it.

Neither a mousepad nor a wristpad is expensive, and you can get creative with a mousepad. Kinko's has a process in which you can put your kids' pictures (or pictures of your cats, if you don't like kids) on your mousepad.

Power Strip

Not until you start putting together your computer and all its various gadgets does it occur to you that homebuilders truly underestimate the need for wall outlets.

You have to plug in your computer, printer, modem, scanner, lamp, clock, and answering machine. The list can get pretty long, and you're probably looking at one, maybe two, plugs to accommodate all this stuff.

Power strips are like short extension cords, except that they have several outlets to accommodate your computer paraphernalia.

- ✔ Never use an extension cord to plug in all your computer stuff. They're inefficient and are too easy to trip over and unplug. It's just not a good idea.

- ✔ Never use one of the power splitter do-jobbies that turn one plug into three. Bad idea.

- ✔ Computers must be *grounded,* which means that they have three prongs that must be plugged in. Power strips provide that for you.

- ✔ Kinsington SmartSockets is a brand of power strip that has a large, wide area that allows more room for the AC converters that often come on computer peripherals. I recommend this brand.

Surge Protector

A *surge protector* is merely a dooded-up power strip. It's like a power strip with a fuse to even out the electricity in times of power glitches, which can crash your computer and make you lose everything you've been working on.

- ✔ A power strip can also be a surge protector. Some just have extra outlets. Others have surge protection in them, like the SmartSockets mentioned in the preceding section.

- ✔ The more you pay for a surge protector, the better the protection. The highest level of protection is *spike protection,* which protects your computer from lightning strikes.

- ✔ Sorry — you can't get any "wrath of God" protection.

UPS

UPS (not the delivery service) stands for *Uninterruptible Power Supply.* It keeps the computer on (for a while) during a power outage.

By plugging your computer and monitor into the UPS, you have enough time to safely save and close all your documents before turning off your computer. The UPS also has surge protection, but you don't really have to plug *everything* into it. After all, who cares whether your modem or your printer goes off during an outage? The data in your PC is more important, and that's what the UPS protects.

- ✔ If you plug too much stuff into a UPS, your computer doesn't have enough power to last long enough to save any of your work. Plug just the computer and monitor into the UPS.

- ✔ Never plug a laser printer into a UPS; printing can wait until after the power comes back on.

- ✔ Most UPS systems are good for at least five minutes, so don't dawdle! Save your work, and then turn off your PC!

Printer Cable

Printers don't come with printer cables, which has always amazed me because you can't get your printer to work unless a cable connects your printer to your computer. It's like buying a television without a cord to plug into the wall. Ugh.

The only thing you need to worry about with printer cables is that your printer can be no farther than 20 feet away from your computer. Information tends to get lost at that distance. The most common length for printer cable is 6 feet.

Because all printer cables are made basically the same, by the way, you can buy any brand for your PC.

Printer Paper

Paper. Gotta have it for the printer, or else the darn thing is kind of useless. Only a few rules apply when it comes to paper:

- ✔ Don't use *bond* paper in a laser printer. Bond paper may have a dust on it, which clogs up the printer.

- ✔ Don't use erasable typing paper. This type of paper is good for manual typewriters, where you have to erase all your typing mistakes.

- ✔ Buy a whole box when you go to buy paper. You'll use it. Nothing is more frustrating than printing a report, running out of paper in the middle of it, and then realizing that you don't have any more.

More Ink Stuff

Printers, like Bic pens, run out of ink — except with a pen, you're more likely to throw the darn thing away and buy another one. You don't want to do that with a printer. That could get costly. Instead, you have to buy more ink.

Printer ink comes in various containers and exists in various states, depending on your printer.

- ✔ Ink printers use little containers of ink that are really super-easy to change.

- ✔ Laser printers use a drop-in toner cartridge. These cartridges are fairly easy to install if you follow the directions.

- ✔ Impact (or dot matrix) printers use a ribbon.

Because all these printers require you to handle the ribbon or cartridge, you run a risk of getting this stuff on your hands. Be careful! It's ink. It doesn't come off easily. It kind of wears off more than it washes off. To help prevent that, wear some rubber gloves when you change the toner or ribbon in your PC.

Modem Cable

You need a modem cable only if you have an *external* modem. The cable hooks the back of your modem to your computer. Internal modems don't use a cable.

As with the printer cable, you can find a modem cable at your local computer store or Radio Shack.

 You probably need a 9-pin to 25-pin serial cable. This cable is often called an *AT modem cable.* Modems have a 25-pin, female D-shell connector on their rump. PCs have a 9-pin, male D-shell connector.

Floppy Disks

Even though your hard drive has a huge capacity to store information, you still need floppy disks. You use them for transferring information from one computer to another.

This advice is one of those tie-a-string-around-your-finger things. Because you're right there in the computer store, you may as well buy a box of disks. Some stores may even give them to you if they're run by nice people. The reason I mention it is that too many people take home a computer system and then realize that they have no floppy disks. I did.

- ✔ Make sure that you get the proper-size disks $3^1/_2$-inch 1.44MB floppy disks. Try to buy them preformatted if possible.
- ✔ You can find floppy disks in all computer stores and in stores that specialize in business and office supplies.
- ✔ It's perfectly acceptable to buy disks in bulk. No shame there.

Backup Tapes

Most tape-backup units come with one tape, just as kind of a tease. You need at least two other tapes, for a total of three. Take the sample tape with you to the store to make sure that you buy the right size and capacity for your tape-backup drive.

Why three tapes? Because you want to rotate them as you back up. Label the tapes A, B and C. Put your first backup on tape A. Your second backup goes on tape B. The third backup goes on C. Then start over again with A. This system makes it easier to keep track of old data. If one of the tapes goes bad, you have a third backup handy.

A Roll of Paper Towels

Paper towels? You're surprised, right? Even though one of the rules for computer use is that you don't eat or drink by your computer, you will. It's inevitable. You'll succumb to temptation and grab a cup of coffee to keep you company.

Paper towels are for those times when you spill your beverage of choice. Spilling liquid of any kind can cause havoc with your computer, so either don't drink and compute or keep those paper towels close by.

Getting your keyboard wet fries the keyboard (metaphorically speaking — it's not like smoke and stuff willows out of the keyboard). You can try to let it dry out or use those paper towels to try to wipe up the liquid before it does too much damage.

Chapter 25
Ten Tips and Suggestions

• •

In This Chapter

▶ Your computer's clock

▶ Get a second phone line

▶ Reread your manuals

▶ Put a timer on the Internet

▶ Get Internet software for your kids

▶ Subscribe to a computer magazine

▶ Join a users' group

▶ Buy some computer books

▶ Don't let the PC ruin your life

▶ Have fun!

• •

*N*o one wants any surprises when they start to use a computer. Imagine buying a new car, signing your name, being handed the keys, and then the salesperson saying, "Oh, I forgot to tell you — this thing runs only on 110 octane multigrade" or "Always hold your steering wheel with your left hand because the car pulls to the right." Fortunately, owning a computer doesn't involve many surprises along those lines.

This chapter contains a list of ten items. I give you some suggestions here, plus tips and a few warnings. They're nothing major; they're just some last-minute items you may not know about — by-the-way sort of things to wrap up this book.

Your Computer Has a Clock

You may not notice at first, but your computer keeps track of the time. And it remembers the time, even when you turn off the computer or unplug it. The reason is that the computer has a battery that helps it remember the time as well as a few other items.

Someday, in about five years, your PC's battery will die. You'll notice it because not only will your PC have lost track of the time but you'll also see an error message when the computer starts up — something like "Invalid setup" or "Missing hard drive." When that happens, phone your dealer and get a new battery installed.

A PC makes a lousy clock. No two computers can keep track of the same time. Some PCs are fast; most are slow. You have to reset your system's clock every month or so. If not, your PC could be lagging by as much as 20 or 30 minutes by the end of the year.

Get a Second Phone Line

If you plan to use a computer and a modem at all, do yourself and everyone else a favor and get the computer its own phone line. I tried to phone up a friend one night, and his phone was busy for *three hours*. He was on the Internet and utterly unaware that anyone was trying to call.

Oh, and forget about call waiting. If you have call waiting on your phone, it disconnects your computer from the Internet whenever someone calls. Just be logical and get another phone line.

After a Spell, Reread Your Manuals

Although computer manuals are horrid, they may make sense in a few weeks after you use your computer. Use any program for a while, and try to figure it out at first. Then go back and read the manuals. Not right away; take some time and do something with the program. Learn how it works. After that, for some reason, the manual tends to make sense. I follow this simple advice, and for some reason everyone thinks that I'm a computer genius.

Put a Timer on That Internet

If you plan to be on the Internet, set a clock! The Internet sucks up time faster than a black hole in space. Limit yourself to 30 minutes or an hour for your Internet browsing, or else you'll see the sun rise some morning.

Get Internet Antiporn Software

If you have kids, get some special Internet software that prevents them from wandering into places no sane parent would let their kid wander into. Programs such as Surf Watch and Net Nanny are good at filtering those nasty places from young eyes.

Visit http://www.surfwatch.com for a copy of Surf Watch.

Refer to http://www.netnanny.com for information about Net Nanny.

Subscribe to a Computer Magazine

Now that you have a computer, it makes sense to get a computer magazine. That's where you find advice, tips, and information about computer things. The magazine keeps you up-to-date and informed better than do dealers and developers, who put their own interests over yours.

Several levels of computer magazines are available, from novice magazines to hard-core nerd publications. Most bookstores have racks full of them, so take a few minutes to browse and pick up a few of the ones that interest you.

Join a Computer Users' Group

Sociologists tell us that injured people tend to cluster after a catastrophe. It's a force of nature. Just like those walking wounded, computer users — dazed and bewildered — gather in small groups in cities across the land. They discuss. They share. They learn.

Refer to your local newspaper events column to see when and where any computer groups meet in your area.

Buy a Great Book

I can't recommend buying books enough! Some great titles are out there to help you find out about just about anything you can do on a computer. When your dealer support craps out, when the developers admit that they loathe the customer, and when you've exhausted your friends and computer buddies, buy a good book.

As with magazines, be aware that different levels of books — beginner, intermediate, and advanced — are available for different computer users: You can get reference books, and you can get tutorial books. Buy what suits you best.

Don't Let the Computer Ruin Your Life

The biggest problem most new owners have with their PC is taking it too seriously. Life is just too important to take anything seriously, especially a computer.

Above all, never think that it's your fault when something goes wrong. If you always blame yourself, you have a horrid time computing. The truth is that computers are dumb. They foul up all the time. It's not your fault.

Don't Let the Computer Run Your Life

Computers are *not* a big deal. They're tools. You use them to extend your own abilities. They are not important. Human beings do not live to serve the computer.

If you find yourself overly enamored with your computer, make it a point to take a break every so often. Walk outside. Get some fresh air. Talk to a human being. If the universe has a center, it's not powered by a microprocessor.

Have fun.

Appendix
Commonly Asked Questions and Their Answers

● ●

Software

Q: What's the difference between Version 1.2 and Version 1.3 in software?

A: Version 1.3 lacks all the bugs that were in Version 1.2. Likewise, when Version 1.4 comes out, it will have fixed all the bugs found in Version 1.3. Other improvements may come along the way as well, though they're usually presented in the major version releases, such as Version 1.4 up to 2.0.

Q: I have some old software. Can I get Windows to use my software?

A: Windows runs all older DOS software, or so it claims on the box.

Q: How about integrated software? If I buy one package for $700, isn't that better than buying the individual software applications for $300 each?

A: Only if you plan to use *all* the applications. For example, buying Microsoft Office when you need only Microsoft Word is a waste of money.

Q: I can't get my program to run. Help!

A: Reading the manual helps. You can also get a good book on the subject because computer book authors have more time and are willing to put more into their work.

Q: I don't have the manual because a friend gave me a copy of his disks.

A: This is theft. You should never use this type of software. You wouldn't think of going into the software store, taking the disks from the package, and walking out the door without paying, would you? Also, this type of "freebie" is how computer viruses are spread.

Q: Should I worry about computer viruses?

A: Sadly, computer viruses are a fact of computing life. They are mischievous little programs that sneak on to your computer to either amuse, annoy, or curse you. Special programs called *virus utilities* can be used to check your system for signs of infection and remove the viruses. If you use only shrink-wrapped, store-bought software, however, you'll never have anything to worry about.

Operating Systems

Q: Which version of Windows do I need?

A: Always get the latest version. After you have it, however, don't bother upgrading unless the next version offers some features you really need or your software suddenly requires.

Q: Can I upgrade to the next version of Windows when it comes out?

A: Yes, but I don't recommend it. Upgrading Windows tends to lead to incompatibilities with your current software — a risk you probably don't want to take. It's better to wait until you need a new computer, which will have the latest version of Windows on it.

Q: Should I buy OS/2?

A: Only if you absolutely need software that runs under OS/2, which probably won't happen for several years. Another consideration is if you have a computer at home and, suddenly, your office computer manager decides to switch to OS/2. To be compatible with the office setup, you should use the same computer and operating system at home.

Bits and Bytes and RAM

Q: What's the difference between expanded and extended memory?

A: *Expanded memory* is extra memory for DOS programs. It's rarely used today. *Extended memory* is now just called *memory* because it's the memory Windows and all Windows programs use.

Disk Drives

Q: Can I add a second floppy disk drive to my PC?

A: Yes. A good reason to do that is if you back up to floppy disks. Few people do that anymore, however, so having a second floppy drive really isn't necessary.

Q: Can I add a second hard drive to my computer system?

A: Yes. Most PCs have room for two hard drives. If yours does, you can add a second, larger hard drive quite easily either by yourself or by having your dealer do it for you.

Monitors and Keyboards

Q: Does a bigger monitor display more colors?

A: No. It's not the monitor that's in charge of the colors; it's your video adapter card. You can plug the card into any size monitor and it doesn't change how the card's circuitry displays colors. The only thing a bigger monitor gives you is a bigger image.

Q: My eyes hurt after computing. The wife says that it's because of my computer's monitor. Is there anything I can do?

A: The problem is caused more by the lights in the room than by your monitor. The lights reflect off your computer screen, and that's what causes eye irritation. I recommend buying a nylon screen for your monitor. It cuts down on the glare and provides more contrast for a better image.

Q: Speaking of my wife, she says that the computer will ruin my eyes. Is that true?

A: Not at all! Using your eyes does not cause them to go bad. Your eyes may get fatigued. When they do, get up and stare out a window for a while. Changing focus is the best way to relieve your tired eyes.

Q: What's a Dvorak keyboard?

A: It's a specially designed keyboard that supposedly enables you to type faster. They keys are laid out in a logical order rather than in the mechanical order on current keyboards. Although Dvorak keyboards never really caught on, some computers allow you to activate a "Dvorak option" if you want to try it out.

Printers and Peripherals

Q: Can I use my typewriter as a computer printer?

A: That works only if the typewriter is designed for that purpose. Normally, a typewriter is a stand-alone device and doesn't talk with your computer. It would be nice, though (and slow as a frozen river).

Q: How can I print 10-foot-long banners on my printer?

A: Banners are normally printed on dot-matrix printers, which use continuous form-feed paper. On laser and ink printers, you usually print the banner a sheet at a time and then tape them together.

Q: My PC's printer doesn't print at all.

A: You probably have two printer ports on your computer. Nothing is wrong with that, except that both ports are fighting over which one comes first. A PC can have as many as four printers, named LPT1 through LPT4. You have to tell one of your printer ports that it's LPT2, and then everything will work fine.

Q: Can I have two printers at a time hooked up to my PC?

A: Yes. You have to buy a second printer port, LPT2. Hook one printer to LPT1 and the other to LPT2. Most programs automatically send their output to LPT1. You have to read your software manual to find out how to send output to the second printer on LPT2.

Q: Can my CD player play music?

A: Sure, as long as you have the proper multimedia software that lets your computer's CD-ROM drive play a musical CD disc.

Q: If I have a modem, can someone call up my computer and steal information?

A: Only if you let them. First, in order for someone to call your computer, you must run special software that lets them do that. Furthermore, you must tell the software that the person can steal information from your computer. If this ever does happen, it's because you let it happen. Your computer will never answer the phone unless you have software that tells it to do so *and* you set it up that way.

Q: Can I hook up my fax machine to my computer?

A: Only if it's designed to do so.

Q: Will my computer receive faxes if it's turned off?

A: No, your computer doesn't do anything if it's turned off. It can receive faxes if you're not there, but you must have a fax/modem installed, and the software that's required in order to receive the fax must be running. External fax machines can receive faxes when the computer is turned off, but the machines must be turned on.

Computer Systems

Q: Should I buy only Intel microprocessors?

A: If it makes you feel better, do so. Otherwise, no major problems have been found with the microprocessors manufactured by others. If problems did exist, the manufacturers probably wouldn't sell many of the chips — which isn't the case.

Q: Do you recommend IBM equipment?

A: Just like the preceding Intel microprocessor question, if buying IBM stuff makes you feel better, do it! Otherwise, when you peel back the outer wrapper, you'll see that all PCs contain basically the same innards.

Q: I want to write letters and balance my checkbook. Will a Pentium computer fill this need?

A: Fit the computer to meet your needs. Look for your checkbook-balancing software *first*. Then match that software's lust for hardware, and that's how you tell what type of computer you need. This basic method is what this book offers. If, in the end, all indicators point to a Pentium, you can buy it.

Q: Should I pay extra for an "Intel motherboard?" My dealer says that they're better.

A: For a Pentium computer, I would get an Intel motherboard, if I had a choice. The reason is that Intel knows how to make the motherboard for its own microprocessors and for the *PCI bus*. It's worth the extra cost (if any), in my opinion.

Q: What's a "flash programmable BIOS?"

A: It's a special chip that can be upgraded without removing the computer's cover. The *BIOS* is your PC's personality chip, and often manufacturers upgrade the BIOS to make it happier with newer PC components. In the olden days, you had to upgrade the chip by physically pulling out the old one and replacing it. With a flash BIOS, you can do the job by running a program on your computer. It makes the job simple.

Q: I've seen deals on refurbished equipment offered without a warranty but at very low (ridiculous) prices. Tell me what's wrong.

A: You have no warranty, and you're taking a stupid risk. Don't mess up your first computer experience by being cheap.

Q: What's a *clone,* and what's a *compatible*?

A: These terms have no concrete definitions, though they seem to have fallen out of favor as the dominance of IBM fades. Traditionally, a *clone* was a no-name, locally assembled computer. A *compatible* was a national brand. Compatibles are usually more expensive and more reliable, and they come with a better warranty (because it's honored by service departments across the country). The warranty on a clone is usually only good in one place: the store where you bought it.

Q: I want to buy one computer and hook up ten monitors and ten keyboards. Can I do that?

A: Not the way you think. What you really need is a file server and several workstations. One PC alone cannot manage such a feat and certainly not cheaply.

Q: What about those dedicated word-processing machines? Because all I want to do is write, why shouldn't I get one of those instead of a computer?

A: Don't! Those dedicated machines are slower, much slower than similarly priced and equipped PCs. Don't let the price fool you. A computer can be had for the same cost, plus you get your choice of word-processing software, a faster printer, and a path to future upgrades and more software options. Those dedicated word-processing machines are a sucker's buy. Don't be lured.

Q: I'm interested in picking up a used computer system. How can I tell whether it's any good?

A: First, I don't recommend a used computer system for your first computer purchase. You're definitely cutting off your service and support, not to mention any warranty. For a second or third purchase, used computers are a deal; most of them still operate and are decent machines. Just take along some software to test drive, and "kick the tires" by trying out the keyboard and monitor and turning the unit on and off a few times.

Q: If this computer comes in green, can I get it in blue?

A: Computer colors are generally white, off-white, and beige. If any colors are available, great. Otherwise, you have to spray paint your system on your own and at your own risk.

General

Q: What does $CALL mean?

A: It means that they can't print the price because the manufacturer won't let them or some other strange reason (such as to foil the "we'll beat any advertised price" crowd). It may also be a ruse to get you to phone up the company to see how much the doojobbie costs. In fact, that's the "call" part of $CALL.

Q: Can I set my computer on the floor? Will it leave a grease spot?

A: The only important thing about setting a computer anywhere is giving it breathing space, as discussed in Chapter 20. Make sure that you don't set the computer on carpet that can clog any breathing slats. If you didn't buy a tower-style computer, consider getting a little stand to help stand your computer up on its side. And, no, no grease is inside a computer to make a spot.

Q: Why doesn't someone make a computer that has every processor in it and can use every operating system?

A: They did. No one bought it. It did everything, but, like any jack-of-all-trades, it didn't do everything well. The cost of the computer was more expensive than buying each of the other computers separately.

Q: I have an old PC that isn't upgradeable. Can I do anything?

A: Sell it — if you can. Or donate it to a school or charity. They may grouse about it, in which case you can always find another school or charity that won't look a gift horse in the mouth.

Q: My computer runs hot — sometimes it shuts itself off. What can I do?

A: Buy a new power supply or, better still, take your system to an authorized repair service.

Q: If I want to learn how to program my computer, where should I start?

A: Buy a book about programming. Many excellent tutorials are out there that let you work at your own pace. For a programming language, I recommend BASIC. Sounds easy enough.

Q: Can I play Nintendo game cartridges on my PC?

A: Nope.

Q: I want a question answered that hasn't been covered in this book. Where can I go for help?

A: First, try your dealer. You paid him money; he should give you the support and answer your question. He may redirect you to the software manufacturer if the problem is with your software. Second, try a local users' group or a friend who is computer-knowledgeable. Third, you can also try writing away to those "Ask Dr. Computer" columnists in the national computer magazines. You can always find both help available for computers and people who are willing to help you.

Software Worksheet

Category: Office   Word processing   Spreadsheet
Recreation   Database   Graphics
Utility   Communications   Internet
Education   Programming   Personal finance
Multimedia   Reference   Productivity

Product name: _____

Developer: _____

Price: _____

Type of support: Vanilla   Chocolate   Carob   Fudge

Operating system: Windows 98   Windows NT   Version: _____
Windows 95   Mac   OS/2
Windows 3.1   DOS   Other: _____

Microprocessor: 486/better   Pentium MMX   Pentium: _____

Speed:_____ MHz

Memory needed: _____ Megabytes

Hard disk storage: _____ Megabytes

CD-ROM: Yes   No

Graphics: SVGA   No special requirements   Other: _____

Graphics memory: _____ Megabytes

Sound: SoundBlaster   AdLib   None   Other: _____

Special printer: Nope   Recommended:_____.

Special peripherals: Scanner   Modem   Microphone
MIDI   Joystick   Special mouse: _____

Other stuff: _____

Software Worksheet

Category: Office   Word processing   Spreadsheet
                  Recreation   Database   Graphics
                  Utility   Communications   Internet
                  Education   Programming   Personal finance
                  Multimedia   Reference   Productivity

Product name: _____

Developer: _____

Price: _____

Type of support: Vanilla   Chocolate   Carob   Fudge

Operating system: Windows 98   Windows NT   Version: _____
                      Windows 95   Mac   OS/2
                      Windows 3.1   DOS   Other: _____

Microprocessor: 486/better   Pentium MMX   Pentium: _____

                   Speed:_____ MHz

Memory needed: _____ Megabytes

Hard disk storage: _____ Megabytes

CD-ROM: Yes   No

Graphics: SVGA   No special requirements   Other: _____

                Graphics memory: _____ Megabytes

Sound: SoundBlaster   AdLib   None   Other: _____

Special printer: Nope   Recommended:_____

Special peripherals: Scanner   Modem   Microphone
                      MIDI   Joystick   Special mouse: _____

Other stuff: _____

Software Worksheet

Category: Office   Word processing   Spreadsheet
Recreation   Database   Graphics
Utility   Communications   Internet
Education   Programming   Personal finance
Multimedia   Reference   Productivity

Product name: _____

Developer: _____

Price: _____

Type of support: Vanilla   Chocolate   Carob   Fudge

Operating system: Windows 98   Windows NT   Version: _____
Windows 95   Mac   OS/2
Windows 3.1   DOS   Other: _____

Microprocessor: 486/better   Pentium MMX   Pentium: _____

Speed:_____ MHz

Memory needed: _____ Megabytes

Hard disk storage: _____ Megabytes

CD-ROM: Yes   No

Graphics: SVGA   No special requirements   Other: _____

Graphics memory: _____ Megabytes

Sound: SoundBlaster   AdLib   None   Other: _____

Special printer: Nope   Recommended:_____

Special peripherals: Scanner   Modem   Microphone
MIDI   Joystick   Special mouse: _____

Other stuff: _____

Software Worksheet

Category: Office   Word processing   Spreadsheet
Recreation   Database   Graphics
Utility   Communications   Internet
Education   Programming   Personal finance
Multimedia   Reference   Productivity

Product name: _____

Developer: _____

Price: _____

Type of support: Vanilla   Chocolate   Carob   Fudge

Operating system: Windows 98   Windows NT   Version: _____
Windows 95   Mac   OS/2
Windows 3.1   DOS   Other: _____

Microprocessor: 486/better   Pentium MMX   Pentium: _____

Speed:_____ MHz

Memory needed: _____ Megabytes

Hard disk storage: _____ Megabytes

CD-ROM: Yes   No

Graphics: SVGA   No special requirements   Other: _____

Graphics memory: _____ Megabytes

Sound: SoundBlaster   AdLib   None   Other: _____

Special printer: Nope   Recommended:_____

Special peripherals: Scanner   Modem   Microphone
MIDI   Joystick   Special mouse: _____

Other stuff: _____

Software Worksheet

Category: Office   Word processing   Spreadsheet
Recreation   Database   Graphics
Utility   Communications   Internet
Education   Programming   Personal finance
Multimedia   Reference   Productivity

Product name: _____

Developer: _____

Price: _____

Type of support: Vanilla   Chocolate   Carob   Fudge

Operating system: Windows 98   Windows NT   Version: _____
Windows 95   Mac   OS/2
Windows 3.1   DOS   Other: _____

Microprocessor: 486/better   Pentium MMX   Pentium: _____

Speed:_____ MHz

Memory needed: _____ Megabytes

Hard disk storage: _____ Megabytes

CD-ROM: Yes   No

Graphics: SVGA   No special requirements   Other: _____

Graphics memory: _____ Megabytes

Sound: SoundBlaster   AdLib   None   Other: _____

Special printer: Nope   Recommended:_____

Special peripherals: Scanner   Modem   Microphone
MIDI   Joystick   Special mouse: _____

Other stuff: _____

Software Worksheet

Category: Office   Word processing   Spreadsheet
              Recreation   Database   Graphics
              Utility   Communications   Internet
              Education   Programming   Personal finance
              Multimedia   Reference   Productivity

Product name: _____

Developer: _____

Price: _____

Type of support: Vanilla   Chocolate   Carob   Fudge

Operating system: Windows 98   Windows NT   Version: _____
                     Windows 95   Mac   OS/2
                     Windows 3.1   DOS   Other: _____

Microprocessor: 486/better   Pentium MMX Pentium: _____

                   Speed:_____ MHz

Memory needed: _____ Megabytes

Hard disk storage: _____ Megabytes

CD-ROM: Yes   No

Graphics: SVGA   No special requirements   Other: _____

             Graphics memory: _____ Megabytes

Sound: SoundBlaster   AdLib   None   Other: _____

Special printer: Nope   Recommended:_____

Special peripherals: Scanner   Modem   Microphone
                        MIDI   Joystick   Special mouse: _____

Other stuff: _____

Software Worksheet

Category: Office   Word processing   Spreadsheet
Recreation   Database   Graphics
Utility   Communications   Internet
Education   Programming   Personal finance
Multimedia   Reference   Productivity

Product name: _____

Developer: _____

Price: _____

Type of support: Vanilla   Chocolate   Carob   Fudge

Operating system: Windows 98   Windows NT   Version: _____
Windows 95   Mac   OS/2
Windows 3.1   DOS   Other: _____

Microprocessor: 486/better   Pentium MMX   Pentium: _____

Speed: ____ MHz

Memory needed: _____ Megabytes

Hard disk storage: _____ Megabytes

CD-ROM: Yes   No

Graphics: SVGA   No special requirements   Other: _____

Graphics memory: _____ Megabytes

Sound: SoundBlaster   AdLib   None   Other: _____

Special printer: Nope   Recommended: _____

Special peripherals: Scanner   Modem   Microphone
MIDI   Joystick   Special mouse: _____

Other stuff: _____

Software Worksheet

Category: Office   Word processing   Spreadsheet
Recreation   Database   Graphics
Utility   Communications Internet
Education   Programming   Personal finance
Multimedia   Reference   Productivity

Product name: _____

Developer: _____

Price: _____

Type of support: Vanilla   Chocolate   Carob   Fudge

Operating system: Windows 98   Windows NT   Version: _____
Windows 95   Mac   OS/2
Windows 3.1   DOS   Other: _____

Microprocessor: 486/better   Pentium MMX   Pentium: _____
Speed: _____ MHz

Memory needed: _____ Megabytes

Hard disk storage: _____ Megabytes

CD-ROM: Yes   No

Graphics: SVGA   No special requirements   Other: _____
Graphics memory: _____ Megabytes

Sound: SoundBlaster   AdLib   None   Other: _____

Special printer: Nope   Recommended: _____

Special peripherals: Scanner   Modem   Microphone
MIDI   Joystick   Special mouse: _____

Other stuff: _____

Software Worksheet

Category: Office   Word processing   Spreadsheet
Recreation   Database   Graphics
Utility   Communications   Internet
Education   Programming   Personal finance
Multimedia   Reference   Productivity

Product name: _____

Developer: _____

Price: _____

Type of support: Vanilla   Chocolate   Carob   Fudge

Operating system: Windows 98   Windows NT   Version: _____
Windows 95   Mac   OS/2
Windows 3.1   DOS   Other: _____

Microprocessor: 486/better   Pentium MMX   Pentium: _____
Speed: _____ MHz

Memory needed: _____ Megabytes

Hard disk storage: _____ Megabytes

CD-ROM: Yes   No

Graphics: SVGA   No special requirements   Other: _____
Graphics memory: _____ Megabytes

Sound: SoundBlaster   AdLib   None   Other: _____

Special printer: Nope   Recommended: _____

Special peripherals: Scanner   Modem   Microphone
MIDI   Joystick   Special mouse: _____

Other stuff: _____

Software Worksheet

Category: Office   Word processing   Spreadsheet
Recreation   Database   Graphics
Utility   Communications   Internet
Education   Programming   Personal finance
Multimedia   Reference   Productivity

Product name: _____

Developer: _____

Price: _____

Type of support: Vanilla   Chocolate   Carob   Fudge

Operating system: Windows 98   Windows NT   Version: _____
Windows 95   Mac   OS/2
Windows 3.1   DOS   Other: _____

Microprocessor: 486/better   Pentium MMX   Pentium: _____

Speed:_____ MHz

Memory needed: _____ Megabytes

Hard disk storage: _____ Megabytes

CD-ROM: Yes   No

Graphics: SVGA   No special requirements   Other: _____

Graphics memory: _____ Megabytes

Sound: SoundBlaster   AdLib   None   Other: _____

Special printer: Nope   Recommended:_____

Special peripherals: Scanner   Modem   Microphone
MIDI   Joystick   Special mouse: _____

Other stuff: _____

Software Worksheet

Category: Office   Word processing   Spreadsheet
Recreation   Database   Graphics
Utility   Communications   Internet
Education   Programming   Personal finance
Multimedia   Reference   Productivity

Product name: _____

Developer: _____

Price: _____

Type of support: Vanilla   Chocolate   Carob   Fudge

Operating system: Windows 98   Windows NT   Version: _____
Windows 95   Mac   OS/2
Windows 3.1   DOS   Other: _____

Microprocessor: 486/better   Pentium MMX   Pentium: _____
Speed:_____ MHz

Memory needed: _____ Megabytes

Hard disk storage: _____ Megabytes

CD-ROM: Yes   No

Graphics: SVGA   No special requirements   Other: _____
Graphics memory: _____ Megabytes

Sound: SoundBlaster   AdLib   None   Other: _____

Special printer: Nope   Recommended:_____

Special peripherals: Scanner   Modem   Microphone
MIDI   Joystick   Special mouse: _____

Other stuff: _____

Software Worksheet

Category: Office   Word processing   Spreadsheet
Recreation   Database   Graphics
Utility   Communications   Internet
Education   Programming   Personal finance
Multimedia   Reference   Productivity

Product name: _____

Developer: _____

Price: _____

Type of support: Vanilla   Chocolate   Carob   Fudge

Operating system: Windows 98   Windows NT   Version: _____
Windows 95   Mac   OS/2
Windows 3.1   DOS   Other: _____

Microprocessor: 486/better   Pentium MMX   Pentium: _____

Speed:_____ MHz

Memory needed: _____ Megabytes

Hard disk storage: _____ Megabytes

CD-ROM: Yes   No

Graphics: SVGA   No special requirements   Other: _____

Graphics memory: _____ Megabytes

Sound: SoundBlaster   AdLib   None   Other: _____

Special printer: Nope   Recommended:_____

Special peripherals: Scanner   Modem   Microphone
MIDI   Joystick   Special mouse: _____

Other stuff: _____

Software Worksheet

Category: Office   Word processing   Spreadsheet
Recreation   Database   Graphics
Utility   Communications   Internet
Education   Programming   Personal finance
Multimedia   Reference   Productivity

Product name: _____

Developer: _____

Price: _____

Type of support: Vanilla   Chocolate   Carob   Fudge

Operating system: Windows 98   Windows NT   Version: _____
Windows 95   Mac   OS/2
Windows 3.1   DOS   Other: _____

Microprocessor: 486/better   Pentium MMX   Pentium: _____

Speed:_____ MHz

Memory needed: _____ Megabytes

Hard disk storage: _____ Megabytes

CD-ROM: Yes   No

Graphics: SVGA   No special requirements   Other: _____

Graphics memory: _____ Megabytes

Sound: SoundBlaster   AdLib   None   Other: _____

Special printer: Nope   Recommended:_____

Special peripherals: Scanner   Modem   Microphone
MIDI   Joystick   Special mouse: _____

Other stuff: _____

Software Worksheet

Category:
Office	Word processing	Spreadsheet
Recreation	Database	Graphics
Utility	Communications	Internet
Education	Programming	Personal finance
Multimedia	Reference	Productivity

Product name: _____

Developer: _____

Price: _____

Type of support: Vanilla   Chocolate   Carob   Fudge

Operating system: Windows 98   Windows NT   Version: _____
Windows 95   Mac   OS/2
Windows 3.1   DOS   Other: _____

Microprocessor: 486/better   Pentium MMX   Pentium: _____

Speed:_____ MHz

Memory needed: _____ Megabytes

Hard disk storage: _____ Megabytes

CD-ROM: Yes   No

Graphics: SVGA   No special requirements   Other: _____

Graphics memory: _____ Megabytes

Sound: SoundBlaster   AdLib   None   Other: _____

Special printer: Nope   Recommended:_____

Special peripherals: Scanner   Modem   Microphone
MIDI   Joystick   Special mouse: _____

Other stuff: _____

Software Worksheet

Category: Office   Word processing   Spreadsheet
Recreation   Database   Graphics
Utility   Communications   Internet
Education   Programming   Personal finance
Multimedia   Reference   Productivity

Product name: _____

Developer: _____

Price: _____

Type of support: Vanilla   Chocolate   Carob   Fudge

Operating system: Windows 98   Windows NT   Version: _____
Windows 95   Mac   OS/2
Windows 3.1   DOS   Other: _____

Microprocessor: 486/better   Pentium MMX   Pentium: _____

Speed:_____ MHz

Memory needed: _____ Megabytes

Hard disk storage: _____ Megabytes

CD-ROM: Yes   No

Graphics: SVGA   No special requirements   Other: _____

Graphics memory: _____ Megabytes

Sound: SoundBlaster   AdLib   None   Other: _____

Special printer: Nope   Recommended:_____

Special peripherals: Scanner   Modem   Microphone
MIDI   Joystick   Special mouse: _____

Other stuff: _____

Index

• A •

A drive, 61. *See also* floppy disk drives
Access (Microsoft), 124
access time, 59–60
adding machines, replacing with
    computer, 122
address books, replacing with
    computer, 26, 124
Adobe Illustrator, 125
advertisements
  address not provided, 213
  common tricks, 164–165
  how to read, 161–164
  and industry standards, 211–212
  price grids, 164
  where to find, 162
Airborne Express Web site, 173
airlines, and laptop computers, 107
America Online (AOL), 129
analog-to-digital ports, 78
AOL (America Online), 129
application programs, 33–34, 120. *See*
    also software
architects, software for, 125
artists, reasons to buy a computer, 24,
    124–125
assembling computer. *See* computers,
    setting up
A-to-D ports, 78
AutoCAD software, 125
AUX ports, 79

• B •

B drive, 61. *See also* floppy disk drives
backing up data. *See also* disk storage
 Jaz drives, 64, 157

tape backup drives, 31, 91–92, 157, 219
  Zip drives, 64, 80, 157
balance sheets, creating on
    computer, 122
bandwidth, 70
banks, 49, 51–52. *See also* memory
    (RAM)
banners, printing, 228
Basic Input/Output System (BIOS)
  defined, 31
  and operating system, 33
  upgrading (flash), 229
BASIC programming language, 132, 231
battery life, 107, 222
BBSs (bulletin-board systems), 128–129
Bernoulli drives, 64
BIOS (Basic Input/Output System)
  defined, 31
  and operating system, 33
  upgrading (flash), 229
bond paper, avoiding, 218
books
  buying, 223
  tracking loans with computer, 26
borrowing software, 133, 225
boxes. *See* consoles
brains
  computers, 111–112
  humans, 40
  printers, 95
brand names
  mail-order, 170–171
  recommendations, 8, 229
browsers, 127–128
budgeting software, 124
building your own computer, 171
bulletin boards, 128–129
bulletin-board systems (BBSs), 128–129

bundled software, 126–127
burn-in tests, 184, 195
buyer's guides, 10
buying grids, 164
buying process overview. *See also specific topics*
  common mistakes, 13, 19, 207–210
  common questions, 7–11
  payment options, 20
  reasons to buy, 23–27
  service, 19
  steps, 14, 21, 181
  support, 19
  technology obsolescence, 20
bytes, defined, 47–49. *See also* disk storage; memory (RAM)

• C •

C drive, 58. *See also* hard disk drives
C++ programming language, 132
cables
  external modems, 219
  printers, 96, 217–218
cache, 45
CAD (computer-assisted design), 124–125
calculators, replacing with computer, 24, 122–123
calendars, replacing with computer, 26, 124
$CALL abbreviation, 162, 231
carpal tunnel syndrome, 75, 216
cash, avoiding, 20, 209
CD-R drives, 63–64, 80. *See also* CD-ROM drives
CD-ROM drives
  disks as hardware, 30
  hardware requirements worksheet, 157
  interface to motherboard, 62
  minimum requirements, 146
  multi-CD changers, 63
  music, playing, 62, 228

size, 62
speed, 62–63
storage capacity, 62
upgrading, 199
writeable, 63–64, 80
CD-WR drives, 63. *See also* CD-ROM drives
central processing units (CPUs), 30
Centronics port, 78
charts, software for creating, 123
checkbook software, 124
checks, avoiding, 20, 209
children
  educational software, 26, 130
  game software, 129–130
  reasons to buy a computer, 24–25
chips. *See* memory (RAM)
classes, availability of, 19, 178, 214. *See also* support
clock in computer, 221–222
clones, defined, 230
color monitors, 68, 227
color of console, 230
color printers, 94, 98
COM ports, 79
command-line interface, 33
communications hardware. *See* modems
communications software
  bulletin boards, 128–129
  Internet, 127–128
compatibility
  hardware with software, 34
  operating system with microprocessor, 33
compatibles, defined, 230
computer box. *See* consoles
computer memory. *See* disk storage; memory (RAM)
computer models. *See* consoles
computer user's groups, 223
computer-assisted design (CAD), 124–125

computers, buying process overview
  common mistakes, 13, 19, 207–210
  common questions, 7–11
  payment options, 20
  reasons to buy, 23–27
  service, 19
  steps, 14, 21, 181
  support, 19
  technology obsolescence, 20
computers, old
  donating, 202
  selling, 201–202
  technology obsolescence, 197–198
  upgrading
    costs, 199
    hardware, 198–200
    memory (RAM), 199
    microprocessor, 200
    motherboard, 200
    operating system, 201
    software, 200–201
computers, setting up
  burn-in test, 195
  leaving computer running, 194
  location, 190–191, 231
  manuals, reading, 190, 195, 209
  parts
    finding, 190
    missing, 212–213
  plugging computer into wall, 191–192
  plugging parts into computer, 192
  turning off computer, 193–194
  turning on computer, 192–193
  understanding the system, 195–196
consoles. *See also* laptop computers
  color, 230
  defined, 32
  desktop models, 101–102
  dumb terminals, 102
  footprint, small, 102–103
  minitowers, 101, 104–105
  towers, 101, 103–104

contact management with computers,
  26, 124
contextual help, 140
controlling hardware, 32–33, 112
controlling software, 32–33, 112
copy machine printers, 94
Corel Office, 126
CorelDraw for Windows, 125
CPUs (central processing units), 30
credit cards, 20, 172, 184, 209
curved keyboards, 73–74

• *D* •

D drive, 58. *See also* hard disk drives
daisy-wheel printers, 94
DAT (digital audiotape), 91. *See also*
  backing up data
database software, 123–124
dBase software, 124
dedicated word-processing machines,
  230
delivery time, 183
demo software, 134
deposits, 183, 212
desktop models, 101–102
desktop publishing (DTP) software, 122
Dhrystones speed-rating test, 41
diagnosing problems, 130–131
dialer programs, 128
digital audiotape (DAT), 91. *See also*
  backing up data
digital cameras, 31
Digital Versatile Disk (DVD), 65, 211
Digital Video Disk (DVD), 65
DIMM, 50. *See also* memory (RAM)
DIP, 50. *See also* memory (RAM)
discounts, 166–167
disk drive requirements, 56
  See also CD-ROM drives
  See also disk storage
  See also floppy disk drives
  See also hard disk drives

disk memory, defined, 55
Disk Operating System (DOS), 33, 116, 225
disk storage. *See also* backing up data
  CD-R drives, 63–64, 80
  CD-ROM drives
    disks as hardware, 30
    hardware requirements worksheet, 157
    interface to motherboard, 62
    minimum requirements, 146
    multi-CD changers, 63
    music, playing, 62, 228
    size, 62
    speed, 62–63
    storage capacity, 62
    upgrading, 199
    writeable, 63–64, 80
  CD-WR drives, 63
  choosing, 65
  defined, 55
  disk drives, defined, 56
  disks, defined, 56
  DVD drives, 65, 211
  external disk drives, 80
  floppy disk drives
    adding, 227
    hardware requirements worksheet, 156
    required, 61–62
    upgrading, 199
  hard disk drives
    access time, 59–60
    adding, 58, 227
    choosing, 182
    controllers, 60–61
    fixed, 58
    hardware requirements worksheet, 155–156
    interface to motherboard, 57, 60–61
    multiple, 57
    price, 57
  removable, 64, 80, 157
  size, 57–59
  speed, 57, 59–60
  storage capacity, 57–59
  terminology, 58
  upgrading, 199
  Jaz drives, 64, 157
  magneto-optical drives, 64, 157
  versus memory (RAM), 55
  permanent, 56
  RAID drives, 64
  RAM drives, 64
  required types, 56
  units of storage, 55
  Zip drives, 64, 80
disks, defined, 56
docking stations, 107
documentation. *See* manuals
donating computers, 202
DOS (Disk Operating System), 33, 116, 225
dot pitch, 70
dot-matrix printers, 94, 98–99, 218
Dr. Seuss software, 130
DRAM, 50. *See also* memory (RAM)
drawing software, 124–125
drinking at the computer, avoiding, 220
Drive A, 61. *See also* floppy disk drives
Drive B, 61. *See also* floppy disk drives
Drive C, 58. *See also* hard disk drives
Drive D, 58. *See also* hard disk drives
DTP (desktop publishing) software, 122
dumb terminals, 102
DVD (Digital Versatile Disk), 65, 211
DVD (Digital Video Disk), 65
Dvorak keyboards, 227

• *E* •

eating at the computer, avoiding, 220
ECC (Error Checking and Correction), 50
ECP/EPP ports, 78
ED (Extended Density) drive, 62

EDO (Extended Data Out), 50
educational software, 26, 130
EISA expansion slots, 84
e-mail software, 26, 127
engineers, software for, 125
entertainment, 26
erasable typing paper, avoiding, 218
ergonomic keyboards, 73–74
Error Checking and Correction (ECC), 50
Eudora, 128
Excel (Microsoft), 123
expanded memory, 226
expansion cards
  defined, 82
  laptop computers, 84–85
  network, 85
  PCI, 85
  PCMCIA, 84–85
  SCSI, 81–82
expansion slots
  defined, 82–83
  EISA, 84
  ISA, 83
  laptop computers, 84–85
  MCA, 84
  NuBus, 84
  PCI, 83
Extended Data Out (EDO), 50
Extended Density (ED) drive, 62
extended memory, 50, 226
extended-service policies, 177
external disk drives, 80. *See also*
  backing up data
external modems
  cables, 219
  choosing, 89
  defined, 88
  plugging into computer, 192
eyestrain, 227

• F •

fax capability, 88, 228–229
fax printers, 94, 99–100

Federal Express Web site, 173
financial software, 124
FireWire ports, 83
fixed disks, 58. *See also* hard disk drives
flash programmable BIOS, 229
flat-screen monitors, 68
floating-point unit (FPU), 44
floppy disk drives
  adding, 227
  hardware requirements worksheet, 156
  required, 61–62
  upgrading, 199
floppy disks, 30, 56, 219
fonts, 95
footprint, small, 102–103
forms. *See* hardware requirements
  worksheet; software requirements
  worksheet
486 or later microprocessors, 43
FPU (floating-point unit), 44
Fractal Design Painter, 125
free software, 132–133
frequency, defined, 70

• G •

G (gigabytes), 48
game controller ports, 81
games
  operating system recommendation,
   115
  software, 129–130
GB (gigabytes), 48
genealogy, 26
general ledger, creating on computer,
  122–123
gigabytes, 48
graphical interface, Windows, 33
graphics accelerator, 72
graphics adapters
  choosing, 69–72
  defined, 68
  hardware requirements worksheet, 157

(continued)

graphics adapters *(continued)*
  minimum requirements, 146
  video controller, 67
  video memory, 69–70
graphics card. *See* graphics adapters
graphics software, 124–125
graphs, creating, 123
grids (prices), 164
grounded, defined, 216

• *H* •

haggling, 166
handheld computers, 105–106
hard disk drives
  access time, 59–60
  adding, 58, 227
  backing up, 64
  choosing, 182
  controllers, 60–61
  fixed, 58
  hardware requirements worksheet,
      155–156
  interface to motherboard, 57, 60–61
  multiple, 57
  price, 57
  removable, 64, 80, 157
  size, 57–59
  speed, 57, 59–60
  storage capacity, 57–59
  terminology, 58
  upgrading, 199
hard disks, defined, 58
hard drive controllers, 60–61
hard drives. *See* hard disk drives
hard file, defined, 58
hardware. *See also specific hardware*
      types
  compatibility with software, 16, 34
  controlling, 32–33, 112
  defined, 29–30
  list of devices, 31–32
  microprocessors, 30

mistakes, common, 208
  upgrading, 198–200
hardware requirements worksheet
  blank form, 18, 151–153
  CD-ROM drives, 157
  example, 160
  floppy drives, 156
  graphics adapters, 157
  hard drive storage, 155–156
  Jaz drives, 157
  memory, 154–155
  mice, 158
  microprocessors, 154
  MO (magneto-optical) drives, 157
  modems, 158
  monitors, 158
  operating systems, 153
  ports, 158
  printers, 158–159
  removable drives, 157
  SCSI requirements, 156
  sound requirements, 158
  tape backup, 157
  Zip drives, 157
Hayes-compatible modems, 88
headphones, 90
help. *See* support
high-speed line printers, 94
hobbies, 26
home budgeting software, 124
human interface, 33

• *I* •

IBM equipment, 229
IDE (Integrated Drive Electronics)
      controllers, 60–61
Illustrator (Adobe), 125
impact printers, 94, 98–99, 218
ink, for printers, 218
ink printers, 94, 98, 218
inports, 78
input devices, 32

Input/Output (I/O), 32
Integrated Drive Electronics (IDE)
    controllers, 60–61
integrated software, 225
Intel microprocessors, 39–40, 229. *See
    also* microprocessors
Intel motherboards, 229
IntelliMouse, 74
interface to motherboard, 60–61
interlaced monitors, 70
internal modems, 88–89
Internet
    browsers, 127–128
    communications software, 127–128
    computer sales, 172–173
    limiting time on, 222
    pornography, filtering, 223
Internet Explorer (Microsoft), 127
Internet Service Provider (ISP), 127
I/O (Input/Output), 32
ISA expansion slots, 83
ISP (Internet Service Provider), 127

• *J* •

Jaz drives, 64, 157. *See also* backing up
    data
joysticks, 81
Jumpstart software, 130

• *K* •

K (kilobytes), 48
K6 microprocessors, 40
KB (kilobytes), 48
keyboard ports, 78
keyboards
    choosing, 72
    curved, 73–74
    defined, 31
    Dvorak, 227
    ergonomic, 73–74
    handheld computers, 106
    multiple, 230
    nonstandard, 73–74
    101-key Enhanced, 73
    plugging into computer, 192
    ports, 78
    price, 72
    spilling liquid on, 220
    standard, 73
kids
    educational software, 26, 130
    game software, 129–130
    reasons to buy a computer, 24–25
kilobytes, 48
Kinsington SmartSockets, 216

• *L* •

laptop computers
    airline use, 107
    battery life, 107
    bundled software, 126–127
    case, 107
    docking station, 107
    expansion cards, 84–85
    expansion slots, 84–85
    history of, 108
    memory, 84
    modems, 84
    monitors, 106
    network adapters, 84
    price, 107
    weight, 106–107
    when to buy, 9, 107
laser printers, 94, 97, 218
line printer 1 (LPT) ports, 78
Linux operating system, 116
lists, replacing with computer, 123–124
local computer stores, 168–169
location of computer, 190–191, 231
Logitech mouse, 74
Lotus 1-2-3, 123
LPT (line printer 1) ports, 78
luggables, 108

• *M* •

M (megabytes), 48
Macintosh operating system, 114, 116
magazines, 10, 223
magneto-optical (MO) drives, 31, 64, 157
mail-order, 170–171
manuals
  missing, 214
  for setting up computer, 190, 195, 209
  for software, 141, 222, 225
math coprocessors, 44
MB (megabytes), 48
MCA expansion slots, 84
McAfee virus scanner, 131
megabytes, 48–49
megahertz (MHz), 40–41
megastores, 170
memory. *See also* disk storage; memory
    (RAM)
  bytes, 47–49
  cache, 45
  hardware requirements worksheet,
    154–155
  laptop computers, 84
  monitors, 70
  operating system requirements, 50
  permanent storage, 47
  temporary storage, 47
  units of storage, 49, 55
memory cards, 51
memory (disk), 55. *See also* disk storage
memory (RAM)
  adding more, 51–52
  banks, 49, 51–52
  choosing, 182
  configuration, 51–52
  defined, 31
  versus disk storage, 55
  expanded memory, 226
  extended memory, 50, 226
  installed by manufacturer, 51

megabytes, 49
memory cards, 51
minimum requirements, 146
monitors, 69
price, 53
printers, 95
required amount, 49–50
self-check, 50
speed, 50
standard quantity, 49
temporary, 47
terminology, 50
units of memory, 49
upgrading, 199
MHz (megahertz), 40–41
microphones, 90
microprocessors
  about, 30
  cache, 45
  choosing, 45, 182, 229
  defined, 30
  486 or later, 43
  hardware requirements worksheet, 154
  Intel, 39–40, 229
  K6, 40
  math coprocessors, 44
  MHz (megahertz), 40–41
  minimum requirements, 146
  MMX Technology, 41–42
  names, 30
  non-Intel, 40
  numbers, 30, 42–43
  and operating systems, 33, 111–112
  OverDrive chip, 44
  Pentium, 39–40, 43
  Pentium II, 39–40, 43
  Pentium or later, 43
  Pentium Pro, 39–40
  686, 40
  speed, 40–41, 44
  tests, 41
  386 or later, 42, 43

turbo mode, 44
upgrading, 43, 200
Microsoft Access, 124
Microsoft Excel, 123
Microsoft Internet Explorer, 127
Microsoft Money, 124
Microsoft monopoly, 113
Microsoft mouse, 74
Microsoft Office, 126, 146–148
Microsoft Visual BASIC programming
  language, 132
Microsoft Word, 121
MIDI ports, 81
milliseconds (ms), 59
minimum requirements, 146
minitowers, 101, 104–105
mistakes, common, 13, 19, 207–210
MMX Technology, 41–42
MO (magneto-optical) drives, 31, 64, 157
modem ports, 79
modems
  cables, 219
  choosing, 87–88
  defined, 31
  external, 88–89
  fax capability, 88
  hardware requirements worksheet, 158
  Hayes compatible, 88
  internal, 88–89
  laptop computers, 84
  and phone bills, 88
  and phone lines, 88, 222
  plugging into computer, 192
  ports, 79
  security of, 228
  speed, 89–91
  upgrading, 199
Money (Microsoft), 124
monitors
  bandwidth, 70
  choosing, 182
  color, 68, 227

defined, 31
dot pitch, 70
eyestrain, 227
flat-screen, 68
frequency, 70
graphics accelerator, 72
graphics adapters
  choosing, 69–72
  defined, 68
  hardware requirements
    worksheet, 157
  minimum requirements, 146
  video controller, 67
  video memory, 69–70
handheld computers, 106
hardware requirements worksheet, 158
interface to motherboard, 67
interlaced, 70
labels, reading, 71–72
laptop computers, 106
memory, 69–70
MPEG, 72
multiple, 230
multiscanning, 70
multisync, 70
non-interlaced, 70
plugging into computer, 192
scan rate, 70
screen, defined, 68
size, 68–69
speed, 70, 72
SVGA (Super VGA), 69
3-D graphics adapters, 69
TV set not a substitute, 68
upgrading, 199
VGA (Video Gate Array), 70
video controller, 67
video memory, 69–70
vision-impaired people, 69
WRAM, 71
XGA, 70

motherboards
  Intel, 229
  interface to
    CD-ROM drives, 62
    hard disk drives, 57, 60–61
    IDE controllers, 60–61
    monitors, 67
    SCSI controllers, 60–61
  upgrading, 200
mice. *See* mouse
  defined, 31
  hardware requirements worksheet, 158
  IntelliMouse, 74
  Logitech, 74
  Microsoft, 74
  minimum requirements, 146
  mousepads, 215–216
  nonstandard, 75
  pen, 75
  plugging into computer, 192
  ports, 78–79
  software, 76
  standard, 74
  stylus, 75
  touch-sensitive pad, 75
  trackball, 75
mouse ports, 78–79
mousepads, 215–216
movies, software for writing, 121
MPEG monitors, 72
ms (milliseconds), 59
multi-CD changers, 63
multiscanning monitors, 70
multisync monitors, 70
music
  playing on CD-ROM drive, 62, 228
  reason to buy a computer, 26
  and sound cards, 90

• *N* •

nanoseconds (ns), 50
national chain stores, 169

Net Nanny, 223
Netscape, 127–128
network adapters
  laptop computers, 84
  ports, 80
network expansion cards, 85
Nintendo, 231
non-interlaced monitors, 70
Norton SI speed-rating test, 41
Norton Utilities, 130
notebook computers, 106–108
ns (nanoseconds), 50
NuBus expansion slots, 84

• *O* •

Office (Corel), 126
Office (Microsoft), 126, 146–148
office suite software, 126
101-key Enhanced keyboards, 73
online help, 140
online sales, 172–173
on-site service, 176
open architecture, 82
operating systems
  about, 32–33, 111–112
  choosing, 112–113, 117
  defined, 32–33, 111
  DOS, 116
  ease of use, 114–115
  hardware, controlling, 112
  hardware requirements worksheet, 153
  Linux, 116
  Macintosh, 116
  memory requirements, 50
  and microprocessors, 33, 111–112
  multiple, 231
  non-Windows, 116
  OS/2, 116, 226
  shells, defined, 115
  software, controlling, 112
  software base, 113–114
  32-bit applications, 115

UNIX, 114, 116
upgrading, 201, 226
Windows version, choosing, 113,
    115, 226
organizational charts, creating, 123
OS/2 operating system, 116, 226
output devices, 32
OverDrive chip, 44

● *P* ●

PageMaker software, 122
pages per minute (ppm), 95
painting software, 124–125
palmtops, 106
paper for printers, 96, 98, 218
paper towels, 220
parallel ports, 78
parity, 50
parts, mail-order, 171
PC models. *See* consoles
PCI bus, 83
PCI expansion slots, 83
PCI network cards, 85
PCMCIA (Personal Computer Memory
    Card International Association)
  cards, 84–85
  ports, 84
PDA (personal digital assistant), 106
pen mice, 75
Pentium II microprocessors, 39–40, 43
Pentium microprocessors, 39–40, 43
Pentium or later microprocessors, 43
Pentium Pro microprocessors, 39–40
performance, improving, 130–131
peripherals, 32
permanent storage, 47. *See also* disk
    storage
Personal Computer Memory Card
    International Association (PCMCIA)
  cards, 84–85
  ports, 84
personal digital assistant (PDA), 106
personal organizer software, 124

phone bills, 88
phone lines, 88, 222
photographic paper, 98
plays, software for writing, 121
plugging computer into wall, 191–192
plugging devices into computer, 192
pointing devices. *See* mice
pornography, filtering, 223
portable computers, 105–108. *See also*
    laptop computers
ports
  analog-to-digital, 78
  A-to-D, 78
  AUX, 79
  Centronics, 78
  choosing, 78
  COM, 79
  defined, 77
  ECP/EPP, 78
  external disk drives, 80
  FireWire, 83
  game controller, 81
  hardware requirements worksheet, 158
  inports, 78
  joysticks, 81
  keyboards, 78
  LPT, 78
  mice, 78–79
  MIDI, 81
  modems, 79
  network adapters, 80
  parallel, 78
  PCMCIA, 84
  printers, 78–80
  RS-232, 79
  SCSI, 81–82
  serial, 79–80
  sound synthesizers, 80
  USB, 83
  video-capture units, 80
PostScript printers, 97
power strips, 192, 216

ppm (pages per minute), 95
printer ports, 78–80
printers
  brains, 95
  cables, 96, 217–218
  choosing, 93–94, 100
  color, 94, 98
  copy machine printers, 94
  daisy-wheel printers, 94
  defined, 31
  dot-matrix printers, 94, 98–99
  fax printers, 94, 99–100
  fonts, 95
  hardware requirements worksheet,
    158–159
  high-speed line printers, 94
  impact printers, 94, 98–99
  ink, 218
  ink printers, 94, 98
  laser printers, 94, 97
  memory (RAM), 95
  mistakes, common, 209
  multiple, 228
  paper, 96, 98, 218
  plugging into computer, 192
  ports, 78–80
  PostScript printers, 97
  ppm (pages per minute), 95
  price, 94
  print quality, 95
  scanner printers, 94
  speed, 95
  thermal printers, 94
  types of, 93–94
  typewriters as, 228
  will not print, 228
processors. *See* microprocessors
programming languages, 131–132, 231
programs, defined, 33–34, 120. *See also*
    software
public-domain software, 133

• *Q* •
Quicken software, 124
quotes, 166

• *R* •
RAID drives, 64
RAM drives, 64
RAM (Random Access Memory). *See*
    memory (RAM)
Random Access Memory (RAM). *See*
    memory (RAM)
Read-Only Memory (ROM), 49. *See also*
    memory
refab computers, 9
refurbished computers, 9, 167, 230
Remember icon, 2
removable disk drives, 64, 80, 157. *See*
    also backing up data
repairs. *See* service
repetitive tasks, identifying, 25
ROM (Read-Only Memory), 49. *See also*
    memory
RS-232 ports, 79

• *S* •
salespeople
  commissions, 167
  warning signs, 213
Saturday sales, avoiding, 184
scan rate, monitors, 70
ScanDisk utility, 131
scanner printers, 94
scanners, 31
screen, defined, 68
SCSI (Small Computer System Interface)
  devices, list of, 82
  expansion cards, 81–82
  hard drive controllers, 60–61
  hardware requirements worksheet, 156
  ports, 81–82
security of modems, 228
selling computers, 201–202

serial ports, 79–80
service. *See also* support
  defined, 19
  extended-service policies, 177
  importance of, 19
  questions to ask seller, 176–177
  used computers, 203
Sesame Street software, 130
setting up computer. *See* computers,
    setting up
shareware, 133–134
shells, defined, 115
SIMM (single in-line memory module),
    50. *See also* memory (RAM)
single in-line memory module (SIMM),
    50. *See also* memory (RAM)
SIP, 50. *See also* memory (RAM)
686 microprocessors, 40
small businesses, reasons to buy a
    computer, 24
Small Computer System Interface (SCSI)
  devices, list of, 82
  expansion cards, 81–82
  hard drive controllers, 60–61
  hardware requirements worksheet, 156
  ports, 81–82
small-footprint models, 102–103
software
  application programs, 33–34, 120
  borrowing, 133, 225
  boxes, how to read, 142–143
  bundled, 126–127
  categories, 120
  choosing, 16, 137–138, 150
  communications
    bulletin boards, 128–129
    Internet, 127–128
  compatibility with hardware, 16, 34
  controlling, 32–33, 112
  databases, 123–124
  defined, 32
  demos, 134

desktop publishing (DTP), 122
discounts, 166
DOS, running in Windows, 225
educational, 26, 130
free, 132–133
games, 129–130
graphics, 124–125
help, 140
importance of, 23, 34–35
integrated, 225
manuals, 141, 222, 225
mice, 76
minimum requirements, 146
operating systems, 32–33, 111–112
price, 209
programming languages, 131–132
programs, 33–34, 120
public-domain, 133
reasons to buy a computer, 23–27
requirements, how to read, 142–143
shareware, 133–134
spreadsheets, 122–123
support, 140–142
text editors, 121
tools, 130–131
trying before buying, 138–139
upgrade versions, 143
upgrading, 143, 200–201
user-friendly, 139–140
utilities, 130–131
versions, 143, 225
viruses, 226
writing your own, 131–132
word processors, 120–122
software base, 33, 113–114
software requirements worksheet
  blank form, 17, 148–149
  Fractal Design Painter example,
      144–145
  Microsoft Office 97 example, 146–148
sound cards, 90, 158
sound synthesizers, 80

SoundBlaster compatible sound
    cards, 90
speakers, 90
speed
    brains, human, 40
    CD-ROM drives, 62–63
    computers, 9
    human brain, 40
spike protectors, 217
spreadsheet software, 122–123
storage. *See also* disk storage; memory
    (RAM)
    permanent, 47
    temporary, 47
    units, 47–49, 55
stylus mice, 75
Super VGA (SVGA) monitors, 69
support. *See also* service
    defined, 19
    importance of, 19
    questions to ask seller, 177–178
    software, 140–142
    used computers, 203
    where to get, 10, 232
Surf Watch, 223
surge protectors, 217
surge suppressors, 192
SVGA (Super VGA) monitors, 69
swap meets, 168

• *T* •

tape backup drives, 31, 91–92, 157, 219
Technical Stuff icons, 2
technology obsolescence, 20, 197–198.
    See also computers, old
telephone, dialing with computer, 26
telephone support, 140–141, 177–178.
    See also support
temporary storage, 47. *See also*
    memory (RAM)

terabytes, 49
text editors, 121
thermal printers, 94
32-bit applications, operating system
    recommendation, 115
3-D graphics adapters, 69
386 or greater microprocessors, 42
386 or later microprocessors, 43
tickler systems, 26, 124
Tip icons, 2
toner cartridges, 218
tools, software, 130–131
touch-sensitive pad, 75
towers, 101, 103–104
trackball mice, 75
tracking mail order packages, 172–173
training, 19, 178, 214. *See also* support
turbo mode, 44
turning off computer, 193–194
turning on computer, 192–193
TV set not a substitute for monitor, 68
typewriters
    as printers, 228
    replacing with computer, 25, 120–122

• *U* •

Uninterruptible Power Supply (UPS),
    193, 217
United Parcel Service (UPS) Web
    site, 173
units of storage
    bytes, 47–49
    disk storage, 55
    memory (RAM), 49
Universal Serial Bus (USB) ports, 83
UNIX operating system, 114, 116
upgrade versions, 143
upgrading
    BIOS, 229
    CD-ROM drives, 199
    costs, 199

floppy drives, 199
hard drives, 199
hardware, 198–200
memory (RAM), 199
microprocessors, 43, 200
modems, 199
monitors, 199
motherboards, 200
operating systems, 201, 226
software, 143, 200–201
video adapters, 199
UPS (Uninterruptible Power Supply),
    193, 217
UPS (United Parcel Service) Web
    site, 173
USB (Universal Serial Bus) ports, 83
used computers, 9, 167, 202–203, 230
user-friendly software, 139–140
user's groups, 223
utilities, 130–131, 226

• *V* •

versions, software, 143, 225
VGA (Video Gate Array) monitors, 70
video adapter cards. *See* graphics
    adapters
video controller, 67
Video Gate Array (VGA) monitors, 70
video memory, 69–70
video-capture units, ports, 80
viruses, 131, 133, 226
vision-impaired people, 69
Visual BASIC programming language
    (Microsoft), 132
Vulcan software, 124

• *W* •

Warning! icons, 3
warranties, 176, 203
Web browsers, 127–128
What You See Is What You Get
    (WYSIWYG), 122

Whetstones speed-rating test, 41
Winchester disk, 58
Window RAM (WRAM), 71
Windows 98 *versus* Windows NT, 115
Windows NT *versus* Windows 98, 115
Windows operating system
  DOS software, running, 225
  ease of use, 114–115
  graphical interface, 33
  minimum requirements, 146
  monopoly, 113
  version, choosing, 113, 115, 226
Winstones speed-rating test, 41
Word (Microsoft), 121
word processors
  machines, 230
  software, 120–122
WordPerfect, 121
WordStar, 121
World Wide Web. *See also* Internet
  browsers, 127–128
  sales, 172–173
WRAM (Window RAM), 71
wristpads, 215–216
writeable CD-ROM drives, 63–64
writers, reasons to buy a computer,
    24, 121
WYSIWYG (What You See Is What You
    Get), 122

• *X* •

XGA monitors, 70

• *Z* •

Zip drives, 64, 80, 157. *See also* backing
    up data

Notes

Notes

Notes

Notes

Notes

Notes

Notes

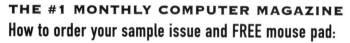

IDG BOOKS WORLDWIDE
BOOK REGISTRATION

We want to hear from you!

Register This Book and Win!

Visit **http://my2cents.dummies.com** to register this book and tell us how you liked it!

✔ Get entered in our monthly prize giveaway.

✔ Give us feedback about this book — tell us what you like best, what you like least, or maybe what you'd like to ask the author and us to change!

✔ Let us know any other *...For Dummies*® topics that interest you.

Your feedback helps us determine what books to publish, tells us what coverage to add as we revise our books, and lets us know whether we're meeting your needs as a *...For Dummies* reader. You're our most valuable resource, and what you have to say is important to us!

Not on the Web yet? It's easy to get started with *Dummies 101*®: *The Internet For Windows*® *95* or *The Internet For Dummies*®, 5th Edition, at local retailers everywhere.

Or let us know what you think by sending us a letter at the following address:

...For Dummies Book Registration
Dummies Press
7260 Shadeland Station, Suite 100
Indianapolis, IN 46256-3945
Fax 317-596-5498

BUSINESS AND GENERAL REFERENCE BOOK SERIES FROM IDG

COMPUTER BOOK SERIES FROM IDG